1st and Ten

1st and Ten

Duffy Daugherty

Head Football Coach
Michigan State University
East Lansing, Michigan

Clifford B. Wilson, II

Professor, Department of Physical Education
State University College
Brockport, New York

Second Edition

WM. C. BROWN COMPANY PUBLISHERS
Dubuque, Iowa

Preface to Second Edition

The purpose of the revision is to "modernize" the book. Football as an athletic event has not changed in any dramatic way. The basic techniques and strategies remain consistent as would be expected due to their long history of development. The name of the game is still rugged physical and strategic competition.

The professional style of football play has had an impact on college performance; this in turn effects all lower levels of football participation. It is only reasonable that athletes should possess aspirations of becoming pros considering the lucritive pay possibilities now available. The influence of professionalism coupled with an increase in player size in general created some coaching problems. The running game, while still primary, had to be heavily supplemented with a diversified passing attack. Team personnel and defensive strategy made scoring consistency by the rush alone rather meager. As the ball became "air-borne" more frequently, the defensive array had to adjust and the four man defensive line returned to popularity. This was true particularly at the pro level with the 4-3 defense the rage. The use of the 4-man line causes great coaching stress to be put on linebackers.

The style of offensive football had one dramatic alteration in the 1960's. The introduction of the I-formation really captivated the imagination of the college and high school coaches to the point where few teams do not have some I-formation plays in their repertoire. Another formation change, though less dramatic in its impact due to severe personnel demands, was the Y or Wishbone formation. The triple option concept developed from this offense set caused much consternation for the defense.

Clifford B. Wilson, II
Duffy Daugherty

Preface to First Edition

The purpose of this book is the provision of a functional foundation for the student of modern football. It certainly does not include all the fundamental and strategic possibilities of football coaching and the myriad "tricks of the trade." To be exhaustive in nature, the book's writing would probably necessitate the endless perseverance of a "team" of highly skilled coaches. The authors do not presume to possess that capacity. There does seem to exist a pressing need for a comprehensive instructional football book, however. This is particularly true when professional courses attempt to adequately indoctrinate future public school physical education teachers in the intricacies of modern football.

To the Instructor

The prospective public school physical educator does not necessarily possess personal football experience when admitted to the professional physical education curriculum. A limited understanding of football seems the rule rather than the exception in students admitted to professional courses of study in physical education. As a result it becomes a course concept that primary experience with football for the mass of physical education major students will be the professional course in football coaching. This poses an instructional problem of course completeness.

As many educators have discovered, it is difficult for the experienced, highly-trained teacher to instruct at the basic fundamental level without assuming some knowledge on the part of the student. The authors realize that even this attempt to write about the fundamental knowledge of football is sprinkled with unavoidable assumptions. The book does try to make the game of football as fundamentally simple as possible, however.

The book is organized as an instructional sequence of material which takes the reader from the fundamental beginning of the game to its strategic climax. Such an arrangement necessitated some partial repetitions, which the authors attempted to hold to a minimum. An attempt to maintain a fundamental practicality has been made throughout the book.

To the Student

You are being exposed to the game of football for the primary purpose of teaching you how to coach a football team. Although some of you may never fulfill this purpose, and others may never desire to do so, it is essential that you adequately comprehend the game. There are two reasons for this statement. First, the physical education curriculum of the public schools invariably devotes a unit or units to the game of touch football, which uses many of the regular football game techniques. Second, and more important, a physical educator inevitably is considered to be an authority on games and sports by the school and community societies. They look to him as a prime source of information, and he must be prepared.

The learning of sufficient knowledge for an eventual assignment as football coach may appear as an insurmountable task. Football may appear vastly more complicated than many of the other games you have learned, or are, or will be learning. You must remember, however, that football is just another game. It would seem that football could be more easily understood if you would methodically digest its mechanics from the fundamentals of individual and small group play on to total team play. This book is organized in such a way as to lead you step-by-step through the maze of techniques and strategies that make up the total game of football. It is designed to serve as an immediate instructional tool and a future resource book.

It is quite true that simply reading a book will not make you an expert on the subject. To prepare properly for coaching football, it is highly desirable that you yourself experience the various skills and techniques of the game. This personal experience can be a part of your course, or of your participation as a football squad member. Once you understand the basic nature of the game, observation of team play (high school, intercollegiate, and professional) will greatly add to your background of knowledge. Football is changing continuously as defensive strategies result in modifications of offensive strategies; this also can work in reverse, but normally does not. To be an effective teacher you must keep up-to-date in your chosen field of endeavor.

To the Spectator

The fact that you have selected this book to read indicates that you are caught up by the excitement and appeal of the very interesting game of football. There is no reason why this interest must remain on the purely emotional level. Football contests consist of carefully pre-arranged strategic plans. A series of successful individually performed team assignments results in a successful total team offensive or defensive effort. The breakdown in any individual player assignment usually results in the failure of the total team effort.

To truly enjoy and appreciate football, the spectator should have a basic understanding of what the individual members of the competing teams are attempting to do. The first six chapters of this book systematically cover individual player assignments. The remaining chapters of the book give detailed accounts of the task of strategy formation undertaken by the coaching staff.

It is hoped that this book will indicate to you, the spectator, the challenges facing both the football team members and the coaching staff. It is the authors' hope that reading this book will make the game of football more meaningful and, as a consequence, more enjoyable, for you. Football is indeed a fascinating game.

Clifford B. Wilson, 2nd
Duffy Daugherty

Contents

Chapter 1. THE GAME OF FOOTBALL, 1

What Is Football?, 1

How Did Football Start?,1

What Playing Equipment Is Used?, 1

What Is the Size of the Football Playing Field?, 2

What Are Some of the More Important Rules of the Game?, 2
Length of the game. Number of players and position names. Substitutions. How is the game started. The 25 second count. Yards to gain. Who is eligible to catch a forward pass? Line of scrimmage. Methods of scoring and points for each. Touchdown. Try-after-touchdown. Field Goal and Safety.

Officials and Their General Duties, 4
Referee. Umpire. Linesman. Field Judge.

Various Offensive Formations, 4

Chapter 2. INDIVIDUAL FUNDAMENTAL PLAY (GENERAL), 7

Stance, 7

The Three Point Stance, 7
Position of the legs and feet. Position of the arms and hands. Plane of the hips, back, shoulders and head. Weight distribution. Coaching tips.

Blocking, 9

The Shoulder Block, 9
Making contact. Keeping contact. Coaching tips. Corrective drill.

The Screen Block, 11
Coaching tips. Corrective drill.

The Brush Block, 12

The Cross Body Block, 12
Making contact. Keeping contact. Coaching tips. Corrective drill.

The Reverse Body Block, 14

The Single Leg or Crab Block, 14

The Roll Block, 16
Coaching tips. Corrective drill.

Tackling, 16

Head-on Tackling, 16

Side Tackling, 17

Tackling from the Rear, 17
Coaching tips. Corrective drill.

Fumble Recovery, 18
    Falling on the Ball, 18
    Picking up the Ball, 18
        Coaching tips. Corrective drill.

Chapter 3. INDIVIDUAL FUNDAMENTAL PLAY (BACKFIELD), 20

Part I, Offense, 20
    Passing, 20
        The grip. The throwing position. The release. The follow through. Coaching tips. Corrective drill.
    Receiving the Pass, 21
        Coaching tips. Corrective drills.
    Punting, 24
        The grip and ball release. The parallel hand method. The palm method. The steps. The knee snap. The follow through. Coaching tips. Corrective drill.
    The Quick Kick, 27
    Catching Punts, 28
        Corrective drills.
    Place Kicking, 28
        Holding the ball. Kicking the ball. Coaching tips. Corrective drill.
    Kick-off, 29
        Rolling kick-off. Outside kick-off.
    Stance, 30
        Upright. Semi-upright. Three point.
    The Split-T, 32
        Split-T stance. Quarterback stance. Parallel stance. Staggered stance. Quarterback hand positions.
    Ball Carrying, 34
        Receiving and holding the ball.
    Eluding Tacklers, 36
        Set-up the opponent for blocks. Shifting the ball. Cross step. Side step. Stiff arm. Pivot. Change of pace. Power through. Individual techniques.
Part II. Defense, 41
    Pass Defense, 41
        Covering a man. Intercepting the ball. Knocking down the ball. Coaching tips. Corrective drill.

Chapter 4. INDIVIDUAL FUNDAMENTAL PLAY (LINE), 46

Part I. Offense, 46
    Alignment, 46
    Stance, 46
    Charging, 46
        Step charge. Lunge or recoil charge. Blocking a man head-on, or slightly to the inside or outside. Coaching tips. Corrective drill.
    Centering the Ball, 47
        Single wing center. T-formation center. Coaching tips. Corrective drill.
Part II. Defense, 49
    Stance, 49
    Defensive Charges, 49
        Hand shiver. Forearm shiver. Straight shoulder charge. Submarine. Over-the-top. One against two. The split. In-and-out. Limp leg. Roll out. Against the trap play.
    Defensive Pursuit, 59
    Defensive End Play, 60

Chapter 5. FUNDAMENTAL OFFENSIVE TEAM PLAY (BACKFIELD), 61

Backfield Alignments, 61
    Backfield Maneuvers, 62

T-Quarterback, 62
   The step-out. Reverse-out. Roll-out. Coaching tips.
Spinning Back, 63
   Forward step. Drop step.
Hand-off, 65
   Taking the hand-off. Fake hand-off deception. Coaching tips.
Lateral Passes (Pitch-outs), 66
   Coaching tips.

Chapter 6. FUNDAMENTAL OFFENSIVE TEAM PLAY (LINE), 68

Formation Alignments, 68
   Offensive Line Maneuvers, 68
   Pulling Out of the Line, 68
      Lead step. Drop step. Cross-over.
Trap Blocking, 69
      Coaching tips.
   Double Team Blocking, 72
      High-low. Post-power. Coaching tips.
   Cross Blocking, 72
      Coaching tips.
   Quick Trap, 73

Chapter 7. GETTING THE BALL INTO PLAY, 74

Numbering Systems, 74
   Numbering of offensive players. Numbering of zones or lanes.
   Signal Systems, 75
      Number system. Word System. Combination of words and numbers.
   The Huddle, 77
      Open huddle. Closed huddle.
   The Shift, 78
   The Starting Count, 79
   Automatics, 79
   Check Signals or Play Changes, 81
   The Quick Play, 81

Chapter 8. POPULARLY USED OFFENSES, 82

Single Wing Formation, 82
      Key running plays. Key pass plays.
Double Wing Formation, 86
      Key running plays. Key pass plays.
Short Punt Formation, 89
      Key running plays. Key pass plays.
   T-Formation, 91
   Tight-T Formation, 91
      Key running plays. Key pass plays.
   Winged-T Formation, 93
      Key running plays. Key pass plays.
   Slot-T Formation, 96
   Split-T Formation, 96
      Key running plays. Key pass plays.
   Tandem-T Formation, 99
      Key running plays. Key pass plays.
   Double Winged-T, 101
      Key running plays. Key pass plays.

I-Formation, 104
    Key running plays. Key pass plays.
Y or Wishbone-T Formation, 107
    Key running plays. Key pass plays.
Supplements to the T Formation, 110
    The split line. The man-in-motion. The wide split end and/or flanker.
Spread Formation, 111
    Key running plays. Key pass plays.
Multiple Offense, 114

Variable Offense, 115

CHAPTER 9. TEAM OFFENSIVE PLAY (THE RUNNING GAME), 116

Basic Line Maneuvers, 116
    Double team blocking. Trap blocking. Man-for-man blocking. Cross blocking. Variations and combinations.
Basic Play Patterns, 120
    The straight ahead play. The off tackle play. The end run.
Supplementary Play Patterns, 121
    Cross-buck. Trap plays. Reverses. Counters. Sweeps. Quarterback sneak. Bootlegs. Draw plays. Special plays. Sally Rand. End-around play. Statue of Liberty play.
Rule Blocking, 134
    Defensive alignment techniques. Number system. Zone or area play.
Rules for Dive Right Play, 138
    Player options.

Chapter 10. TEAM OFFENSIVE PLAY (THE PASSING GAME), 142

Passing Concepts, 142
    Pass Protection, 142
        Cup blocking. Individual blocking.
    The Running Pass, 145
        Optional pass. Button hook passes. Screen passes. Quick passes.
    Straight Passes, 147
        V-out pattern. Flag and post passes. Sideline cut. Out-and-in or in-and-out passes. Button hook passes. Zone flooding. Cross passes. Flair passes. Screen passes. Trailer or check-out passes. Over-loading the deep territory. Straight deep pass (Fly). Look-in pass. Delay pass.

Chapter 11. THE KICKING GAME, 155

The Kick Off, 155
    Kicking off. Returning the kick off.
The Punt, 162
    Punt protection. Blocking the punt. Returning the punt.
Field Goal and Extra Point Kick, 170
    Field goal and extra point protection. Blocking the field goal or extra point.

Chapter 12. TEAM DEFENSE, 171

Defensive Theory, 171
    Desire to stop the opponent. Fundamentals. Properly placed defensive personnel.
Selecting the Defense, 172
Teaching the Defense, 173
Defensive Huddle, 174
Pass Defense, 174
    Zone defense. Man-for-man defense. Combination pass defense.
General Rules, 176
Standard Defenses, 177
    The eight- and nine-man front. The odd and even defenses. The monster or rover defensive man. Backfield rotation. On off tackle runs. Defensing the split end(s) and/or wide flanker(s). Split ends (balanced back-

field). Weakside flanker (regular ends). Strongside flanker (normal ends). Weakside flanker and split end. Strongside flanker with both ends split. Split ends double wing. Use of linebackers. Four-man line. Five-man line. The 5-4-2 five-man line. Six-man line. The six-three-two line. Split-six-man line. Overshifted six-man line. The six-five goal line defense. Seven-man line. Eight-man line. Nine-man line.

Stunting Defenses, 199
Looping. Slanting. Converge. Small group stunts. Shifting or stemming defenses.

Chapter 13. SCOUTING, 204

Who Scouts, 204
What to Scout For, 205
Pre-Game warm-up information. Game information. Post-game information.
How to Scout, 206
Offensive charts. Defensive charts.
What to do with the Information, 208
Personnel charts. Statistical chart. Running offense. Pass plays. Running plays. Pass plays. Punting. Kick off. General information.
The Scout's Report, 215

Chapter 14. STTRATEGY, 216

The Team Captain, 216
Duties during the season. Duties during the game. Duties during the off-season.
The Offensive Quarterback, 217
General items. Specific items.
The Defensive Quarterback, 219
To Kick Off or Receive, 220

Chapter 15. ADMINISTRATION, 221

Staff Assignments, 221
Team Managers, 221
Physical Examinations and Insurance, 222
Training Rules, 222
Conditioning, 223
Early fall conditioning.
Conditioning During the Season, 223
Practice Plans, 223
Game Plans, 224
Pre-game warm-up. Bench management. Substitutions.
Game Statistics, 225
Offense. Defense. Season totals. Offensive information. Defensive information. Additional chart (offense and defense).
Movies, 227
Review by the coaches. Review by the team.
Team Meetings, 228
Off Season Organization, 228
Equipment and supplies. Planning for the next season. Personal improvement.

Postlude, 229

Glossary, 231

Index, 235

Legend for Plays

◯ Offensive player

◑ Players who handle the ball but do not end up with it

● Ball carriers

Ⓧ Center

▦ Pulling or downfield blocking assignments (linemen)

∨ Defensive lineman

X Defensive linebacker or halfback

S Safety

⟶ Path of player other than ball carriers

⟿ Path of ball carrier

------➤ Lateral or forward pass

—‖— Backfield fake

Chapter 1

The Game of Football

Football is an extremely popular American sport. Its popularity probably is due to the high emotional appeal generated within the player and spectator; however, the criteria for successful coaching consist of considerably more than mere emotional appeal. To adequately understand football, the future coach needs to know the background of the game. He must be familiar with the general aspects of the sport before he can properly comprehend the specifics of the game—namely, fundamentals and team strategy. It is the purpose of this chapter to expose the newcomer and reacquaint the "old timer" with the game called football.

What Is Football?

Football is a rugged contact sport in which the 11 members of one team attempt by strength, speed, skill, and deception to out-score their 11 opponents during a prescribed period of time.

How Did Football Start?

The first recorded intercollegiate football game in the United States was played November 6, 1869, between Rutgers and Princeton Universities. The game at this time was a combination of rugby and soccer. Each team consisted of 25 men. No formal coaching or protective equipment were used, and Rutgers emerged victorious by a score of 6-4. Each goal was scored as one point. Return matches were played between these two schools until Rutgers finally challenged Columbia College in 1870, after which Columbia introduced football to Yale University.

The idea of intercollegiate competition spread rapidly among the few established colleges and universities. On November 23, 1876, representatives of Columbia, Harvard, Princeton, and Yale met and organized an intercollegiate football association. The British Rugby code of rules, with but few exceptions, was adopted. Yale voted to reduce the number of players from 15 to 11, but was outvoted and decided to drop from the association. Walter Camp, Yale captain, took Yale back into the association at the convention held in 1879. Camp proposed many rule changes at the convention held in 1880. Most notable of these changes was the reduction of the number of players from 15 to 11: thus, American football came into existence. From that time on, football was stream-lined and modernized until it became the game we know today. The modifications and alterations included the wearing of protective equipment, as well as rule changes.[1]

What Playing Equipment Is Used?

Football players wear the following protective equipment:

Helmet—face mask usually attached
Shoulder pads
Hip pads
Thigh pads
Rib pads—worn by some of the players, usually those with heavy blocking assignments

---

[1]Allison Danzig, *The History of American Football*, First Edition, (Prentice-Hall, Inc. 1956).

Special shoes with attached cleats
Jerseys—usually in the particular school's color, with numbers
Pants—with pockets for thigh pad insertion
Socks—usually heavy woolen
Athletic supporter—a metal cup is worn by some players

What Is the Size of the Football Playing Field?

The football playing field is rectangular in shape. The length is 300 feet and the width is 160 feet from the inside edge of the boundary markers. The area inclosed by the side lines and end lines is "inbounds," and the area surrounding and including the side lines and end lines is "out-of-bounds."

The goal line extends the full width of the field. An end zone is established at each end of the playing field. This end zone is 160 feet wide and 30 feet deep.

Goal posts are erected on the end line of the end zone. Goal posts consist of two uprights extending 20 feet above the ground with a connecting horizontal cross bar, the top of which is 10 feet above the ground. The uprights, at the high school level, are 18 feet 6 inches apart above the cross bar, inside to inside, and not more than 19 feet 2 inches apart, outside to outside. At the college level, the inside to inside measurement is 23 feet 4 inches, and the outside to outside measurement is to be not more than 24 feet. (This is the first time the cross bar width has been altered, a rule established for the college level with the beginning of the 1959 season. Probably the high school level also will adopt this change in the near future.)

Flags with flexible staffs are placed at the inside corners of the four intersections of the goal lines and the side lines.

Inbound lines, "hash marks," are marked perpendicular to the 10 yard markers which run across the field. These inbound lines are made at a distance of 53 feet 4 inches from the respective side lines.

What Are Some of the More Important Rules of the Game?

Length of the game. A game of high school football consists of four 12 minute quarters, with a minute intermission between the first and second quarter (first half) and between the third and fourth periods (second half). A period of 15 minutes of intermission is taken between the halves. An additional three minutes of intermission may be allowed for warm-up activities.

A game of intercollegiate football consists of four 15 minute quarters, with a minute intermission between the first and second periods (first half) and between the third and fourth periods (second half). An intermission of 15 minutes is taken between halves, unless extended or shortened by mutual agreement.

Number of players and position names. A football game is played between 11 players on one team and 11 opponents. For convenience, a player is referred to by his position. (The diagram on page 3 shows one of the many possible offensive formations.)

Substitutions. In high school football there is a rule allowing unlimited substitutions. The rule states that, between downs, any number of eligible substitutes may replace players, provided the substitution is completed and the replaced players are off the field before the ball becomes alive.

In collegiate football, two eligible substitutes of each team may enter the game at anytime before the ball is put in play. Any number of eligible substitutes for each team may enter the game between periods, after a score or try, when Team B is awarded a first down, or when, following a kick Team A is awarded a first down.

How is the game started? Each half starts with a kick off. Three minutes before the scheduled starting time the referee tosses a coin in the presence of the field captains of the opposing teams, first designating which field captain shall call the fall of the coin. The winner of the toss chooses one of these options:

1. To designate which team shall kick off.
2. To designate which goal line his team will defend.

The loser of the toss exercises the remaining option. Before the start of the second half, the choosing of options is reversed.

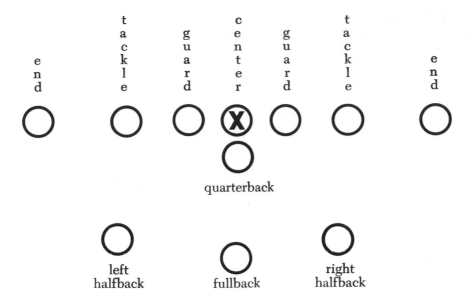

Between the first and second periods, and also between the third and fourth periods, the teams exchange goal lines.

The 25 second count. The ball must be put into play within 25 seconds after it is declared ready-for-play, unless, during that interval, play is suspended by the referee.

Yards to gain. A series of four consecutive scrimmage downs in which to advance the ball to, or beyond, the line-to-gain is awarded to the team which is next to put the ball in play by a snap following a free kick, touchback, fair catch, or change of team possession.

The line-to-gain for a series is established 10 yards in advance of the ball's most forward point. If this line is in the opponents' end zone, the goal line becomes the line-to-gain.

Who is eligible to catch a forward pass?. Each player who is in an end position on his scrimmage line, unless he is a center, guard, or tackle in such position while a teammate is in a position which is outside of and behind him, is eligible to catch a forward pass. In addition each player is eligible who is legally in his backfield and who is not in position to receive a hand-to-hand snap from the center. (A backfield man is any man who is not on the line of scrimmage.)

Line of scrimmage. The scrimmage line for each team is the yard-line and its vertical plane which passes through the point of the ball nearest its own goal line. A player is "on the scrimmage line" when he faces his opponents' goal line with the line of his shoulders approximately parallel thereto, and with his head within 12 inches of that scrimmage line.

Methods of scoring and points for each. The point value for various methods of scoring is as follows:

Touchdown .... 6 points   Try-after-touchdown:
Field Goal .... 3 points   High School .... 1 point
Safety .... 2 points   Collegiate .... 2 points if by run or pass
                                                                  1 point if by kick

Touchdown. A touchdown is scored for the team whose player is legally in possession of the ball while any part of it is on, above, or behind his opponents' goal line.

Try-after-touchdown. High School—A try-for-point is an opportunity given to the team that has scored a touchdown to score one additional point while time is out. The opportunity is a scrimmage down from any point between the inbound lines on or behind the opponents' 2 yard line. The point is scored if the try-for-point results in what would be a touchdown, field goal, or safety under rules governing play at other times.

Collegiate—A try-after-touchdown is an opportunity given to the team that has scored the touchdown to score an additional point or points while time is out. The opportunity is a scrimmage down from any point between the inbounds lines on or behind the opponents' 3 yard line. Two points are scored if the try-after-touchdown results in what would be a touchdown under rules governing play at other times. One point is scored if the try-after-touchdown results in what would be a field goal under rules governing play at other times. (Adopted Jan. 1958—first scoring change since 1906).

Field goal. A field goal is scored for the kicking team if a drop kick or place kick, other than at kick-off, passes over the cross bar or directly over an upright of the receiving team's goal before it touches the ground or a player of the kicking team.

Safety. When the ball is out-of-bounds behind a goal line (except for an incomplete forward pass), when the ball becomes dead in possession of a player behind his own goal line, or when a penalty leaves the ball on or behind that line, it is a *touchback* if the attacking team is responsible for the ball's being on or behind that goal line; if the defending team is responsible, it is a *safety*.

The team responsible for a ball's being on, above, or behind a goal line is the team whose player carries the ball to or across that goal line; imparts to the ball an impetus which forces it to go across that line; or incurs a penalty which leaves the ball on or behind that line.

Officials and Their General Duties

There are four officials designated to enforce the rules of football: the Referee; the Umpire; the Linesman; and the Field Judge.

Referee. The referee has general oversight and control of the game. He is sole authority for the score, sole judge of forfeiture of the game by rule, and his decision is final on all matters not specifically under the jurisdiction of other officials. He has the responsibility for declaring the ball in play and/or dead. He must spot the ball where play is to resume. From scrimmage plays the referee's normal position is behind the offensive team.

Umpire. The umpire has primary jurisdiction over the equipment and conduct of the players. In each scrimmage the umpire is responsible for keeping line play free from fouls, but he must also cover open play which develops after linemen make their initial charge. For scrimmage plays the umpire's normal position is behind the team on defense, but he must adjust his position to the defensive formation and avoid interfering with the vision or movement of defensive players.

Linesman. The linesman has primary jurisdiction over the neutral zone and infractions of the scrimmage formation. The linesman marks the progress of the ball and keeps an accurate count of the downs, under the supervision of the referee. For a scrimmage formation the linesman's normal position is in the neutral zone, well clear of the players.

Field Judge. The field judge has primary jurisdiction over the timing of the game. He must provide himself with a whistle and act for the referee on downfield play. For a scrimmage, the position of the field judge is on the side of the field opposite the linesman, either on or beyond the scrimmage line.

Various Offensive Formations

Modern football offenses consist of a wide variety of player formations. Each formation has many individual variations. These variations are adaptations made by various coaches to better fit the offensive pattern to their particular player material. Often coaches utilize some key plays from several of the various standard patterns. The following player formations are given only as a means of better familiarizing the new or prospective coach with the variety of offensive patterns available. Most of these particular formations will be dealt with in detail in Chapter 8.

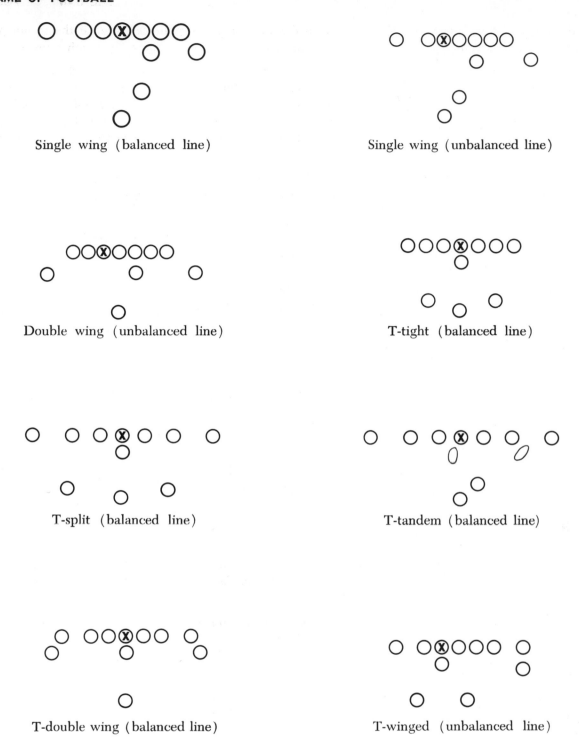

Single wing (balanced line)

Single wing (unbalanced line)

Double wing (unbalanced line)

T-tight (balanced line)

T-split (balanced line)

T-tandem (balanced line)

T-double wing (balanced line)

T-winged (unbalanced line)

Figure 1. Offensive Formations

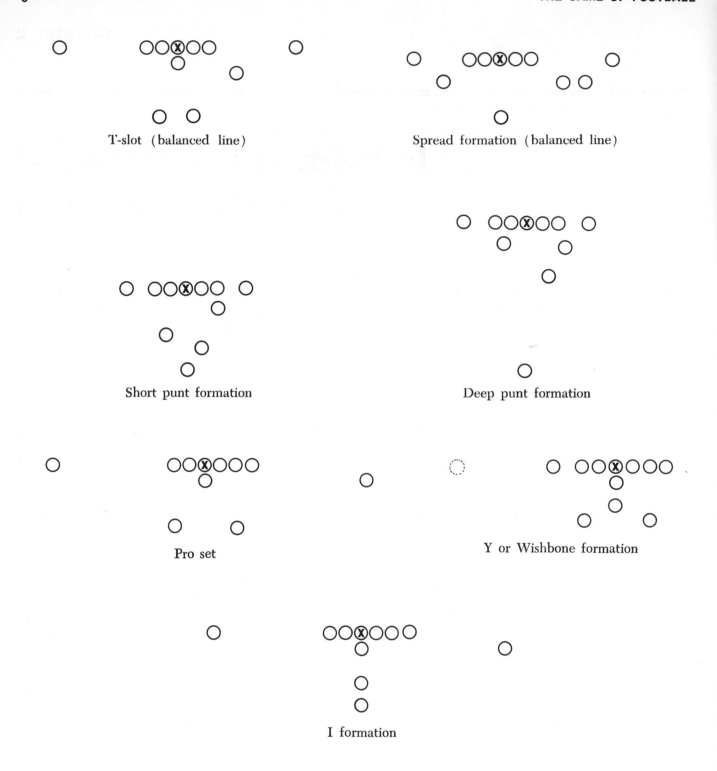

T-slot (balanced line)   Spread formation (balanced line)

Short punt formation   Deep punt formation

Pro set   Y or Wishbone formation

I formation

Chapter 2

Individual Fundamental Play (General)

It is essential that all the players on the football squad learn some common basic fundamentals, namely blocking, tackling, and fumble recovery. These maneuvers are basic to all 11 positions on the football team. They are vital requirements for team play, and equally important as excellent physical conditioners for pre-season and weekly practice sessions.

STANCE

The Three Point Stance

A house is no better than the foundation upon which it is built. This principle holds true for football players. To have maximum power and mobility, to be an effective performer, the football player must assume an efficient starting position. There are several stances used in modern football, however, a basic starting position that will teach the players correct body control for efficient performance is desirable. The three point stance most effectively meet this requirement. It is recommended that all players, regardless of their particular playing position, be taught this fundamental position. When this basic stance is perfected and understood by the players, the fundamental blocking and tackling maneuvers can be introduced with relative ease.

There are four basic parts of the three point stance: (1) position of the legs and feet; (2) position of the arms and hands; (3) plane of the hips, back, shoulders, and head; and (4) weight distribution.

Position of the legs and feet. The primary concerns here are comfort and maneuverability. The position used most frequently has the feet slightly staggered. The toe of one foot (the right foot for a right hander) is in a line with the instep of the left foot. The toes are pointed straight forward with the weight on the balls of the feet. The spread between the feet is about equal to the shoulder width of the player. The knees should be in a straight line with the feet. A line drawn through the foot and knee of the player should be perpendicular to the line of scrimmage.

Position of the arms and hands. The right arm and hand (right handed player) form the apex of the tripod position. The arm should be straight and in line with the right foot and knee. The right hand should contact the ground perpendicular to the line of scrimmage and directly under the right shoulder. The hand can be opened or closed. Many coaches recommend a closed fist for finger protection; however, this is probably a needless precaution as the hand is moved from the ground the moment the ball is put into play.

Plane of the hips, back, shoulders, and head. The most popular position in use today is that with the hips, back, shoulders, and head in the same plane. This affords maximum impact power. The plane of the body is parallel to the ground. Some coaches recommend a position in which the hips are slightly lower than the shoulders, feeling this position better enables the player to drive up and through the opponents when making contact. The parallel position is highly regarded as the most mobile position for movement in any direction. Both shoulders should be "square" and parallel to the line of scrimmage. This position is very effective when used with the lunge charge.

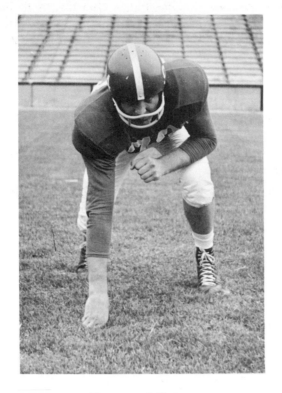

Front View

Right side View

Rear View

Left side View

Stance - (Refer to page 7)

Weight distribution. Three concepts of weight distribution are popular today. One idea is to have most of the weight forward on the hand that is on the ground in order to afford maximum straight ahead driving power. This is recommended by coaches who use almost exclusively straight ahead type blocking with no trap blocking or pulling by linemen.

A second idea is to have only a portion of the weight on the extended arm. This has the advantage of keeping the player from being over-balanced forward. It is thus possible to utilize the step charge when playing against loose or drifting defensive men. It also affords a position of excellent mobility for "pulling" linemen.

The third theory of weight distribution is to have most of the weight back at the hips with little or none on the extended arm. Coaches feel that this position makes the player highly mobile for play in any direction. A disadvantage of this position, however, is that the player must "gather" himself before being able to move forward. This position, while highly mobile, is apt to be slightly slower for forward motion than the positions previously described.

Probably the most popular position has little or no weight on the hand.

Coaching Tips

Problem	*Correction*
1. When pushed from the side, the player loses his balance.	1. Check spread of feet—probably too close together. Check alignment of legs—probably not in line with the feet.
2. When pushed from the front, the player loses his balance.	2. Check placement of hand on the ground—probably too close to his feet. Check weight distribution—probably too much weight on his feet due to a squatting position with low hips.
3. No forward driving power.	3. Check alignment of feet—may have toes turned out rather than pointing straight forward. Check the position of his hand on the ground—may be too far forward to allow for rapid motion. Check stagger of feet—may have one foot so far back that the hips are dropped too low and the knee is too close to the ground.
4. The player is indicating to the opponent the direction he plans to charge.	4. Check placement of his hand on the ground—this is frequently a cause of "pointing."

BLOCKING

The Shoulder Block

The most frequently used block in football is the straight shoulder block. The shoulder block has four primary uses in football: (1) to move an opponent; (2) to screen an opponent from the path of the ball; (3) to check an opponent on the weak or off side of the line, or in pass protection; and (4) to apply power to a two-on-one block.

Making contact. As heretofore pointed out, it is essential that the potential blocker assume a correct starting position. The three point stance is highly practical due to its all-around maneuverability potential. The blocker attempts to make contact at about the belt-buckle of his opponent for proper opponent control. This contact is effected by a low hard charge. The charge is low, to dip under the opponent's hands and hard, to beat the opponent in making contact. The objective is to drive the broad surface of the shoulder into the opponent. Additional force is achieved by driving the upper arm up with power on the contact side. This

Left Shoulder

Left Shoulder
Follow Through

Shoulder Block - (Refer to page 9)

forces the opponent into a vise-like grip caused by the neck, shoulder, and upper arm. The forearm is brought to the chest to avoid illegal use of the hand. At the moment of contact, the feet of the blocker will be spread slightly more than shoulder width apart, with toes straight forward or turned in slightly. The leg opposite the side making contact will be well under the blocker's body. The moment contact is made, the leg on the side of the shoulder contact comes forward in a driving action. The driving force, forward and up, tends to lift the opponent and deprive him of traction for resistance. The action will cause the hips to be lower than the shoulder, but the back should maintain a straight line at all times. The angle of the back should be about 45 degrees.

Keeping contact. Once contact is made with the opponent, driving power is necessary to keep him under control. This driving action consists of taking rapid, short, driving, digging steps with feet well spread and under the body. Pressure is applied between the upper arm and neck to maintain constant contact. *Remember, a well executed shoulder block takes aggression and much perseverence.*

Coaching Tips

Problem	*Correction*
1. Does not keep contact with opponent.	1. Check movement of feet—probably does not follow through after making contact by short digging steps. Check point of contact—he may be hitting the opponent too far out on his shoulder without forearm drive to compensate; also, he may be

contacting opponent too low, thus sliding to the ground. Check direction of driving force—the force may not be lifting the opponent to his toes, thus giving the opponent the controlling position.

2. Does not make solid contact with opponent.

2. Check position of head—he may be looking at the ground and losing sight of his opponent. Check line of charge—he may be aiming at where the opponent was, rather than anticipating where the opponent will be. Check stance—poor stance may be the cause of slow forward motion which is allowing the opponent to make contact first.

Corrective drill. Place bell-bottom dummies 5 yards apart. Have one player hold the dummy while his teammates block. Three blockers and one holder are ideal. After each block, the blocker becomes the new holder of the dummy. The coach can circulate among the blockers, making corrections as deemed necessary.

The Screen Block

The screen block is essentially a straight shoulder block. The fundamental difference occurs after contact has been made. The blocker now drives his forearms up toward the head of the opponent. This movement is to make the defensive man stand up straight. The elbows of the blocker force the arms and hands of the opponent up into a useless position. All that is required by this block is to render the opponent defenseless at the spot where he is located. There is no wish on the part of the blocker to move the defensive man. After contact, the blocker maneuvers his body between the opponent and the hole where the ball carrier is to run.

Screen Block-Left

The Screen Block

Coaching Tips

Problem

1. Opponent reaches over blocker and makes grabbing tackles.

Correction

1. Check position of blocker's arms and elbows—he may not be keeping his arms bent and elbows up under the arms of his opponent.

| *Problem* | *Correction* |
| 2. Opponent smothers blocker with his weight and strength. | 2. Check angle of block—he may be blocking down at the mid-section of his opponent, thus allowing the opponent to fold over on top of him. The taller the opponent, the higher the initial contact. |

Corrective drill. Have several players hold air dummies. Teammates use screen blocks against the air dummies. Have the players take turns holding the dummies. Hold air dummies at different heights to simulate varying player heights.

The Brush Block

The brush block, like the screen block, is basically a straight shoulder block. The purpose of the blocker is momentarily to delay the forward movement of the defensive man; the brush block consists of a shoulder block contact with almost immediate release. The defensive man is contacted with the initial impact of the shoulder charge and then let go.

This block frequently is used by ends before going out on a pass receiving pattern. It is used also by the offside (side of the line opposite the actual path of the ball carrier), tackle and guard. This maneuver momentarily checks the defense, allowing the offensive men to proceed downfield as blockers against defensive halfbacks.

Brush Block

The Cross Body Block

The cross body block is another kind of block often used in football on the line of scrimmage, on linebackers, and downfield on the defensive halfbacks and safety. Its basic use is to cut off opponents who are on their feet moving toward the play. This block is used also as a part of the double team block where two offensive men block one defensive man.

Making contact. The object of this block is to put the body between the opponent and the path of the play. To execute the block, run directly at the opponent as if to use a straight shoulder block. When within a stride of the opponent, throw the body across his legs at the thighs almost waist high by snapping the

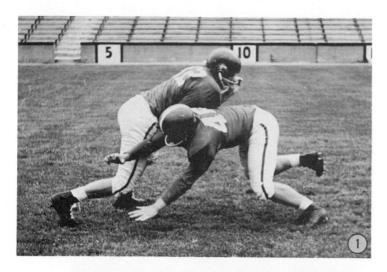

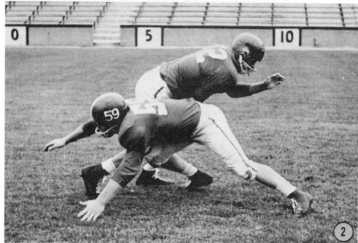

Single

Leg
or
Crab

Block

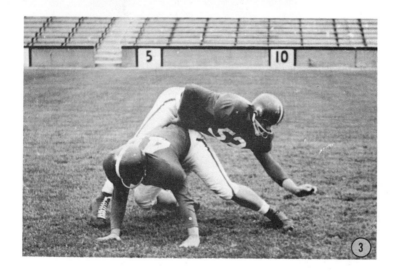

Cross Body Block - (Refer to page 14)

hips, knee, and upper leg hard against him. If the body snap is sufficiently hard, or if the opponent did not see the blocker approach, he will go down to the ground. Otherwise, immediately upon making contact with the opponent, go into a four point position. The arms are extended with the hands or fists on the ground; the leg that was driven into the opponent continues through to the ground.

Keeping contact. From the four point position, the opponent is kept under control by a crab-like movement. The blocker keeps his back high and moves sidewise on all fours. To make a successful block, *the blocker must not go to the ground.* Only the hands and feet are in contact with the ground at all times. It is important to keep both hands on the ground or it is possible that the elbow will hook the opponent or the hand will grab him, both of which are illegal.

Coaching Tips

Problem	*Correction*
1. Does not maintain contact.	1. Check point of contact—he may be hitting the opponent too low, allowing opponent to drive him to the ground. Check tripod points—one of the points may be missing or located at the wrong spot. Check action after contact is made—he may not be following through with a crab-like action.
2. Bounces off the opponent.	2. Check drive of the forward leg—he may not be snapping his leg on past the opponent with enough force, or he may have the leg raised too high. Check contact point on blocker's body—he may be hitting too high on his side, or too low on his thigh.
3. Misses opponent.	3. Check position of head—he may be looking away just before executing the block. Check point at which block is started—he may be starting the block too soon, allowing the opponent time to counteract.

Corrective drill. Have one man hold a bell-bottom dummy while his teammates execute the cross body block. Replace the heavy dummy with an air dummy once the fundamentals seem to have been mastered. Finally, replace the air dummy with a live opponent. Have players rotate positions.

The Reverse Body Block

The reverse body block is a variation of the cross body block with some deception added. It is used effectively against opponents who are doubling back into the play, and against linemen, especially ends, who are charging on a sharp converge path—a straight line from their original defensive position to the deepest man in the offensive backfield.

This block varies from the cross body block in that the blocker, at the moment prior to impact, reverses his body so that the hips, rather than the head, are between the opponent and the play. In most instances, the blocker will be looking at his own goal line at the conclusion of the block.

The Single Leg or Crab Block

An effective block against an opponent who is strong, and knows how to use his hands effectively on defense, is the single leg block. This block is a variation of the cross body block. The objective of the block is to drive through the front extended leg of the hand fighter. The basic principles of the cross body block are used with one exception: the up knee is driven between the legs of the defensive man. The force of this block will cause the leg to buckle and the opponent will be taken to the ground. If the block does not take

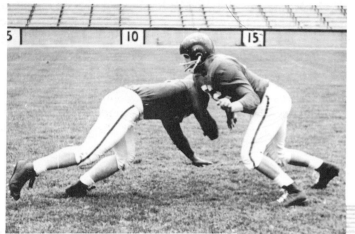

Reverse Body Block
(Refer to page 14)

**Reverse Body Block
Left**

**Reverse Body Block
Right**

Straight Cross Body Block
(Refer to page 12)

the opponent down, the blocker immediately crabs around his opponent, keeping his inside foot stationary but digging with his outside leg. It is imperative that a good head and eyes fake be made upward prior to contact in order to raise the opponent's hands. The upward motion of the opponent will allow room for the blocker to slide under the opponent's hands for the execution of the block.

The Roll Block

The roll block is used primarily by offensive men against secondary defenders downfield. Some coaches prefer a straight shoulder block or screen block downfield; however, the defender has considerable room to out-maneuver a shoulder blocker. This type of block is effective when the ball carrier is running close to his blocker. The roll block is effective no matter where the ball carrier is. It makes the defensive man pay strict attention to the blocker in his endeavor to escape the roll block.

The roll block is executed while the offensive man is running at full speed. He runs directly at the defensive man or at the cut-off spot where he expects to find the defender. When about 3 yards from the opponent, the roll blocker clenches his fist and cocks his arm on the side with which he intends to block. The blocker now drives his cocked arm past the midsection of the opponent. The opponent will be contacted by the back of the blocker's shoulders. At the moment of contact, the blocker extends his arms, body, and legs to their fullest. While maintaining full muscular tension, the blocker continues to roll into and through his opponent and should not relax until three full body turns have been completed.

Coaching Tips

Problem	*Correction*
1. Blocker usually ends up behind opponent and cannot block him without illegally clipping.	1. Check speed of release from line—blocker may be slow in getting free from the line of scrimmage. Check direction of downfield travel—blocker may be moving to the spot where the opponent was, rather than to the spot where he can expect to meet him.
2. Blocker does not gain contact with his opponent.	2. Check speed of blocker's run—blocker may be lessening speed and "dancing" with his opponent. Check distance of "take-off"—blocker may be going into his block too soon. The correct distance of the "take-off" is about 1 yard.
3. Blocker does not remove opponent from play after contact.	3. Check roll of blocker—he probably is not continuing an aggressive roll after making contact.

Corrective drill. Place three dummies in a line 10 yards apart. Station a player at each dummy to stand up the dummy after the block. A player roll blocks through the first dummy, recovers immediately and proceeds on through the other two dummies. The men stationed at each dummy stand them up and then move up to the next dummy. The blocker takes his place at the last dummy.

TACKLING

One of football coaches' major problems is teaching the players how to tackle. The mechanics of the tackle are not exceptionally complicated; however, it takes a great deal more than well executed fundamentals to make a successful tackle. The tackler must be alert and full of "desire," if any success is to be achieved. If any one phase of football playing takes more courage than all the others, tackling should certainly head the list. It is at this point in football playing that the "men are separated from the boys."

Head-on Tackling

The fundamental movements of the shoulder block hold true for this type of tackle. The position of the legs, the feet, the plane of the hips, back, neck, and head, and the upward follow-through are all identical with the movements in the shoulder block. (See page 10). The difference lies in the fact that this is a defensive maneuver and the hands can be used legally. At the moment of contact, the arms are driven hard around the opponent in an attempt to grasp hands in a locked position behind him. This arm action will cause the opponent to be locked in a vise between the tackler's neck and arm, and will cause the opponent to feel the full force of the shoulder impact. The follow-through of the tackle is up to lift the man off his feet and then down to drive the opponent to the ground. The opponent's legs are immobilized by the squeezing force of the tackler's arms. The tackler should end up on top of the ball carrier, if the tackle has been well executed.

The major error made by the tackler is his tendency to lower his head just before contact has been made, which causes the trajectory of the tackle to be low and down. The ball carrier need only step high to avoid the tackler. It is almost impossible to hold a spinning ball carrier with this type of approach. The lowering of the head causes the tackler to lose sight of the opponent, making firm contact almost impossible. The tackler must learn to keep his head up and should try to drive his helmet into his opponent's crotch to assure full shoulder contact, should the ball carrier attempt to side step just before the tackle.

Side Tackling

Most of the tackles made in football are actually side tackles: seldom do tackler and opponent meet head on. The objective of the side tackle is to get the tackler's body between the opponent and the tackler's goal line. The ball carrier is approached as if to execute a shoulder block. To make contact the tackler drives his head in front of the ball carrier, driving his arms around each side of the opponent. The tackler attempts to grab his own wrist as contact is made. The ball carrier is then turned by a vigorous body twist in the direction the ball carrier is heading. This action will cause the tackler and the ball carrier to roll, and the tackler should end up on top of the ball carrier. The locking of the arms around the ball carrier is essential in order to prevent the opponent from spinning free. *Remember, it is the ball carrier's momentum that causes him to go to the ground.*

Tackling from the Rear

There are times during a football game when an opposing back can be caught from behind by a lineman or a back. To execute a tackle from this position, the tackler aims about waist high on the opponent. The shoulder is driven into the ball carrier with the arms driving around him. The tackler then immediately slides down the body of the ball carrier and powerfully encircles the runner's legs. He does not take a running dive at the ball carrier, as this usually results in taking the runner's flying heels in the tackler's face. He does not jump on the runner's back either, as the runner will be able to carry him down the field. A desperation tackle can be made from the rear of a ball carrier by diving at his feet and slapping the back foot hard toward the opposite foot. Frequently this will cause the opponent to trip and fall.

Coaching Tips

Problem	*Correction*
1. Misses man on head-on tackle.	1. Check position of head and eyes—he may be looking down when executing this tackle, causing a downward trajectory. Check length of stride—he may be taking long strides rather than shortening his stride as the opponent nears him, thus taking himself out of balance. Check driving power of tackler—he may be relaxing upon contact, thus allowing opponent's momentum to knock him loose from the tackle.
2. Misses or loses man on side tackle.	2. Check position of head at point of contact—he may be putting his head behind the ball carrier. Check body action at moment of contact—he may not be rolling his opponent, thus allowing him to counteract the force of the tackle with a wide spread of his legs. Check line of flight of tackle—he may be too low, thus allowing the opponent to step past him.

Corrective drill.   For head-on tackling, warm up on tackling dummy. Place two dummies 5 yards apart. Have the ball carrier come straight through between the two dummies. The defensive tackler meets the ball carrier head-on between the dummies. Have tacklers and blockers change positions if desired.

For side tackling, place a dummy on a yard line. Have the ball carrier approach the dummy on a line parallel to the one on which the dummy stands. The ball carrier turns the corner around the dummy. The tackler comes up to meet the ball carrier as he starts around the dummy. The ball carriers can change with the tacklers, if desired.

FUMBLE RECOVERY

Possession of the ball is all important in football. The team that can recover its own fumbles, and the fumbles of its opponent, stands the best chance of winning. The ability to recover fumbles will go a long way toward developing the determination and alertness desired for efficient team play.

Falling on the ball.   Most fumbles occur around the line of scrimmage amid the mass of players. This is due sometimes to poor ball handling by the offensive players, and sometimes to defenders who tackle hard or try to knock the ball out of the opponents' grasp. Recovery, therefore, becomes dependent upon alertness and speed. The primary object is to gather in the ball securely before the opponent recovers. This means not picking up the ball, but rather falling on the ball. To fall on the ball properly, the player actually dives for the loose ball. He leaves his feet at least the length of his body from the ball. The dive is low, dragging the hip close to the ground. One hand and arm are extended to gather in the ball, by scooping it with the extended hand so that it comes into the pocket formed by the player's legs and body. The free hand clamps the ball securely to the player's body. The drawn-up knees help to protect the player from the impact of the other players who are also after the loose ball. *Remember, the ball is not picked up, but is scooped in.*

When practicing the recovery of fumbled balls, it is advisable to allow the players to roll over after scooping in the ball. This rolling action, which is caused by a vigorous scooping action of the extended arm, will lessen the possibility of landing on the point of the shoulder, causing damage and possible shoulder separation.

Picking up the ball.   Under most circumstances, it is advisable to fall on the ball; however, there are situations in which the player is in an excellent position to pick up the ball and advance it. To pick up the ball, the player should take a long stride with the foot opposite the hand that will pick up the ball. The stride foot should be placed just beyond the ball and close to it. The knees are then bent and the hand is placed under the ball with the palm of the hand up. The ball is lifted by one hand and immediately covered by the other hand to insure possession.

There is a familiar situation on the playing field that requires teamwork in recovering a fumble. When an opponent is closer to the ball, it is necessary and advisable to attempt to block him away from the ball to allow your own teammate to recover the fumble.

Coaching Tips

Problem	*Correction*
1. Players do not take immediate possession of fumbles, but continually miss them.	1. Check the line of approach—the players may be "high diving" after the ball rather than using a low approach. Check method of taking the ball—players may be attempting to pick up the ball rather than scooping it in.
2. Players know how to recover fumbles, but rarely do so in the game situation.	2. Players are not fumble conscious. To develop alertness for fumbles, make the players "hit the ball" on every fumble in practice, whether during a

drill or during a scrimmage. A tour around the football field makes an excellent penalty for slow reactions.

Corrective drill. Use two lines, one on each side of the coach. The coach tosses the ball ahead and the players fight for it. One player at a time goes from each line. The coach should use various spins on the ball and vary the depth of the throw. The use of the underhand toss is the most satisfactory. High competitive action can be introduced by having team competition, one line against the other.

Chapter 3

Individual Fundamental Play (Backfield)

PART I   OFFENSE

It is a policy of many coaches to consider the ends primarily as backfield men. This is desirable, as the ends have the responsibility for catching passes and running with the ball. Additionally, ends frequently are punters and in many situations put and kick-off receivers. Consequently, ends are considered as backs in this discussion of fundamental backfield play.

Passing

Modern football places considerable emphasis upon the execution and completion of forward passes. Completed passes eat up yardage quickly with relative ease. Completed passes also cause the defensive team to "loosen up," making the running offense much more effective. The offenses of successful teams usually inter-mix passes with the running game. One supplements the other.

The desirable attributes of a passer are: (1) the ability to locate his receivers; (2) the ability to get the ball to the receivers; and (3) the ability to run with the ball when the receivers are effectively covered.

The ability to get the ball to the receiver is usually the easiest thing to teach the passer. The technique of passing consists of four basic parts: (1) the grip; (2) the throwing position; (3) the release; and (4) the follow through.

The grip.   The most popular method of gripping the football is to spread the fingers over the laces of the ball. This is done by contacting the laces with the fingers. The ball is generally held slightly back of center. The exact placement of the hand on the ball will depend upon the structure of the particular hand. Some passers like to place the thumb on the laces; others disregard the laces. The object is to have a grip that will be secure and will cause the ball to spiral with its nose slightly up. This is known as a "light ball."

The throwing position.   Immediately upon receiving the ball and preparatory to the pass, the ball is brought up with both hands to the throwing position just behind the ear. At this point, the non-passing hand is moved away and in front of the ball. The upper passing arm is approximately parallel to the ground. The side of the body is facing the intended receiver. The legs are spread about shoulder width apart. The weight is partially on the back foot.

The release.   The ball is thrown from behind the ear with wrist snap, similar to the catcher's throw to second base. As the ball leaves the hand, the wrist action is applied by vigorously turning the palm down toward the ground. The drag of the fingers across the ball causes the ball to spiral. The power of the pass comes from the following rhythmical action: the body weight shifts from the back foot to the front foot; the shoulders are vigorously snapped to face the receiver; the elbow is extended; and the wrist is snapped with the fingers pointing toward the receiver and the palm pointing down.

The follow through. The important part of the follow through is to keep the passing arm from going down across the body too quickly. The downward action of the arm tends to cause the ball to travel with its "nose down," resulting in what is known as a "heavy ball." Try to make the hand follow the ball to the spot where you wish it to go.

Coaching Tips

Problem	*Correction*
1. The ball is difficult for the receivers to handle.	1. Check grip on the ball—he may be holding the ball so as to cause it to travel with the nose down. Check release point—he may be releasing the ball too late to allow the nose to stay up. Check speed of the pass—he may be throwing short passes with too much force.
2. Cannot get distance into the pass.	2. Check throwing action—he may be using all arm action and no shoulder and body action. The body weight should shift from the back foot to the front foot as the ball is about to be passed.
3. Throws without enough lead.	3. Check position of front foot at the moment of release—he may be pointing the foot at or behind the receiver, rather than out in front where he wants the ball to go. Check the follow through—he may be crossing in front of the body, rather than at the spot where the ball is intended to go.

Corrective drill. Hang automobile tires between the goal posts. Have the passers throw the ball through the tires, first at 5 yards. Increase the distance progressively by 5 yards until the passers are 40 yards from the tire. Have the players move back toward the tires 5 yards at a time. Competition can be arranged by giving five points for a ball going through the tire and three points for the ball that hits the tire.

Receiving the Pass

The actual receiving of the pass is a simple technique. The problem is to be rid of the defenders and to be at the right spot at the right time. In addition, the receiver must know what to do immediately after the ball is caught. All too frequently, he is thinking of the the opposition rather than concentrating on catching the ball. *Remember, you cannot run with the ball until you have it in your possession.*

Ideally, the pass will come over the receiver's shoulder, so that the receiver can catch the ball without breaking his running stride. To catch the ball over the shoulder, the receiver extends his hands so that the palms are facing the ball with the little fingers almost touching each other. The elbows should be close together: the hands and elbows actually form a basket, and passes which are not cleanly handled will fall into the basket. Passes that are on the finger tips can be deflected down into the basket. The hands give with the force of the ball as a fielder gives with a hard hit baseball. This "give" lessens the impact of the ball and makes it easier to hold. If it is necessary to leap into the air for the ball, the receiver takes off from one foot and lands on the opposite foot. The action is that of a hurdler clearing a hurdle. The objective is to get height without "breaking the running stride." *Remember, watch the ball until it is securely held in your hands.*

To receive a ball that is thrown low, the receiver points his fingers to the ground, again with the little fingers together. A ball that is thrown behind the receiver can often be batted by the hand nearest the ball into the formed basket. On button hook passes where the receiver stops and faces the passer, the ball is caught in the hands with the thumbs together, unless the ball is below the waist, at which time the little fingers will be together.

Ball Over Shoulder

Receiving the Ball - (Refer to page 21)

Coming to Ball - Low Ball

Receiving the Ball - (Refer to page 21)

Coaching Tips

| Problem | Correction |

1. The receiver fumbles the ball.

2. Receiver cannot seem to get open.

3. Cannot evade defenders once he catches the pass.

1. Check the position of the eyes as the ball contacts the hands—probably the receiver is not watching the ball until he has firm control of it. Check the position of the hands and arms—the receiver may be blinding himself at the last moment with his arm. Check receiver for tension—he may be tensing rather than relaxing as the ball comes to him. Check runner's speed—he may be moving too fast to be under control.

2. Check speed of pass receiver—he may be too slow for the job. Spot passes may increase his efficiency. Check maneuvering leg of his run—the receiver may not be using eye deception. The receiver should make eye-to-eye contact with his defender so that his fakes will be more effective. Check maneuvers of receiver—he may be running in a straight line.

3. Check the tucking away of the ball—he may take too long moving the ball into a desirable running position, giving the defenders a chance to over-take him.

Corrective drills. Have the pass receivers stand in two parallel lines 10 yards apart. One line has footballs and the other line turns so that their backs face their teammates. The receiver now looks back over his shoulder and raises his arms and hands ready to receive the pass. The pass is thrown into the formed basket. The receivers then become the passers and the passers the receivers.

Mark out a few different maneuvering patterns with chalk on the practice field. Have the players run the course. Plain lines can indicate areas where receivers are to run full speed. Cross marks can indicate the area where head and shoulder fakes are used and a slower speed maintained.

Have the ends practice the same evasion drills used for the running backs.

Punting

There are arguments as to whether the punt is an offensive or defensive weapon. In reality, it matters little which emphasis is given, as punting is a part of every football game. Better arguments can be given from the defensive point of view. The only times most teams punt are when they cannot gain the yards necessary for a first down, or when they are in serious trouble. Actually, the punt cannot rightfully be considered an offensive weapon, since the punting team does not retain possession of the ball. The primary purpose of football offense is to retain possession of the ball as long as possible. If you must give up the ball by kicking, make it as difficult as possible for the opposition to maneuver with the ball. Put the ball out-of-bounds within the opponents' 10 yard line, if possible. An alternative is to put the ball far enough and high enough to forestall run back opportunities.

The art of punting can be broken down into four basic elements: (1) the grip and ball release; (2) the steps; (3) the knee snap; and (4) the follow through.

The grip and ball release. There are many ways of holding the football prior to the punt. The way the ball will be held depends to a great extent upon the ability of the player to release the ball properly. Two popular methods of holding the ball will be described—the parallel hand method and the palm method.

Across Field, Ball Thrown in Front of Receiver

Receiving the Ball - (Refer to page 21)

The parallel hand method. To receive the ball from the center, extend the arms waist high with the palms parallel and facing each other. The left hand will very lightly hold the back half of the ball. Place the right middle finger along one of the seams of the ball. The thumb of the right hand should lie along the top seam of the ball, adjacent to the seam under the middle finger. The point of the ball should be in heel of the right hand. The middle finger of the left hand is placed along a seam directly opposite that of the right middle finger. The heel of the left hand rests lightly upon the ball at about the middle of the ball. The fingers of the left and right hand are now placed lightly upon the ball and are spread slightly apart. Only enough pressure is applied by the two hands to keep the ball from falling out of the hands. There should be an equal amount of pressure at all points of hand-ball contact.

The palm method. The ball is received again from the center waist high with the palms facing each other. Once possession of the ball is assured, the right hand will turn so that the palm is facing up and the ball is resting on the palm. The middle finger should be running along one of the seams of the ball. The left hand is held lightly against the left side of the ball and acts as a steadier. The desired elevation or depression of the nose of the ball can be effected by raising or lowering the middle finger of the right hand.

To release the ball, hold it about waist high with a slight bend of the right elbow to keep it directly over the kicking foot. The right forearm should not be parallel with the ground. It is essential that the hand be a little lower than the elbow. The wrist must be straight in line with the forearm. The ball is now pointing slightly downward and slightly to the left. To release the ball, simply remove all points of contact simultaneously by drawing the arms apart by action of the shoulders rather than by arm action. This motion is used most advantageously with the parallel hand grip method. With the palm method of holding the ball, pull the right hand down sharply to release it from the ball. The ball, when allowed to contact the ground, should strike it with the nose down. The bounce of the ball will be back past the right foot.

The steps. Professional and college punters frequently utilize a three step approach when kicking the ball. This is permissable only if the kicker can be at a distance of about 15 yards from the line of scrimmage. Most high school centers are not proficient at that distance, nor are the kickers powerful enough to sacrifice the extra 5 yards. It is recommended that the punter be placed at a distance of 10 yards from the line of scrimmage. This position necessitates use of the two step kick in order to get the ball off before the on-rushing defensive linemen can block it.

The parallel foot stance usually is used by the punter; however, he may achieve greater efficiency by using a staggered stance. This is most frequently done by having the right foot 6 or so inches behind the left foot. In reality, it is a way of compensating for the third step, which was discontinued. The weight should be slightly more on the back foot.

The step is taken first with the right foot. It is essential that this step be fairly short and directly at the spot where the ball is to go. As in bowling, it is absolutely necessary that these steps be taken in a direct line, with no body sway. The length of the left foot stride is slightly longer than that of the right foot. Punters should practice these steps blindfolded until they are certain that the step will be in a straight line. This is one of the prime essentials of punting.

The knee snap. As the left foot goes forward, the right foot is "cocked" by bending the right knee. The ball is released just about the time the left foot hits the ground. The punting power is now produced by a vigorous snap of the right leg at the knee. The toe is pointed down, and the ball is contacted on the instep of the right foot, slightly to the right of center. *Remember, watch the foot kick the ball.*

The follow through. As the ball is met by the foot, the arms are extended sidewards, the head is down, and the body weight is on the ball of the left foot. With the punting power coming from the right knee snap, the punter keeps his left foot in contact with the ground. Many excellent punters drive their right foot down to the ground immediately after the knee snap has been fully expended. This insures knee snap in the punt rather than a "leg" kick. Punting the ball by having the power come from the hip will be ineffective, and will cause the left foot to be lifted off the ground. *Remember, power comes from knee snap.*

To kick the ball high, desirable with a trailing wind and with plenty of distance to go, the ball should be released slightly higher than normal. To kick the ball low, desirable when punting into the wind, the ball is released lower than normal. To punt out-of-bounds, the punter takes his two steps directly at or slightly up field from the desired point at the side line, depending upon how much lateral drift he gets on his spiralled ball.

Coaching Tips

Problem	Correction
1. Cannot get a spiral on the ball.	1. Check ball release—he is probably dropping the ball incorrectly. Check toe depression—he may not have the toe pointing down. Check steps—he may not be progressing along a straight line.
2. Does not get maximum power.	2. Check knee snap—he may be a "leg" kicker. Check point of ball contact—he may be meeting the ball too soon or too late.
3. Ball goes too high without adequate distance.	3. Check leg follow through—he may be allowing his leg to follow up after the ball is contacted. Try to instill the idea of kicking out. Check position of the ball at the moment of contact—the ball may be too close to the kicker's body.
4. Can kick best with three steps.	4. Move the kicker farther back from the scrimmage line. If the center cannot handle this added distance, teach the kicker the "rocker step" (see below) or have him start by placing his left foot a full stride behind the kicking foot.

Corrective drill. Mark a straight line on the field. Place the kicker so that his punting foot is on the line. The punter then practices moving down this line as though to kick an imaginary ball. Repeat this action many times. Add the real ball after sufficient practice. Warn the punter not to try for distance, but merely to meet the ball. After several kicks, add the centering of the ball to the kicker. End up the drill by having the punter try five or six full power punts. As the kicker's skill improves, decrease the number of trials of no ball and easy kicking and increase the number of full power kicks.

The Quick Kick

The quick kick is used primarily to catch the defensive team by surprise. It is usually made on the first or second down while still in the offensive team's territory. The object of the kick is to have the ball travel over the safety man's head so that it will roll toward the opponents' goal line. The quick kick can be made from a short punt formation or from the team's standard offensive formation. The offensive line must not allow any penetration by the opponents.

Usually the quick kick is preceded by a backward movement on the part of the kicker, designed to take him a little deeper from the line of scrimmage. As the ball is about to be snapped from center, the kicker takes backward steps, generally three. Assuming the kicker to be right-footed, the first backward step is taken with the non-kicking foot. The three steps when completed will leave the kicker in a position with his non-kicking foot one full stride behind his kicking foot. The body weight will be primarily on the back foot. Now the weight is shifted forward to the kicking foot by taking a short step with the right foot. A full stride is then taken with the non-kicking foot. The knee snap of the kicking foot is now applied. (This total action from the third backward step to the completion of the punt is known as the "rocker step." It is used with considerable success by some punters in regular kicking position.)

The ball can be spiralled or kicked end-over-end. To make the ball travel end-over-end, the back half of the ball must be contacted with the exact center of the instep flush along its long axis. This type of ball action will cause the ball to roll a greater distance than will a spiralled ball. Usually a punter can get more total yardage from an end-over-end punt. The reason it usually is not used is that the ball will not travel as far in the air as will a spiralled ball.

Catching Punts

The safety man has a tremendous responsibility because he usually has sole responsibility for catching punts made by the opponent. The halfbacks also are responsible, at times, for catching punts; particularly short distance punts. It is desirable to teach all of the backs the technique of punt catching. The mechanics of catching punts is relatively simple. To know when to catch the ball, when to let it roll, when to make a "fair catch," where and how to run with the ball when caught are the problems that make punt catching difficult.

It is better to catch the ball while running toward the opponents' goal than to make the catch while standing still or backing up. The punt receiver should play deep enough to be able to come up and meet the ball, rather than finding it necessary to retreat as the ball sails along. With practice, the punt receiver can learn to time the descent of the ball so that he will arrive at the receiving spot at the same instant that the ball arrives. The ball should be caught in the hands with the little fingers almost touching. It is best to learn to catch the ball in the hands. This prevents a break in the receiver's running stride. A bouncing ball should be watched carefully in an attempt to determine when the ball will bounce high. Usually a ball will tumble over several times before it bounces high. It won't go high until it starts to lose its momentum. The receiver should not stand and wait for the ball; rather he should charge it. The chances of getting the ball before the opponents' arrival will be greatly increased if the ball is played aggressively. If the bounce of the ball is quite erratic, it should be left alone. *Remember, a ball touched by the receiving team is a "free ball."*

On wet days or nights, it is usually better to catch the ball with caution. A slippery ball is difficult to hand handle. It is better to form a pocket by putting the elbows close to the body, extending the forearms in front of the body with partially bent elbows, and palms turned up with little fingers close together. The ball can now be cradled to the body. The receiver should reach up slightly to meet it as the ball arrives and guide it into the pocket. This will tend to erase some of the force so that the ball can be "eased in."

Corrective drills. Have the passers throw the ball at the punt receivers. Throw some high and short, high and long, low and short, low and long, to the left, and to the right of the receiver. Follow this drill by having the punters kick the ball.

Form two lines of players, one on each side of the punter. As the ball is punted, the first man in each line goes downfield to tackle the receiver. The receiver uses a "fair catch," or runs the ball back. Do not change the receiver until he brings the ball all the way back to the punter.

Place Kicking

Place kicking is used under two circumstances: to kick the try-after-touchdown and to kick field goals. A kick-off is quite similar to the place kick and will be covered in the next section.

Place kicking requires the coordination of two men, the kicker and the man who holds the ball. On place kicks, most kickers use a specially designed kicking tee to elevate the ball about 1 inch above the ground.

Holding the ball. Frequently the quarterback is assigned the responsibility for holding the ball. This is usually a good rule to follow. It keeps the quarterback out of the heavy contact and makes available a passer in case of a fake kick play. The description following will be for a right foot kicker.

The person to receive the ball from the center takes a position 7 to 9 yards behind the center. The distance is dependent upon the ability of the center, the ability of the line to restrain the opposition, and the height and distance of the kick. The person who is to hold the ball has his left knee on the ground at the spot where the ball is to be placed down. The kicker should have the responsibility for selection of the kicking spot. The right leg of the holder is extended forward and slightly to the right. The right foot is flat on the ground with the right knee slightly bent. The hands are extended forward with a slight forward lean of the body. The palms are perpendicular to the ground with the fingers turned slightly outward. The ball is taken by the two hands and eased directly to the spot where the ball is to be placed down. The end of the ball is placed on the pre-arranged spot with two hands. The fingers of the left hand hold the top end of the ball and the right hand is removed. The person holding the ball now has one job, which is to concentrate on holding the ball in the desired position with no movement. The ball holder should not be aware of the kicker until after the ball has been kicked.

Kicking the ball. The kicker has the responsibility for deciding where the ball is to be placed and the particular angle of the ball. The ball can be kicked off the ground or off a kicking tee. The advantages of the tee are that it will give a smooth surface for the ball and will tend to cause the ball to rise more rapidly. The backward lean of the ball can be determined by trial and error. The objective is to have the ball rise rapidly without losing its forward force. You certainly want the ball to travel over the cross bar!

After the placing of the ball has been determined, the kicker assumes his stance about one step away from the ball. The exact distance is again an individual matter. The kicker should have his feet together with a partial forward body lean. His eyes are looking directly at the spot where the ball is to be placed down. As the ball comes into the holder's hands, the kicker takes his first and only step toward the spot with his left foot. The objective is to place the left foot a little to the left of the ball and slightly in back of the ball. The exact distance can be determined by trial and error. As the step is taken, the right or kicking force comes from the snap of the right knee driving the toe of the foot into the lower half of the ball. The leg follow through is up toward the cross bar. The foot is held in a rigid flexed position. Some kickers prefer a hard toe shoe. The head is held down so that the eyes watched the foot meet the ball. The head is kept down until the ball is well on its way. The arms are raised sidewards to maintain balance. Some kickers find that they can meet the ball more squarely by placing their left foot as much as 6 inches behind the ball. *Remember, snap the knee and keep the head down.*

Coaching Tips

Problem	*Correction*
1. Kicks the ball too close to the bottom, does not get power.	1. For a right foot kicker, move the spot where his left step ends back farther from the ball. Check toe position—he may have his toe depressed.
2. Kicks the ball off to the side.	2. Check step—he may not be moving in a straight line. Check eyes and head of kicker—he may be looking at the onrushing defenders. Check holder—he may have the ball tilted laterally.
3. Does not get power into the kick.	3. Check body position—he may not be in a bent position. Check knee snap—he may be a "leg" kicker. Check spot of non-kicking foot—he may be stepping too close to the ball.

Corrective drill. Have the kicker try several short distance kicks. Then move him back by 5 yard distances until he is at his maximum effective distance. Now take him back to the desired extra point spot and make him kick with the same force he used at his maximum distance.

Kick-off

The actual mechanics of the kick-off are quite similar to the extra point kick. The ball is usually placed on a specially made kicking tee. This tee will hold the ball in the desired kicking position. The object of the kick-off is to make the ball go high and deep to the opponent. The higher and deeper the kick, the less will be the runback opportunities.

The basic difference between this kick and the field goal or extra point kick is in the approach. The kicker usually starts at a spot seven to nine strides from the ball, when taking the first step with the left foot. The distance is lessened to six to eight strides when taking the first step with the right foot. (This is based on a right foot kicker.) The exact placement of the non-kicking foot in relation to the ball is again an individual matter. Some kickers achieve greater distance and height by placing the foot close to the ball; others achieve the desired results by placing the foot more to the rear of the ball. Once the exact spot is located, the kicker should learn to pace-off the exact approach distance in strides. The kicking foot drives through the ball and toward the opponents' goal line with less up swing than that used for the extra point kick. *Remember, start from the same spot each time and learn to approach in a straight line.* Practice will correct the natural tendency for the kicker to veer to the right on his approach.

Rolling kick-off. Some coaches like the ball kicked in such a way that it will bounce and roll crazily in the opponents' territory, feeling that such a ball will be difficult for the opponent to handle. This may result in one of two advantages for the kicking team. The receiving team may fumble, thus allowing the kicking team an opportunity to gain posession of the ball. The other outcome may be that the receiving team is so busy trying to gain possession of the ball that team members completely disrupt their run back plan.

To kick a rolling ball, the kick-off man uses the same step approach mentioned above. The only difference lies in the placement of the ball on the ground prior to kicking it. The ball is usually placed right on the ground with its long axis parallel to the yard lines, and is kicked right at its mid-section. A tee can be used.

Onside kick-off. The onside kick-off is used primarily when the kicking team must gain possession of the ball. This usually occurs late in the game when the opponents have the score advantage. It is used as an element of surprise at other times during a game. This second circumstance must take into consideration the relative strengths of the two opponents. The assumption is that the opponents will not be able to advance the ball if they do gain possesison of it, and the kicking team can move the ball out of their own deep territory, if the opponent punts accurately.

The onside kick-off can be executed in two different ways. One method is to have the regular kick-off man do the actual kicking. Instead of kicking the ball hard and fairly low, he meets the ball high and kicks fairly easily. He directs the kick-off toward one of the sidelines.

The other technique is to have the kick-off man proceed as if he were going to kick the ball. Just prior to kicking the ball, he stops and the teammate next to him actually kicks the ball. This kicker comes diagonally at the ball and kicks it gently toward the sideline. *Remember, in each situation, the ball must cross the opponents' restraining line before the ball is a "free ball."*

Stance

The stance used by the backfield players varies with each position, with the particular style of offense, and with individual characteristics. Three basic halfback stances will be described. After these descriptions, variations will be pointed out. The three basic stances are the upright, semi-upright, and the three point.

Upright. The upright stance was made popular by the straight T-formation. It is used by the "deep" back in the I-formation also. The backs stand with their feet parallel and about shoulder width apart. The knees are partially flexed with the palms of the hands resting on the knee caps. The head is up and the back is straight. The weight of the body is slightly forward on the balls of the feet. Two major disadvantages of this stance are (1) the backfield man tends to take a step backward before moving forward, thus losing some of his starting quickness, and (2) the backfield man will tend to "hit the line" in an upright position, thus losing some of his hitting power.

Semi-upright. This stance is used widely with the single wing formation. The backfield men stand with their feet parallel and about shoulder width apart, as in the upright stance. The knees are flexed so that the forearms of the players rest on the legs just above the knee caps. The head is up, back straight, and hands apart as to receive the ball. The weight is slightly forward on the balls of the feet. This is an excellent position for backs who have to spin after receiving the ball. The tendency to "hit the line" in an upright position is lessened, but not removed.

Semi-upright

Upright Stance

**Upright Stance
Side View**

**3 Point Stance
Front View**

**3 Point Stance
Side View**

Stance - (Refer to page 30)

Three point. The three point stance has become very popular as a result of the split-T formation. The stance is very similar to that taken by linemen. The right foot is staggered slightly with the toe in line with the instep of the left foot. The right arm is perpendicular to the ground, with the hand contacting the ground in a line with the right foot. The left forearm rests on the left leg just above the knee. The head is up with the weight balanced equally on all three points. The advantage of this position lies in the tendency of the backs to "hit the line" in a semi-upright position.

The Split T

The split-T offense utilizes a stance variation which is quite similar to a sprinter's stance. In addition, the quarterback in the T-offense uses different stances from those of the other backs because of his special offensive functions.

Split-T stance. The split-T utilizes a combination of the aforementioned stances with special variations. The right halfback takes a position with his left foot considerably in back of the right foot. The left hand is in the standard three point position. The weight is mainly forward. The stance is acceptable as the right halfback travels on only two routes—straight ahead or to his left. The left halfback assumes a three point stance in reverse of the one used by the right halfback. The right hand is on the ground and the right foot is staggered well behind the left. The routes traveled by this back are either to the right or straight ahead. The fullback uses a standard three point stance. The major variation occurs in weight distribution. The weight is more forward in this stance than in the normally-used three point stance.

Quarterback stance. There are two basic stances for the T quarterback: (1) feet parallel and (2) feet staggered.

Parallel stance. The quarterback assumes a position close to the center with his feet parallel to the line of scrimmage and spread slightly apart. If the ball is to be centered between the quarterback's legs to the fullback on some plays, the foot spread of the quarterback is about shoulder width. The quarterback should have a slight bend at the knees. He attempts to keep his back as straight as possible, holding his head high. This position of the body gives the quarterback a clear view of the defensive alignment.

Staggered stance. The quarterback again assumes a position close to the center. The only variation from the preceding position is in the placement of the feet. The right foot—for a right handed player—is dropped back of the left foot so that the toe of the right foot is about in line with the heel of the left foot. Some players find that they can move more quickly from this position. This is a desirable position for players who tend to take a drop step before moving laterally. If the ball is to be passed to either halfback, the quarterback places one foot directly behind the other. This is necessary if a spinning buck-lateral series or similar series of plays is to be used.

Quarterback hand positions. Four hand positions popularly are used by quarterbacks for the ball exchange in the T formation. One position places the heels of the hands close together with the palms spread apart. The thumbs are up and together. They are placed against the center's "tail" with the fingers pointing straight down. The elbows are spread apart a little to absorb the jar of the ball.

Another position has the back of the left hand under and in contact with the "tail" of the center. The palm of the hand is about parallel with the ground. The heel of the right hand is in contact with the heel of the left hand. The fingers of the right hand are pointing straight down.

A third position is the reverse of the latter. The back of the right hand is in contact with the center, and the left hand is pointing down.

The fourth position, and probably the newest one, is quite similar to the last two-mentioned ones. The back of the right hand is in contact with the center's "tail." The thumb of the left hand is placed along the thumb of the right. The palm and fingers of the left hand are perpendicular to the ground and in such a position as to prevent interference with the exchange. The left hand is really a guide, as the right hand does the work. It is important to keep the fingers of the right hand relaxed, even though the back of the hand is applying pressure to the center's crotch.

Side View

Front View

Split T Stance - (Refer to page 32)

QB's Hand Position T Formation
(Refer to page 32)

Split-T coaches usually prefer the first position described. The ball is centered into the hands point first. The quarterback is now on the move and can hand-off the ball rapidly without fear of having his arm caught in the exchange. The second and third positions are usually used by teams that employ straight-T offenses. The ball is centered in such a way that the quarterback does not need to make any serious adjustments for passing. The fourth position is usually used by teams that employ the multiple of variable type offenses. This particular hand position is considered to be more adaptable to a variety of offenses.

Ball Carrying

Ball carrying consists of receiving the ball, holding the ball, and techniques of running with the ball to elude tacklers.

Receiving and holding the ball. The ball carrier can receive a direct pass from the center, or take a hand-off from a teammate. To receive a ball from the center (deep backs), the ball is caught with the hands slightly spread and palms parallel. The hands are perpendicular to the ground. As the ball makes contact with the hands, it is eased to the player's body. The ball is held close to the chest with the right hand over the end of the ball that is pointing left, and the left hand over the end that is pointing to the right. This is the position of the ball recommended for plays in which the ball carrier is to drive into the line. On end runs, and sometimes on off-tackle plays, the ball is held by one arm and hand. The hand is over one end of the ball, and the other end is up against the player's arm pit.

The usual method of receiving the ball on a hand-off is to have the inside forearm (arm closest to the person who is handing off the ball) across the chest and parallel to the ground. The outside forearm is held a few inches in front of the body (3 inches is recommended), parallel to the body, and with the hand slightly lower than the elbow. As the ball is placed in the formed pocket, the receiver places his hands firmly over the ends of the ball. From this position, it is a simple maneuver to push one end of the ball up into the arm pit so that the ball can be held by one hand.

Single wing coaches usually recommend a different position of the hands and arms for a hand-off. A pocket is formed over, or just below, the belt of the player's trousers. His little fingers should have a space of 2 inches between them, and his thumbs should be pointing in the same direction as his shoulders. The backs of his hands should be 2 inches from his body.

**Deep Back Receiving Ball
From Center**

**Handoff Pocket by H. B.
Taking Handoff**

**Single Wing Handoff Position
H. B. Taking Ball**

Halfback Receiving the Ball

Eluding Tacklers

There are many ways to avoid being tackled in football. The most successful technique, and the ideal, is to have excellent blocking so that no opponent is able to approach the runner. Following are described several methods of eluding tacklers that can be used by the ball carriers.

HB Setting Up Defensive Tackler for Blocker
(Refer to page 37)

Shifting the Ball

Set-up the opponent for blocks. An intelligent runner can be of invaluable assistance to his blockers. It is the runner's responsibility to know where his blockers are supposed to be; then, when the runner is past the line of scrimmage, he can maneuver to pick-up his blockers. Frequently the inexperienced ball carrier tries to out run the secondary, even though blockers are close by. The smart runner maneuvers to draw the opponents to the blockers. This does not mean to greatly slacken speed, as the runner is then in danger of being caught from behind. Rather it means to change direction when necessary to draw the tackler to the blocker. *Remember, good down-field blocks are frequently the result of smart ball carrying.*

Shifting the ball. A standard rule of ball carrying is to have the ball under the "off" arm, on the side farthest from the nearest opponent. To achieve this, it becomes necessary to shift the ball rapidly from one arm to the other and to do so without fumbling. This is done best by sliding the ball across the body with the arm that is holding it. The opposite hand and arm then take possession of the ball by clamping down quickly on it. Momentarily, the ball is held with a hand over each end in the same fashion as in the T hand-off. The

Use of Cross over Step by Halfback

hand nearest the opponent is now released. *Remember, do not let the end of the ball pass across the abdomen so that the ball is perpendicular to the body; rather, slide the ball across.*

Cross step. If the ball carrier wishes to pass to the right of his opponent, he shifts the ball under his left arm. A head and shoulder fake is made to the ball carrier's right as the ball is shifted. The ball carrier then takes a long step with his right foot by crossing it in front of his left foot. The next step with the left foot will carry the runner well to the right of his opponent. *Remember, a head and body fake is essential.*

Side step. To side step to the right of an opponent, the runner carries the ball in the left arm. The right foot is placed directly in front of the tackler as a target. When the opponent starts his tackle, the ball carrier quickly springs to the left. If the head and body fake have taken the tackler on a line to the right of the ball carrier, the runner need only to land on his left foot and take his next right step toward the opponents' goal line. If the tackler has not been fooled, the ball carrier can take a double side step in the form of a lateral hop, or he can allow his right leg to go limp. This limp leg will frequently bounce out of the arms of the tackler. The right leg also could be crossed behind the left leg. *Remember, you have to out-smart the tackler.*

Stiff arm. Cross steps and side steps are frequently accompanied by a stiff arm: this is particularly true when the original maneuver did not fool the opponent. The stiff arm is employed by holding the arm low and close to the body until the stiff arm is applied. Contact is made by stiffening the arm, planting the heel of the hand on the tackler's headgear or neck, and pushing hard toward the ground. The body weight should be partially on the stiff arm. The impact with the opponent will cause the runner to come upright. *Remember, do not punch, but keep the elbow stiff after contact has been made.*

Side Step and Cross Step Combination

Pivot. The pivot is extremely valuable when the opponent is head-on, or when he has a partial hold on the runner. To pivot to the right of an opponent, the ball is held in the right arm, and a head and body fake is made to the runner's right. This deception is used to convince the tackler that the ball carrier is going to the tackler's left. The right foot is planted about in line with the tackler's left foot. The runner's left foot is then placed to the outside of the opponent's right foot. The ball carrier now pushes off his right foot and pivots to the rear by keeping his weight over his left foot. At the same time, the runner uses a left hand stiff arm on the opponent. The pivot is as near to a full 360 degrees as possible, with the runner attempting to place his right foot down in the direction of the opponents' goal line. As the right foot contacts the ground, the left foot is snapped up and around vigorously. This reverse pivot movement will usually pull the legs free from anything but a perfectly executed tackle. *Remember, do not step too far to the left side of the opponent or your spin will present your back as a perfect target for your opponent.*

Halfback Pivot to Elude tackler

Front View   **Side View**

Defensive Backfield Stance

Change of pace. Speed is an essential qualification for an open field runner. Good runners have a sense of timing that enables them to confuse the tacklers by slowing down or accelerating their pace. A change of pace can be caused either by a momentary pause in the run or by changing the length of the running stride. By shortening the stride and then lengthening it, the tackler is frequently left bewildered. The tackler must estimate the spot where the ball carrier will be when he makes his lunge. If, at that precise moment, the runner increases his speed or stride length, the tackler will end up in an arm tackle or a complete miss.

Power through. Despite the attempt of the ball carrier to elude the tackler, there will be situations where a tackle is inevitable. When these occur, the ball carrier should take possession of the ball with both hands and arms, as though he were driving into the line of scrimmage. With considerable bend at the waist, he should drive his knees and legs viciously into the oncoming tackler. Frequently this violent driving power will knock the tackler over and jar the runner free; at least it will prevent the ball carrier's being knocked over backwards, and insure an extra yard or two of advancement. *Remember, lower the boom and "blast."*

Individual techniques. Each backfield man should develop some characteristic movement to confuse and "freeze" the tacklers. These may be a head movement, shoulder sway, hip sway, bob forward and backward—some movement that comes easy and naturally to the runner. This individual deceptive motion, coupled with the stunts before listed, should make it possible for a ball carrier to elude most of the open field tacklers.

PART II   DEFENSE

Individual defensive play will be concerned with individual pass defense. Total pass defense and backfield responsibilities against running plays will be covered in a later chapter.

Pass Defense

Pass defense used in modern football are varied and extensive. They depend upon the capabilities of the defensive backfield and the opponents' passing strength. In all the various pass defense plans, however, cer-

Defensive Position - Pass Interception

42

Defensive Position - Down and out pattern
or Side line pattern

tain basic fundamental techniques are employed by the defensive backs—covering a man, knocking down the ball, and intercepting the ball.

Covering a man. To cover a man heading straight for your position, you must "give ground." It is essential that you keep at least 7 to 8 yards away from the oncoming man. The faster the pass receiver and the slower the defensive man, the more ground must be kept between the two. If the pass receiver is able to get within about 3 yards of the defensive man, his chances of eluding the defender are extremely good. To "give ground," the defensive man should bounce backwards off the balls of both feet almost simultaneously. Bent knees will greatly enhance this movement. Once the offensive man has definitely declared the direction he intends to finally pursue, the defensive man can turn sideways and run with him, still maintaining the safe distance of about 5 yards.

Halfbacks should maintain a position in line with the outside shoulder of the offensive man and perpendicular to the line of scrimmage. This will allow the defensive man to cover the man on a V-out pattern easily, or on any sharply lateral maneuver. If the offensive man turns to the inside, the halfback can still cover him fairly well; however, he will usually have the assistance of linebackers and/or the safety man. When the offensive man changes his course from a straight line down the field to a lateral movement or button hook, the defensive man can then, and only then, afford to move closer to the pass receiver. A distance of about 3 yards is adequate. *Remember, never let the man get in back of you, and allow him a little more running room to the inside rather than to the outside.*

Intercepting the ball. If proper position is maintained as described above, the pass defender will be in an excellent position to intercept passes that are thrown too long or too short. Once the pass defender determines exactly where the ball is going to come down, he should ignore the receiver and concentrate on intercepting the ball on anything but a perfectly thrown pass. Proceed directly to the spot where the ball is to come down and take the ball on the dead run as high as possible. *Remember, if you are going forward to meet the ball, it will hit your hands with considerable force.*

Knocking down the ball. Whenever the possibility arises in which the pass receiver is in a good position to receive the pass, the primary task of the defender is to knock the ball down to the ground. Although a perfect pass is extremely difficult to defend, the correct approach by the defensive man will greatly reduce touchdown possibilities, and will often cause the receiver to lose possession of the ball. The defensive man who has correct position will be moving toward the offensive man. He should drive both hands directly at the football in order to force the ball down to the ground. If the ball is coming into the hands of the receiver, lunge over him with one arm on each side of his head as you go for the ball. Then, if the ball is not knocked free, the defensive man will have a firm hold of the receiver to prevent him from covering additional yardage. You cannot deliberately shoulder, bump, or in any fashion molest the man who is about to catch the ball. This does not mean that contact is illegal. An honest effort to get the ball, which results in contact, is permissable. *Remember, you have as much right to that ball as does your opponent. Do not hesitate and be shy, drive right through him.*

Coaching Tips

Problem	*Correction*
1. Receiver out-runs defender.	1. Defender is probably not analyzing the pass play soon enough. Teach him to give ground the moment a pass is imminent. Watch the ends: they usually tip-off a pass play by the determination of their downfield run. Defenders must analyze the strategy being used by the opposition. This will frequently give a clue as to the situations in which the opponents like to pass.

2. Receiver out-maneuvers defender.

2. Check defender's leg movements—he may be taking cross steps rather than slide steps on lateral movement. Check defender's eyes—he may not be looking at both the ball and the receiver. A gaze at the receiver is safer than a stare into his eyes, or at any one of his deceptive motions.

3. Defender does not intercept the ball.

3. In practice drills, make the defenders concious of interceptions, rather than on knocking down the ball. Have them practice learning how fast they can react. Once this is known, the defenders can hang back from the ball until the last moment, making interceptions much easier.

Corrective drill. Have one defender 10 yards downfield and "head-on" a receiver. The receiver goes down the field and attempts to evade the defender to catch the pass. Add another defender and receiver after each defender has had several chances. Finally, add a third defender to help against the two pass receivers. Intercept the ball at every opportunity.

Chapter 4

Individual Fundamental Play (Line)

There are basic movements and maneuvers that characterize the offensive and defensive play of linemen. This section is concerned only with these common fundamentals.

PART I   OFFENSE

Alignment

Some coaches, noticeably professionals, prefer to have the linemen line-up at the back portion of the scrimmage line with the exception of the center. This places the center's head even with (or over!) the near end of the ball. The remaining linemen are aligned so that their heads are about one foot behind the ball. (See page 3 for definition of scrimmage line.)

The advantage of being aligned tight to the ball is to make quick contact with the opponent: a preferred procedure in quick-hitting offenses, i.e. split-T and Wishbone T. The off-the-line positioning is beneficial for quick trapping (See page 73), for pass protecting, and for getting momentum (contact being made after step forward taken) for fast but light weight players.

Stance

The most popular stance used by linemen is the tripod or three point stance. The details of this stance have already been covered in the section dealing with Individual Fundamental Play (General). Some teams have their interior linemen assume a four point stance, particularly when the offense is primarily quick hitting with man-to-man blocking assignments. This stance is accomplished by assuming the tripod position and then placing the off hand to the ground similar to the down hand.

It is essential to re-emphasize the extreme importance of correct stance. One also must not forget that individual variations in stance are sometimes necessary. Some coaches employ a much greater foot stagger for their linemen than is normally used, particularly when the blocking assignments consist of all straight ahead movements. *Remember, without an adequate stance the linemen will be relatively ineffective in performance proficiency.*

Charging

Charging consists of the movements necessary on the part of the lineman to effectively execute his offensive blocking assignments. Two standard types of line charges are employed in modern football: the step charge and the lunge charge.

Step charge. The step charge is used against opponents who are using a waiting defensive tactic, those who are originally lined up off the scrimmage line, and those who are "floaters." This charge is generally executed by driving forward off the front foot by taking a step forward with the back foot. Usually contact with the opponent will be made as the back foot completes its forward movement. If the opponent is playing deep or is floating, contact will probably be made on the second step. The step action only begins the block. Once this forward momentum is started, variations in further procedures of movement will depend upon the specific type of block to be employed. *Remember, the step is used to develop driving force without the loss of initial balance.*

Lunge or recoil charge. This particular movement is used against hard charging defensive opponents, shifting defensive men, and defensive men who are playing tight to the line of scrimmage. It is a highly valuable charge for explosive quick opening plays. The charge is executed by driving with considerable force off both feet at the same time. This lunge should bring you into contact with your opponent, either before the full extension of the knees has taken place, or just as the full extension has taken place. Immediately upon making contact, the legs are brought up into their original positions. The time lapse between the movement of the trunk and the follow-up of the legs is scarcely noticeable. The moment the feet are in their forward position, a churning driving action is developed by taking short powerful steps. Remember, this is not a "high dive" action. The motion of the trunk is comparable with the initial forward action of a released arrow. Do not leave your feet "at home." They have a vital part to play in the charge. The lunge charge is used primarily with shoulder and screen blocks.

Blocking a man head-on, or slightly to the inside or outside. Shoulder and screen blocking become quite difficult when the opponent plays directly in front of (head-on) the offensive man. This difficulty increases when the defensive man moves to the inside—closer to the intended hole—of the offensive man. The individual block becomes more effective by the use of a lateral movement prior to contact. This lateral motion is effected by taking a 45-degree step forward and lateral with the inside foot. The outside foot is now driven at the defensive man as in the regular shoulder or screen block. *Speed of motion is particularly essential in this blocking maneuver.*

Another method of executing this block is to swing the head and shoulders low and in front of the defensive man. At the same moment, slide or lateral step is taken along the line of scrimmage. This should put the offensive man in blocking position inside the defensive man.

If you wish to block a man in who is playing to your outside, reverse the procedures described above.

Coaching Tips

Problem	*Correction*
1. Slow step charge.	1. Check the stance, particularly the foot stagger and hip level—he may be wasting time raising up rather than moving forward.
2. Does not maintain contact after the lunge charge.	2. Check the trajectory of the charge—he may be moving down toward the legs of his opponent. Check the follow-through of the leg and foot action—he may be hitting and relaxing, rather than hitting and immediately taking short digging steps. Check the play of the opponent—the offensive man may be using lunge charges when the step charge would be more effective.

Corrective drill. Use a Crowther blocking machine or plum dummy, if possible. If the player does not hit these pieces of equipment correctly, the machines will let them know by their rebounding actions.

Centering the Ball

Single wing center. The single wing center, who passes the ball to "deep backs," will use a wide base with his feet spread well apart. The toe of the right foot will be in line with the instep of the left foot. The hips must be low. This is accomplished by a slight bend of the knees. The head will be down so that the center can see between his legs. It is generally desirable to have the center see the target to which he is passing. Only the exceptionally skilled man can center accurately without seeing his target. Both hands are placed upon the ball. The right hand grips the ball with the standard forward pass grip. The left hand acts as a guide. No weight is placed upon the ball. If weight is placed on the ball, the center's body weight will shift to his heels as he passes the ball, leaving him defenseless and inefficient. The ball is snapped back with arm action, followed by strong wrist action. The elbows are held locked so that the arms are straight throughout the actions. The follow-through of the hands should be low in order to keep the ball from rising too rapidly. *Remember, as the ball is passed backwards, the center should have his body weight moving forward.*

T-formation center. The stance used by the T-formation center is more erect and much narrower than that of the single wing center. The feet are slightly staggered, toe to instep. It is incidental whether the left or right foot is forward. Some coaches prefer to have the right foot forward to aid the two guards in their scrimmage alignment. If some of the center's passes are to go past the quarterback, it is preferable to have the right foot back, which will allow the arms of the center to have more follow-through room.

The hips of the center are as high as possible to allow the quarterback to stand almost erect. The grip on the ball is usually the same as that used by the passer. The right hand grips the ball and the left forearm rests on the left knee. The head of the center is up, the same as for all linemen. This position makes the center a more effective blocker than does the single wing position.

The method of snapping the ball will depend upon the position of the quarterback's hands. If the end of the ball is to go back in a straight line, the center drives the ball back and up with no wrist turn. Another method is to make the ball take a half end-over-end turn. To do this, drive the ball back and up with a stiff arm motion so that when it is placed in the quarterback's hands, the back of the center's hand is facing the ground.

To have the ball arrive sidewards with the laces up, the center starts with the laces close to the ground. As he brings the ball back and up with force, he rotates his wrist by turning his fingers to the left as he lifts the ball. To cause the laces to be down, the center starts with the ball placed on the ground with laces up.

The final snap technique is to drive the ball back and up, allowing the hand and wrist to take its natural course. This will cause the ball to take a quarter turn to the left as it is placed in the quarterback's hands.

As the center drives the ball back and up, his body weight starts forward. It is essential that the center does not carry the ball with him in his forward motion, because this will usually result in a fumble. The actual forward motion does not take place until the ball is firmly in the quarterback's hands. The body weight is shifting forward as the ball goes back. As contact with the quarterback's hands is made, the center takes his first step forward. This step is usually made with the right foot. *Remember, do not step and then center the ball; just shift your weight forward.*

If the ball is to be passed to "deep" men, or to the quarterback, it is generally preferred that the center have both hands on the ball, as is recommended for single wing centers. To center to "deep" men, the action becomes the same as in the single wing centering action; to center to the quarterback, the ball is snapped with one hand as in regular T-formation centering action.

Coaching Tips

Problem	*Correction*
1. The center does not block effectively.	1. Check the center's balance—he may be taking himself out of balance when snapping the ball; his weight may be moving backward rather than forward. Try having the center place his left hand on the ground, assuming a four point position.

2. Fumbles occur on center-quarterback exchange.

2. Check movement of center—he may be carrying the ball with him on his first step; the exchange should occur before the step. In addition, the center's snapping action may cause the ball to arrive too low for the quarterback. Check position and movement of the quarterback—he may not have his hands in the proper receiving position; he may be pulling out from under the center before the completion of the exchange. Many coaches prefer to have the quarterback move slightly forward with the center before pulling back.

Corrective drill. Always have a defensive man line up against the center. When the center snaps the ball, he blocks the defensive man. A center should never snap the ball without this forward motion. The defensive man may be holding a blocking dummy.

PART II DEFENSE

Stance

The most common defensive stance used by linemen is the three point stance. (See page 6) Many coaches prefer to keep the defensive men in their offensive stance because it eliminates new teaching. An additional advantage is that the linemen should be more comfortable in a stance that they are using most of the time. Some coaches prefer to have their guards in a four point stance. A general rule followed by many coaches is to have the guards in four point stances, tackles in three point stances, and ends in three point or semi-erect stances. The particular stance used by the linemen will depend, in part, upon the defensive strategy of the moment. A seven- or eight-man defensive line may find all the men in a four point stance; the four- or five-man line may find all the linemen in a three point stance. *Remember, stance is as important in defensive play as it is in offensive play.*

The basic difference between the four and three point stance is that the left hand is on the ground with the right hand. The linemen using the four point position should be cautioned not to let their knees touch the ground. It is a four point stance, not a six point stance.

The weight distribution for defensive three and four point stances varies slightly from that used in offensive stances. Approximately 60 per cent of the weight should be on the down hand(s).

Defensive Charges

The most common charge used by defensive men is the step charge. Some coaches prefer to have the defensive personnel on the right side of the center line up in a three point stance with their outside feet back. This is true also of the personnel on the left side of the line—outside feet back. The step charge employed in this instance is a jab step with the inside foot, as contact is made. Other coaches prefer to have the linemen in a three point stance with the inside feet back. The first step is then made with the inside foot. In either instance the lineman ends up with his outside foot back. The idea is to worry less about the inside attack than about the outside attack.

The direction of the charge and final maneuver of the linemen will depend upon the total defensive pattern being employed. The defense must play it "smart," diagnose, maneuver, and employ all the tricks known. In the final analysis, defensive line play is a matter of hand-to-shoulder contact, strength against strength, and courage and determination against courage and determination. Contrary to the offensive linemen, *the first thought of the defensive linemen is to get contact and lose it.*

There are several ways in which a defensive lineman can determine when to make his initial charge. The rules do not permit forward motion on the part of the defensive linemen (motion into the neutral zone)

Front

Line Backer Stance

Left Side

Rear

Right Side

Defensive Stance - (See page 49)

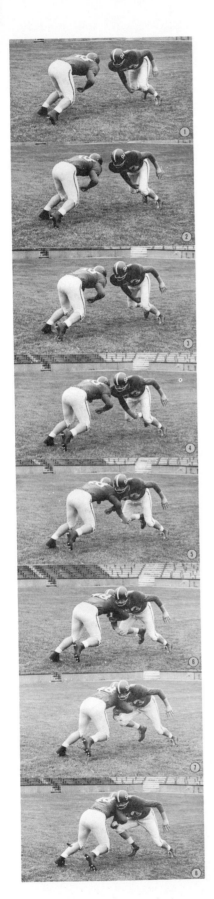

Forearm Shiver

Shoulder Charge

(See pages 49 and 52)

until the ball has been moved by the center. The most popularly used procedure is to permit the guards playing near the ball to watch it for their signal to move. The other players watch the head of the opponent playing in front of them. By watching the head, the defensive man can meet power with power whether it be a high block, low block, reverse head and shoulder block, cross body block, or another play. Some coaches teach the defensive linemen to watch the down hand of the opponent in the belief that the first movement made by the offensive lineman is one of this hand.

It is very important to train defensive men not to listen to the signal calling cadence of the offensive quarterback. *The defensive men take their initial starting signal from what they see, not what they hear.*

Hand shiver. This charge consists of driving the heels of the hands into the opponents' shoulders ending with straightened and locked elbows. The step charge initiates the movement, and short, powerful, chop steps continue the motion. The offensive lineman is straightened up, shoved back, pushed aside, or driven to the ground. At times the lineman maintains contact with the offensive man and controls him while moving laterally toward the direction of the play.

Forearm shiver. The forearm shiver is similar in many respects to the hand shiver. The difference lies in the part of the body that makes contact with the offensive opponent. The elbows are bent to a 90-degree angle, allowing the forearms to make the initial contact with the opponent. Once the initial blow is neutralized with the forearm shiver, the result is the same as that of the hand shiver: the opponent is straightened up and pushed arm's length away from the body of the defensive man. This movement allows the defensive man adequate room for a frequently necessary releasing of the offensive man.

Hand Shiver - (See page 49)

Submarine

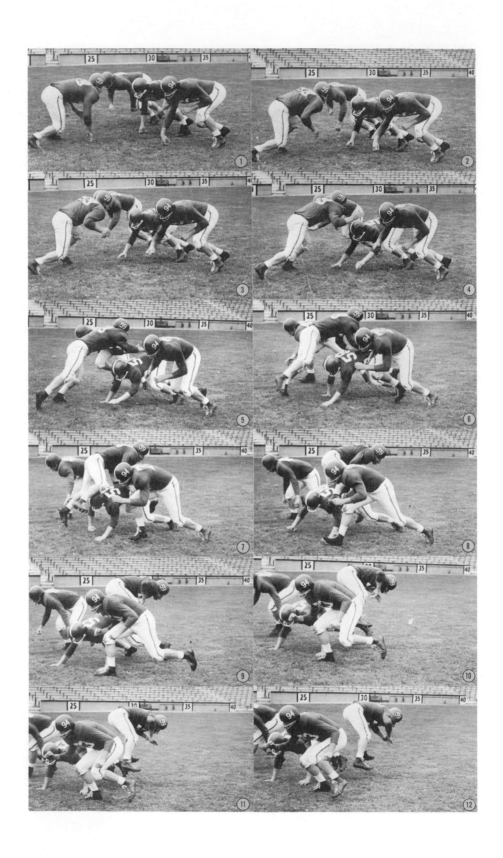

Over the Top - (See page 57)

Roll out - (See page 58)

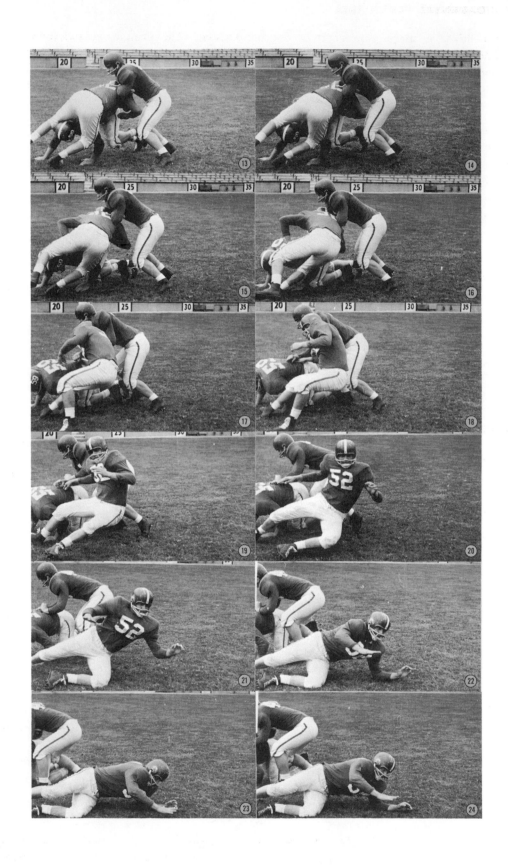

Roll out - (continued)

The forearm shiver is more popular than the hand shiver. The primary reason for this is that the performer of the hand shiver must have exceptional strength in order to insure its satisfactory execution. If the blocker's shoulders are missed with the hand shiver, or if the defensive man does not possess adequate strength, the offensive blocker is immediately invited into the defensive man's body. This, of course, is the offensive man's primary desire.

Straight shoulder charge. A strong, fast-moving lineman can use this charge to advantage. To execute the charge, the lineman uses a step charge, driving his shoulder into the mid-section of the offensive man. The direction of the charge is low and up. If the defensive man beats the offensive man to the charge, he can drive right through him. This will bring the defensive man into the offensive backfield in such a position as to allow the penetrating man to protect his assigned territory.

Submarine. The submarine charge is used for two basic purposes: to penetrate into the opponents' backfield and to pile up the offensive linemen, leaving the ball carrier with no running room. The charge is executed by dropping low on the hands and knees while moving rapidly forward. The shoulders should hit the opponent below the knees. The action is continued by driving forward powerfully and grabbing ahold of all the legs in sight. This action will cause a pile up of the opponents. If the play is to the opposite side or is a pass, drive under and through the opposing lineman and come up to follow the play.

Over-the-top. This maneuver is sometimes employed by guards against low charging opponents. The defensive man places his hands on the backs of the opponents and leap frogs over them. Remember to square yourself away and be prepared to meet the ball carrier, or to continue your forward charge as the situation may dictate.

One against two. Most teams today utilize offensive blocking techniques which have two offensive men responsible for blocking one offensive man. This is particularly common in trap blocking. An example would be a double team block on one guard with a trap block against the other guard. The standard defensive maneuver in a two-against-one situation is playing first one man and then the other. Four types of maneuvers that can be used against two offensive blockers are the split, the in-and-out, the limp leg, and the spin-out.

The split. The defensive man using this technique will drive his shoulder and hip against one of his two opponents and, at the same time, drive his hands against the other. The hands are usually driven into the side of the helmet and shoulder of the opponent in an attempt to re-direct his charging momentum. What actually happens in a properly executed split maneuver is that one opponent is bumped away, the other opponent is shoved away, leaving a gap for the penetration of the defensive man. The defensive man must be quick, strong, and vicious, if he expects to perform this movement successfully.

In-and-out. The in-and-out or out-and-in technique is similar to the split method. If the defensive man is almost certain, because of field and down situation or pointing on the part of the opponents, that the play is going to be made to his outside, he can drive hard off the man to his inside and then immediately react and fight to his outside. He would thus be facing and fighting toward the expected point of attack. *Remember, "jolt" one and hand fight the other.*

Limp leg. This defensive maneuver can be executed by two different methods. Against a single man, extend a leg toward that man. As he drives into the leg relax it and allow the leg to move back under the force of the block. Shove the blocker on past the "limp leg" with the hands and bring the "limp leg" down behind the blocker. Against two blockers, play one viciously with the hands, and allow the leg nearest to the opponent to go "limp" as above. The opponents will be split apart, allowing the defensive man to penetrate to the desirable spot about one yard behind them.

Roll out. A lineman who is outcharged by the opponent(s) and/or pinned between them can use this roll out technique very effectively. Plant the foot nearest the path of the ball carrier and reverse spin quickly on the planted foot. A short drop step before the planting of the foot will allow the defensive man adequate room for the maneuver. It is necessary to give some ground in order to execute the spin; however, the motion will

Trap Reaction

carry the defensive man into the path of the ball carrier. This may turn what appeared to be an obvious long gaining play into only a short gain. The reaction must be rapid with some loss of ground.

Against the trap play. It is necessary for all linemen to know how to react against a trap maneuver by the offensive team. Interior linemen handle a trapper differently than do the ends. These linemen should use a dip shoulder charge into the trapper, placing their heads between the trapper and the hole. The attempt is to drive the would be trapper into the proposed offensive hole. This maneuver is much superior to the older technique of immediately dropping to all fours when allowed free penetration.

The end is generally given outside defensive responsibility against the running offense; therefore, he must play the trapper just the opposite of the interior linemen. The end uses a dip shoulder charge to the blocker's outside in an attempt to force this trapper into the interior, while still being in a position to release to the assigned outside territory. This will put the end into a good defensive position should the ball carrier be forced to change his running direction to the outside.

Defensive Pursuit

Pursuit is the term used to describe the play following action of linemen after they have penetrated to their proper position behind the scrimmage line, or have their immediate opponent under control. Coaches generally feel that the defense is just as strong as its pursuit action. It is almost inevitable that the opponent will advance the ball on some running plays and pass plays; however, these gains can frequently be kept to relatively short ones by the alert pursuing action of the defensive linemen.

The problem in pursuit is following the correct "angle of pursuit." There is some direct path that every man on the team can follow to the ball carrier. A movement along the incorrect pursuit angle immediately removes the player from a possible tackle. A correct "angle of pursuit" will bring the defensive player to, or in front of, the ball carrier, not behind him.

In selecting the correct "angle of pursuit," there are two considerations: the running speed of the defensive man in relation to the ball carrier and the path to follow in order to intercept the ball carrier. The defensive man must rapidly determine his own speed in relation to the ball carrier, and then select a direct line to follow in order to complete the interception. The "angle of pursuit" should not be along an inside arc; rather the angle should be along a straight line or outside arc. (See Fig. 2)

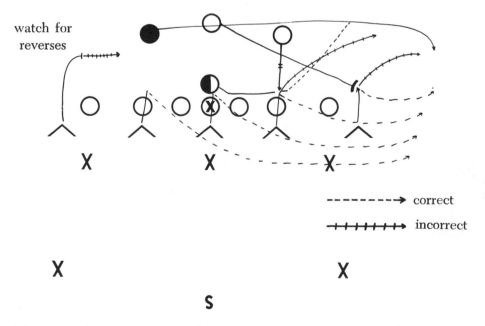

Figure 2.   Angle of Pursuit of Linemen From a Five Man Defensive Line

Drills for teaching pursuit

Spin drill.

Whenever an offensive player (O) has proper position on the defensive player (X), a spin is required.

Slide drill.

Whenever the defensive player (X) has control of the offensive player (O), a slide out is required.

Team pursuit.

This drill can be executed without an offensive team. The coach stands facing the defensive team and gives a hand signal to indicate direction of pursuit. Stress position first—pursuit second.

Reaction to trap and pursuit. Proper execution of this drill is stressed with emphasis on ability to "read" the man opposite you. If he leaves you to the outside, the tackle should turn in quickly, being alert for a trap. If the blocking pressure is from the outside, be prepared to pursue properly.

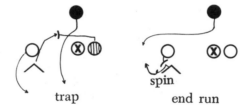

trap   spin   end run

A general defensive rule to remember is that, unless resistance is met, the defensive man is going in the wrong direction.

Defensive End Play

The play of the defensive end will depend primarily upon the total team defensive strategy at the time. From an individual play point of view, however, the end does one of three things: he crashes or slices, drives hard into the offensive backfield and aims at the tailback or passer without any outside responsibility; he waits, takes no more than one step forward and stops to see what is to develop, having flat territory pass defense responsibility; or he drifts or boxes, takes two steps across the line of scrimmage and keeps the offensive play from going to his outside by hand fighting and giving ground.

Chapter 5

Fundamental Offensive Team Play (Backfield)

A backfield is a unit of four men who must work in complete harmony if the play is to be deceptive and successful. As will be shown later, backfield offensive maneuvers lend most of the surprise and deception to the total team offense. The coordinated movements of these backs are an essential and vital part of team play.

BACKFIELD ALIGNMENTS

A clearer understanding of the technical manipulations of the four backfield men can be attained more readily by a picture of the available backfield alignments. The technical maneuvers can be visualized more adequately in relation to the actual player alignments. Only the more popular backfield alignments will be diagrammed; actual spacing will be given in the chapter dealing with team offense.

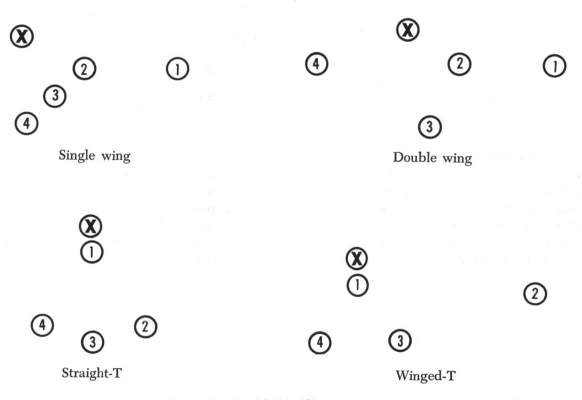

Figure 3. Backfield Alignments

Y or Wishbone T   I-Regular

(The numbers are used to indicate specifically the positioned players as follows:)

        1—right halfback
        2—quarterback
        3—fullback
        4—left halfback

Figure 3.   (Continued)

Backfield Maneuvers

This section will be used to discuss the specific techniques used by the backfield men to give speed, power, and deception to the running and passing offense.

T-Quarterback

The stance and hand placement of the T-quarterback have been previously covered. (See page 32) The problem at hand is to decide specifically what the quarterback can do now that the center has given him the ball. Actually, there are but three basic maneuvers used by the quarterback: (1) the step-out; (2) the reverse-out; and (3) the roll-out. The particular maneuver depends, to a great extent, upon the theory behind the particular play or set of plays.

The step-out.   The quarterback step-out is recommended for teams using the split-T, or quick hitting type of offense. In this style of play, the halfbacks are usually placed close to the line of scrimmage—3 to 3½ yards. The task of the quarterback is to move rapidly enough to get the ball to the halfbacks before they are out of reach: if he does not give the ball to them, at least to fake to them, so that the opposition will think the ball has changed hands. To step-out to the right, the quarterback pushes off the left foot and takes his first step with the right foot. The right foot is placed down at the spot where the right guard's feet were placed. The quarterback then continues running along parallel to the line of scrimmage. A step-out to the left is performed by pushing off from the right foot and stepping with the left foot. Momentum is gained by pushing off from the foot opposite to the direction one wants to travel. *The quarterback should not lean in the direction he wishes to go prior to receiving the ball.*

A variation of the split-T step-out is used in the so-called "belly" series and "sprint-outs." Instead of stepping laterally, the quarterback steps back toward the man he is to "ride" or in the direction of his sprint-out.

Reverse-out.   The reverse-out maneuver is used most frequently with the regular T-formation, or with plays that are relatively slow in developing. An example of a slower developing play is the crossbuck. This maneuver has, for example, the fullback going to the right of center and, after a momentary delay, the right halfback going to the left of center. To execute a reverse-out to the right, the quarterback pushes off with the left foot and pivots to the rear on the ball of the right foot. As the pivot is made, the body weight should be directly over the right foot. The quarterback will have his feet parallel, and approximately shoulder width apart, at the completion of the movement. This will place him in a position parallel to the line of scrimmage, with his back to the opposition. To pivot to the left, a reverse of the movement is used. *Remember, the body weight should be directly over the pivot foot.*

Roll-out. The roll-out maneuver is used for plays hitting to the outside and on some passes. The movement involved is almost identical to the reverse-out. The basic difference is that the quarterback does not come to a stop at the completion of the pivot, but continues to move away from the center. He takes a partial cross-over step with the right or pivot foot. *Remember, the body weight is over the pivot foot only momentarily and is rapidly shifted to the left of the pivot foot.*

Coaching Tips

Problem	*Correction*
1. The quarterback is slow on his step-out.	1. Check the exchange—the quarterback may be waiting for the ball. Check the quarterback's foot movement—he may be stepping laterally in the direction opposite the desired direction on his off foot prior to his first step in the desired direction.
2. Quarterback reverses well to first man, but cannot get back to hand-off the ball to a cross-bucking or countering man.	2. Check position and balance—he may be ending his reverse with his feet spread too wide apart; he may be allowing his weight to shift over or outside his outside foot.
3. Quarterback cannot seem to get the ball to an outside dive man on a reverse-out.	3. Check second step of quarterback—he may be bowing back with his second step away from the scrimmage line.
4. On a "ride" play, the quarterback is taken down or knocked off balance on the "ride" fake.	4. Check position of quarterback—he may be too close to his teammate; he may be "riding" his teammate too long.

Spinning Back

The single and double wing offenses and some of the T-variations use a spinning attack as part of the total offense. Instead of the quarterback's hiding, faking, and/or keeping the ball, the deception is provided by the so-called spinning back. The fullback usually handles the duties of the spinning assignments; however, the right or left halfbacks can also be used. The movement is executed by one of two different methods: the forward step or the drop step.

Forward step. The forward step technique is probably the most popular movement used by spinning backs. It has the advantage of bringing the spinning back, and those to whom he fakes or gives, closer to the line of scrimmage. This speeds up the execution of the total play, and thus adds rapid play to an otherwise relatively slow developing offense. To execute the maneuver, the spinning back must receive the pass from the center at about knee-high level on the side the spinner is to turn. (The center should practice passing the ball to the left and right knee caps of the spinning back.) If the fullback is the spinning back and wishes to fake to the left halfback, the ball should be centered to the left knee cap of the fullback. As the ball starts toward the spinning back, he pivots forward on his left foot. This pivot can result in a quarter turn or a half turn. The quarter turn is executed by placing the right foot down on a line drawn perpendicular from the left foot to the line of scrimmage. (See Fig. 4) The forward step is about shoulder width in length. The body weight shifts to the right foot. The shoulders are allowed to continue their turning action until the back is square to the line of scrimmage. The half turn is executed by continuing the pivot on the left foot until the right foot can be placed down shoulder width distance from the left foot. The two feet are now on a line parallel to the scrimmage line. The spinning back has his back to the center.

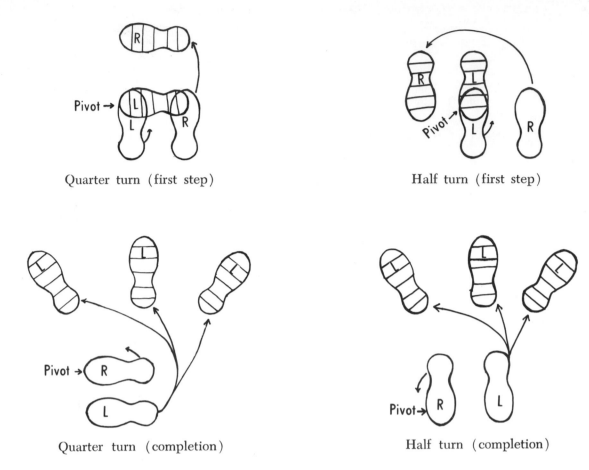

Quarter turn (first step)   Half turn (first step)

Quarter turn (completion)   Half turn (completion)

Figure 4. Backfield Spinning

In either the half or the quarter turn, the spinning back is now in a position to fake to the left halfback. To continue on into the line of scrimmage, the spinning back pivots on the right foot and steps with the left foot in the direction he wishes to travel.

The quarter turn is more desirable than the half turn under most circumstances. As can be seen by the diagrams, the quarter turn takes the spinning back to the scrimmage line much more quickly. The fake can be made also to the left halfback on the quarter turn. This can be followed by a fake or hand-off to the right halfback as the spinning back shifts his weight to the right foot and starts his left foot toward the scrimmage line. This particular action will keep the left and right halfbacks from colliding on reverse plays. *Remember, the spinning back should not straighten up; rather, he should stay low and in perfect balance.*

Drop step. The drop or backward step sometimes is used by spinning backs for formations that have the left halfback a yard or so deeper than the fullback, such as the traditional single wing formation. The maneuver has two disadvantanges, however: the fullback has a greater distance to cover in order to "hit" the scrimmage line, and this method of spinning drives the right halfback or end quite deep for a fake or hand-off to them.

To execute the backward step, the fullback spins on his right foot and drop steps with his left foot. The left foot comes to the ground on a line drawn perpendicular from his right foot to the line of scrimmage. After the fake or hand-off, the fullback moves toward the line of scrimmage by reversing the movement. The forward spin is made on the right foot, and the left foot is stepped forward toward the desired spot in the scrimmage line. (See Fig. 5)

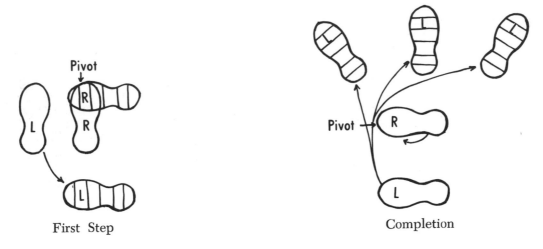

Figure 5. Drop Step Spin

Hand-off

A hand-off occurs whenever one player gives the ball to one of his teammates, excluding the pass from the center. In the modern T-formation, most of the hand-offs are made by the quarterback. Even so, single and double reverses require players other than the quarterback to make hand-offs. A spinning attack requires the hand-off be initiated by the spinning back.

To execute a hand-off, the person making the hand-off can use one of two different methods. The method most peculiar to the T-formation is that in which the hands are on the sides of the ball, perpendicular to the ground and held about waist high. As contact with the teammate is about to be made, the hand nearest the receiver is removed from the ball. The ball is then placed into the desired receiving position by the hand away from the receiver. One hand acts as a steadier and guide while the other makes the hand-off. In most instances, the ball is placed on the far hip of the receiver.

The second method, which is more peculiar to the single wing or spinning attack, is to have one hand on top of the ball with the opposite hand underneath it. The ball is palmed in one hand and steadied and guided by the other. As the passing of the ball is about to take place, the top hand is removed from the ball. The hand-off is finally made by the ball's being held in the hand away from the player who is to receive it. The wrist and arm holding the ball should be relaxed to prevent interference with the man getting the ball.

To "ride" with the receiver as in the "belly series," the quarterback must be slightly behind his man and arm's length away. *Remember, the person making the hand-off has the responsibility for placing the ball in the correct position.*

Taking the hand-off. There are two recommended methods for receiving the ball on a hand-off. One way is to raise the elbow and forearm nearest to the person making the hand-off, while holding the far hand just hip high. The near forearm is raised parallel to the ground and across the upper part of the chest. The far upper arm is held close to the body. The forearm is across the body with the hand slightly lower than the elbow. The position of the far arm will stop the ball from passing right on through. The ball is placed across the body between the two forearms and close to the far arm. As the ball hits into the formed pocket, both arms are clamped down onto the ball. A hand is placed over each end of the ball. The ball is now securely possessed by the new man. This method is peculiar to the T-offense.

The second method recommended for receiving a hand-off is more commonly used with a spinning attack. A pocket is formed over or just below the belt of the trousers. The little fingers should have a space of 2 inches between them, and the thumbs should be pointing in the same direction as the shoulders. The backs of the hands should be 2 inches from the body. After receiving the ball, the runner should lower his inside shoulder and turn his upper trunk slightly toward his own goal line. The away elbow is held tight to his side, and the ball is cradled in the away arm. Running speed is gained by rocking down and up with the upper trunk.

Fake hand-off deception.   There are three current views on ball handling deception. The first is to show the ball at all times, with no attempt to conceal it as fake hand-offs are made. An effort is made to keep the ball in motion and showing at all times. The theory behind this technique seems to be that the opponents will concentrate on the ball rather than on the blockers.

A second, and most commonly-used technique, is to keep the ball hidden at all times. Fakes are executed by concealing the ball next to the quarterback's or spinning back's stomach and using a "dead hand" fake. Fakes can be executed also by having the quarterback and faker brush by each other—no hand fake is made. This technique is based on the notion that the defenders will waste time looking for the ball rather than being concerned about blockers.

The third method, which has gained much popularity since its great success at Georgia Tech, is to "ride" with the faker in a "belly series." As described in hand-offs, the quarterback places the ball next to the stomach of the faker, then allows the faker to pull away from him at the line of scrimmage. The fake is made so late the defense must tackle the faker, or simply guess that he does not have the ball. An option "give" or "keep," according to the strategy of the defense, makes this technique highly potent.

Coaching Tips

Problem	*Correction*
1. Fumbles occur on hand-offs made by the T-quarterback.	1. Check the quarterback—he may be getting to the receiver too late, which results in the ball's being incorrectly placed. The quarterback may not be looking at the receiver. Check the receiver—he may be reaching for the ball. Have the receiver look at the hole where he is to go, not at the ball.
2. No deception in the T hand-off.	2. Check positioning of players—the deep backs may be too close or too far from the line of scrimmage, which might lead to an early or late arrival at the hand-off spot. Check man faked to—he may not be reacting as though he has the ball. Make the men faked carry out the fakes until well beyond the line of scrimmage.
3. Single wing spinning back not deceptive.	3. Check the knee bend on his turn—he may be straightening his knees on each movement, causing an up-and-down action. He may be reaching the ball to the backs, rather than making the hand-off in front of his own body.

Lateral Passes (Pitch-outs)

A lateral pass occurs whenever one offensive player passes the ball to another who is parallel to him or behind him. It differs from a hand-off in that the ball is actually tossed to the other player. A lateral pass from the quarterback to a halfback going wide on end runs is commonly refered to as a pitch-out. Most laterals are made by quarterbacks after a direct pass from the center.

Two different techniques are employed to lateral the ball. One method is to spiral the ball by actually throwing an underhand pass. The ball is held with one hand on each side. In most instances, the right hand actually does the work. The left hand guides the ball as the right hand passes the ball. The fingers of the right hand are pulled up and across the ball as it is released, causing the ball to spin in a spiral fashion. The motion of the right arm and hand is very similar to that of an underhand softball pitch.

Another method of lateralling the ball is to cause the ball to travel end-over-end from the same hand position described for the spiral lateral. The ball is actually passed with both hands. The fingers are lowered toward the ground as the arms swing back. On the forward arm swing, the fingers are raised up by bringing both wrists up at the same time. The ball is released as the wrists reach a plane parallel to the ground. The ball will now travel end-over-end. The ends of the ball will be reversing back toward the person who made the pass. (The ball will be turning on its short axis.)

The spirial pass is used most generally because the ball will travel much faster. The end-over-end pass is used when the receivers do not seem able to handle the spiral pass. In either case *the man to lateral the ball must remember to follow his arms and hands directly at the spot where he wants the ball to go.*

It is quite possible to lateral the ball by making a one-hand toss, as sometimes done by quarterbacks. This maneuver is executed by continuing the near hand on back after receiving the ball on the exchange. A large sure hand is needed to avoid fumbles. The advantage gained by this maneuver lies in giving the quarterback ample time to assist in leading interference downfield.

Coaching Tips

Problem	*Correction*
1. The pitch-out to the right is too poorly timed to be effective.	1. Check the foot movement of the quarterback—he may be stepping incorrectly after making the "dive" fake. On either the step-out or reverse-out maneuver, the quarterback can usually lateral more accurately by preceding the action with a "kick step." This movement is made by crossing the right foot behind the left foot. Such a motion allows the quarterback to get his full shoulder and trunk weight behind his pass without any mechanical interference. Check the pitch-out receiver—he may be moving on a path toward the line of scrimmage, rather than parallel to or away from it.
2. Lateral passes sometimes travel over the receiver's head.	2. Check the follow-through action of the quarterback—he may be allowing his hands and arms to follow up as the ball is being released, rather than extending his arms directly at the spot where he wants the ball to go.

Chapter 6

Fundamental Offensive Team Play (Line)

There are certain basic movements used by linemen for almost all offensive formations. In the next chapters, all the fundamental techniques of line and backfield play will be woven together into team offensive play.

FORMATION ALIGNMENTS

A clearer picture and understanding of fundamental offensive line play can be realized by a simple knowledge of basic line formations. A more detailed description of these alignments will be developed in later chapters. (See Fig. 6)

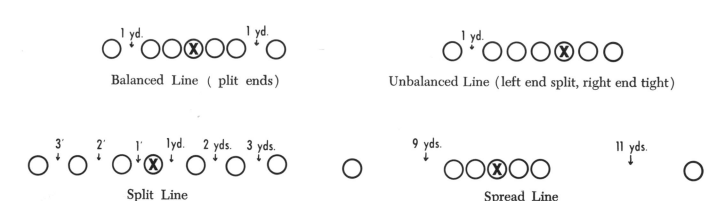

Figure 6. Line Formations

Offensive Line Maneuvers

The offensive line maneuvers of concern here are how to pull out of the line, how to trap block, how to double team block, and how to cross block.

Pulling Out of the Line

A primary task for guards, and sometimes centers and tackles, is to pull out of the line of scrimmage to trap block, or to lead interference on end runs. There are three methods of executing this pulling out maneuver: (1) the lead step; (2) the drop step; and (3) the cross-over.

Lead step. The lead step is used when the lineman must cover a considerable distance, which may consist of long trap blocks, or leading interference on end runs. Speed is fundamental to this particular movement. The lineman takes a short step with the near foot in the direction he wishes to go. If going to his right, the lineman steps laterally with his right foot. The man to the right of the pulling lineman should be out of the way by the time the pulling lineman takes his second step. This maneuver should take the lineman on a path parallel to and a foot or two behind the line of scrimmage. To speed up the movement and cause the trunk to turn rapidly, the near arm is snapped violently in the intended direction of movement. *Remember, the lineman lines up as usual and makes no preliminary movement of the head or eyes prior to the snap of the ball —this is known as pointing.*

Drop step. The drop step is used when the pulling lineman does not have a great distance to cover prior to making his block. This is the case in most trap blocks and in cross blocking. To carry out the maneuver, the lineman takes a step back with the near foot. At the same time, he turns his body in the direction in which he is to move. The first lateral step is now made with the foot that acted as a pivot in the drop step. *Remember, for deception the lineman must stay low in this maneuver.*

Cross-over. For a very agile lineman, this is probably the fastest method of pulling out. The offensive man pivots on the foot on the side to which he is going. At the same moment, he pushes off the extended arm. While still maintaining a low body position, he crosses over the pivoting foot with the other foot and is now facing down the line of scrimmage. *Remember, the lineman does not dip on the extended arm—he just pushes off.*

TRAP BLOCKING

A trap occurs when a defensive lineman is allowed to penetrate behind the offensive line. This man is then blocked laterally—usually by a man from the opposite side of the center. This block is effective especially against a hard charging defensive lineman; however, it can be used with considerable effectiveness against a lineman who has not continued his penetration. The diagram in Fig. 7 illustrates a typical trap block.

Figure 7. Trap Block

The usual step used for the trap blocker is the drop-step, previously described as a method of pulling out of the line. (See page 68) The trap blocker runs on a line directly to the place where the man to be trapped was on the scrimmage line. If the man is on the line of scrimmage, but turned to meet the trapper, the straight shoulder block is used. If the man is on all fours, as many linemen are taught when they meet no resistance in their peneration, the trap blocker smothers the defensive man by driving the knees under and into his side. The force of the contact should roll the defensive man over, or at least the offensive man will be on top of the defensive man, making him ineffective. If, as expected, the defensive man is continuing his penetration, the offensive man turns and uses a reverse body block. If the man has penetrated deep enough, the blocker simply turns and runs along side of him, shouldering the defensive man on toward the defensive goal line. *Remember, the trap blocker should always expect to find the defensive man at the line of scrimmage.*

Coaching Tips

Problem	Correction
1. When pulling out to lead end runs or off tackle plays, the guard penetrates too deeply into the offensive backfield.	1. If using the step-out method, check the force of the forearm drive—he may be causing the body weight to swing back instead of along the scrim-

Pulling left for Trap - (Refer to page 70)

Pulling right for Trap - (Refer to page 69)

Problem	*Correction*

mage line. If using the cross-over technique, check the swing over the pivot foot—he may be over-pivoting, causing the lineman to face the backfield.

2. Man to be trapped beats the blocker to the ball carrier.

2. Check the blocker's movement—he may be pausing after the drop-step to look for his opponent. Check the ball carrier—he may be too close to the scrimmage line.

3. Trap blocker runs past the man to be trapped.

3. Check second step of trap blocker—he may not be stepping at the spot of the hole at the scrimmage line, allowing the opponent to wait in the hole for the ball carrier. Check the drop-step—he may be so far back from the scrimmage line that it is impossible to make the second step correctly.

Post - Power Left   Post - Power Block - Left

Double Team Blocking - (See page 73)

Double Team Blocking

Double team blocking occurs when two offensive men block one defensive man simultaneously. An example of a double team block can be seen in the trap block diagrammed in Fig. 7. The defensive guard playing against the center is being double teamed. Two types of double team blocks are commonly used in modern football: (1) the high-low and (2) the post-power.

High-low. The offensive man nearest the direction in which it is desired to move the defensive man is known as the low blocker. His teammate is the high blocker. The low blocker has the duty of stopping the forward charge of the defensive man, pinning him at the point of contact. This is most effectively done by using a reverse cross body block with the head of the blocker in the direction away from the intended path of the ball carrier. A single leg block can be used effectively also, consisting of a body block across the leg of the defensive man who is away from the hole. *Remember, the low blocker does not go to the ground; he keeps the hips waist high.*

The high blocker uses a straight shoulder block about waist high on the defensive man by stepping with the near leg between the legs of the low blocker. The head of the blocker should be behind the defensive man. This will prevent the man from reversing out of the block. The low blocker primarily checks the onrush of the defensive man and "sets him up." The high blocker applies the power necessary to move the defensive man laterally and away from the play.

Post-power. Post-power blocking is very similar to high-low blocking, with the basic difference in the movement of the post blocker. The blocker nearest the direction it is desired to move the man is the post blocker. His main duty is to check the forward movement of the defensive man by driving the helmet straight into his crotch. It is, in reality, a shoulder block with the head's making contact first. The power blocker reacts the same as did the high blocker mentioned before. He will not be able to step between the legs of the post blocker, however, he must move on an angle that will bring him tight to his teammate, which will close the gap between the post and power blockers. Both blockers continue their charge, which will move the defensive man back and away from his original position.

Coaching Tips

Problem	*Correction*
1. Opponent splits double team apart.	1. Check post or low blocker—he may not be hitting directly into the middle of the opponent. Check the power or high blocker—he may be taking his first step away from the opponent.
2. Opponent driven straight back rather than laterally.	2. Check first step of each blocker—they should be stepping off on the same foot so that the driving power will not be of an antagonistic nature. Check post or low blocker—he should act as a pivot rather than use driving power.

Cross Blocking

Cross blocking occurs when two offensive men change their blocking assignments. Instead of blocking the man in front of them, they block the man in front of or near the teammate with whom they have changed assignments. (See Fig. 8)

Figure 8. Cross Block

The defensive man nearest to the offensive center usually is blocked first. In the example given in Fig. 8, the right tackle makes his block first. The rule followed by many coaches is that the defensive man nearest the path of the ball carrier is blocked first. The tackle in Fig. 8 uses a straight shoulder block or reverse body block. The right guard takes a short drop-step with his right foot and then steps directly at the defensive man with his left foot. If the tackle is fast enough, the guard can take a lateral step rather than a drop-step. To execute the right drop-step, the left foot acts as a semi-pivot foot. The guard now uses a straight shoulder block or a reverse body block, depending upon the depth of penetration by the defensive man.

Coaching Tips

Problem	*Correction*
1. First blocker screens off the second or cross blocker.	1. Check first man—he may not be driving after contact, leaving his legs and feet in the way; he may be too slow due to incorrect fundamentals. Check second man—he may not be taking correct first step, causing him to collide because of no delay.
2. First blocker does not get to his defensive man soon enough, allowing the man to tackle the ball carrier for a loss.	2. Check direction of first man—he may be heading for the place where the man was lined up, rather than where the initial step of the defensive man carried him.

Quick Trap

The cross block made between a guard and the center is referred to often as a quick trap. The change of assignment occurs as in any cross block, however the center usually makes his block first. The first man must step diagonally across the scrimmage line with his near foot and the second man (the trapper) also steps with his near foot. The step of the second man will be to the spot where the first man originally was stationed. The advantage of having the guards and tackles somewhat back of the center in their stance is obvious. (See Fig. 9.)

  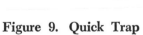 

Figure 9. Quick Trap

Chapter 7

Getting the Ball into Play

Certain basic procedures are used to start the team offense. The coach must have a terminology for the necessary intra-team communications. Numbering systems, signal systems, huddles, shifts, and starting counts are all basic to, and preliminary to, the start of team play. The coach must have a clear cut concept of his proposed team offense before he installs these preliminaries. It seems a good idea to discuss these aspects of team offense before actually investigating the various offenses available.

NUMBERING SYSTEMS

There are many different numbering systems in modern football. In the early days, the numbering of defensive holes was popular. Some coaches still use this technique; however, the modern swing to multiple and complex defensive patterns in general has resulted in the discontinuance of the defensive numbering system. The majority of modern numbering systems are based on the team offensive alignment.

Three concepts of numbering sequences are basic to the numbering systems employed. One concept numbers the holes in sequence from right to left, or from left to right, an idea used by teams that shift from a right to a left formation. The second theory assigns even numbers to holes on the right side of the center, and odd numbers to holes on the left side of the center, using zero for the hole directly over the center. Exponents of this theory believe that it is helpful to the team to know immediately in which direction the play is to develop. The third idea employs the same numbers for both sides of the line, but "right" or "left" designates the direction of the play. The proclaimed advantage of this system is that the team will have to learn only half as many play numbers. The system to be employed is a matter of individual preference, since all three systems are being used successfully. (See Fig. 10)

1 2 3 4 5 6 7 8 9

Left To Right

9 8 7 6 5 4 3 2 1

Right To Left

7 5 3 1 0 2 4 6 8

Even Right—Odd Left

1 2 3 4 5 6 7 8 9

Sequence "right"

9 8 7 6 5 4 3 2 1

Sequence "left"

Figure 10. Numbering Sequences

Numbering of offensive players. This system is very popular in modern football. A number is assigned to each offensive lineman. The number assigned to the end is really a zone number, covering the territory "over" the man and to his outside. When the quarterback calls a hole number, the man with that number knows that he has a primary blocking assignment, and that the play is to be run directly over his position. (See Fig. 11)

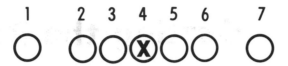

Figure 11. Numbering of Offensive Players Using Sequence System

Numbering of zones or lanes. Another numbering system frequently employed uses the idea of zones or lanes. Areas are numbered which cover the territory "over" a man and the "gap" to his side. An example would be the numbering of the lane provided by the distance from the outside shoulder of the guard to the outside shoulder of the tackle. In this system, a number is assigned to the area "over" the center. (See Fig. 12)

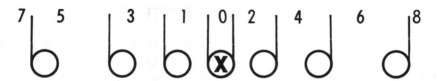

**Figure 12. Numbering of Offensive Lanes Using the Even Right—
Odd Left Number System**

The idea of numbering zones lends itself well to split lines, or to formations which constantly vary the line spacing. In these cases, the numbering of offensive linemen tends to become too confining. The coach may want the play to actually run outside or inside a particular lineman, not just over his position.

Signal Systems

A great variety of signal systems is now used in football. Some employ series of numbers, some words, and some combinations of numbers and words. Examples of these three systems will be given.

Number system. If two or more formations are to be used, coaches usually designate one formation as the "100 series." Other formations are "200," "300," and so on. Numbers from 10 to 19 designate a specific series. An example would be play 134. (See Fig. 13) This would mean that the "100 formation" would be used—in the example this is a balanced line box backfield. The ball is centered to the fullback. The fullback fakes to the left halfback and carries the ball into the the number 4 hole. The 80 to 89 series is usually reserved for pass plays. This system is adaptable particularly to multiple type offenses.

Another popular signal system employs groups of numbers. The first number designates the player who is to receive the ball from the center. The second number determines what backfield man is to carry the ball eventually. The third number indicates what hole the back is to "hit." An example of this system follows: Play number 2-4-1. (See Fig. 14) This means that the quarterback is to receive the ball from the center. The quarterback will give the ball to the left halfback, who will carry through the number 1 hole.

Some coaches prefer to have their teams given their signals while deployed in formation positions at the scrimmage line. This eliminates the more widely-used huddle system. To call numbers from this open forma-

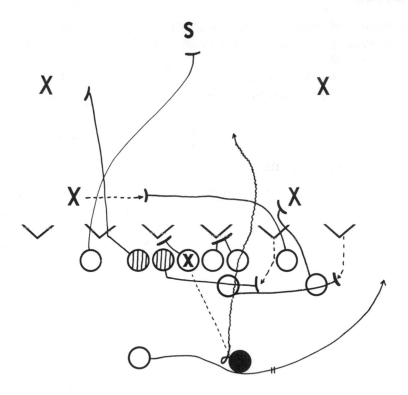

Figure 13. Play 134—Balanced Line Box Formation

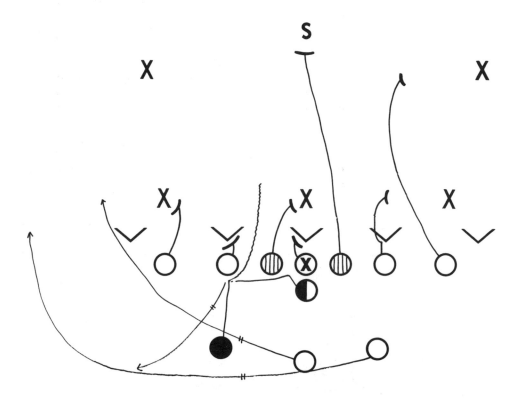

Figure 14. Play 2-4-1 T-Formation, Split Line

tion, there must be considerable disguise in order to confuse the defense. Usually a series of four numbers is used; however, as many as 10 or more series can be employed to "eat-up the clock." An example of this system is 642—344—521—384. As can be noted, this play is identical to the one previously given. The ball is centered to the quarterback, who gives it to the left halfback. The halfback carries the ball through the 1 hole. The ball is snapped on the third count. The placement of the key numbers can be changed at any time, and is frequently done at half time.

A major advantage of a number system is that the quarterback can change the entire play at the last moment. If, on arrival at the scrimmage line, he notices that the defense is so arranged as to forestall a gain by the pre-arranged play, he simply calls the numbers of a new play.

Word system. Some coaches prefer a word system for calling the plays, believing that this causes less confusion for the players. It is not necessary to remember any numbers under this system. The major disadvantage would be that this system could become too time-consuming in the huddle, unless relatively few plays were to be used. An example of this system is as follows: Pitch-out to left half around right end on four. This means a lateral will be made from the quarterback to the left halfback as he circles around right end. The ball will be snapped on the fourth number. This system sometimes uses special names to indicate favorite plays, for example the Sally Rand or the Brockport Special.

Combination of words and numbers. There are many combination signal systems. An example might be T- left half at 7 on 4, which would mean that the T-formation would be used, with the quarterback giving the ball to the left halfback. The back carries the ball through the 7 hole. The ball is snapped on the fourth count. Another variation would be 43-trap. In this variation the four back, or left halfback would carry the ball through the 3 hole. The line was to open the hole by means of trap blocking. As can be seen, any number of combinations can be devised.

The Huddle

Two huddle systems are currently popular: (1) the open huddle and (2) the closed huddle. The choice is a matter of preference. The only reason for the huddle is to have the offensive team hear their play assignments without "tipping off" the defense. Most teams huddle "on the ball" and 5 to 8 yards back of it. The center is responsible for selecting the spot of the huddle.

Open huddle. The open huddle was devised primarily to keep the team members from carrying on a conversation with the quarterback or other team members. An advantage of this system is that it gives the offensive team a chance to look at the defense and think of their particular assignments. The standard procedure is shown in Fig. 14.

In this huddle, all the players stand erect, or the front linemen have their hands on their knees. Some teams vary this open huddle by having all the team members face their own goal line with the quarterback facing them, the reverse of the huddle shown in Fig. 15.

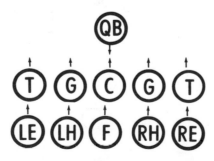

Figure 15. The Open Huddle

Closed huddle. The most popular closed huddle is shown in the diagram in Fig. 16. The advantage of the closed huddle is that it gives the team a chance to pass information on to the quarterback. In addition it gives the linemen a chance to decide on the particular blocking assignments they will use, which is especially valuable for teams that have the linemen select their own method of opening holes. This system prevents the team from revealing the direction of the play. Some players in the open huddle form the habit of immediately looking right at the men they are to block when the quarterback gives the play.

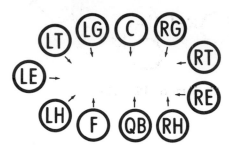

Figure 16.   The Closed Huddle

In this particular huddle, all players have their hands resting on their knees.

A variation of the closed huddle is shown in Fig. 17. The guards and left end have their hands on their knees. All the others stand erect. This system is particularly adaptable to the unbalanced line. The two guards can go to either side of the center after leaving the huddle.

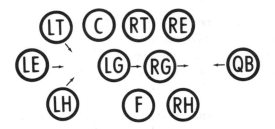

Figure 17.   Variation of the Closed Huddle

The Shift

Many teams line up in a straight T formation at the scrimmage line and then, at times, shift from this formation into a single wing formation, or some other variation of attack. The backfield shift is generally accomplished in three rhythmical movements. (This shift was highly popularized by the late Knute Rockne of Notre Dame University fame.) To maneuver the backfield to their own right, three steps are used. The first step is taken with the "lead" or right foot. The second step is taken with the left foot. The final step is actually a hop off the left foot, landing on both feet in the new position. The count used to teach this maneuver is "step," "step," "hop." Fig. 18 shows the shift of the backfield from the T-formation into the single wing formation.

The players can turn their bodies on the first step so that they are facing the new position, or can maintain a body position facing the line of scrimmage. If the latter system were to be used, the lateral movement would then consist of a side step (right foot), cross step (left foot), and the hop off of the left foot.

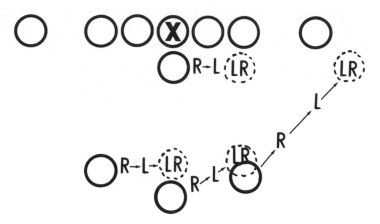

Figure 18. The Shift

The Starting Count

There are several variations of starting counts. As the team assumes its final offensive position, the players usually have their hands on their knees. Some coaches prefer, however, to have their players go right into their three point stances. If the team is not "down," the quarterback begins his starting count by numbers or words designed to move the team into the starting position. "Set down" and "Signals" are used popularly for this purpose.

The starting count can be in a rhythmical cadence or in a halting varied cadence. Most coaches prefer the rhythmical cadence, as it tends to keep the team together in their start. The rhythmical cadence is either a series of consecutive numbers or a combination of words and numbers. An example of the rhythmical cadence system is "Ready hike-one-two-three-four." The pause between the numbers called is identical. The ball is snapped on any one of the numbers as predetermined by the quarterback in the huddle.

Another technique for getting the ball into play by the rhythmical cadence system is to call a combination of word and number in each sequence. An example of this system would be "Signals— hut one— hut two— hut three— hut four" or "Ready— one and— two and— three and— four and." The ball can be snapped on any one of the "huts," "ands" or "numbers." Exponents of this system believe that the additional rhythm afforded by the combination of word and number enhances the uniform starting movement of the offensive team.

A major disadvantage of the very popular rhythmical cadence starting counts is that it can be as effective for the defensive team as the offensive team. The quarterback must be certain that he does not get into a "rut" by having the ball snapped repeatedly on the same word or number. There are a few coaches who prefer an uneven cadence. These coaches believe that such a system tends to give the advantage to the offensive team, as the defense must "guess" as to when the ball will be snapped. An example of the uneven cadence method is "Signals— pause, pause— one— pause, pause, pause— two— three— pause, four." Any variation can be used if there is adequate practice.

The desirable system to use for the starting count is the one that suits the purpose of the coach, and gets the team off without illegal or delayed starts. The starting count, though very important, is merely a device used to get the ball into play.

Automatics

Automatics are used to handle certain peculiar situations that sometimes occur in football, or to take advantage of certain defensive weaknesses. The team must drill in practice sessions so that they will react immediately, usually upon some pre-arranged signal, to the automatic play change.

In Fig. 19, two automatics are diagrammed. The first play is a standard running play against an odd defensive line that automatically has a change occur in several of the blocking assignments when the quarter-

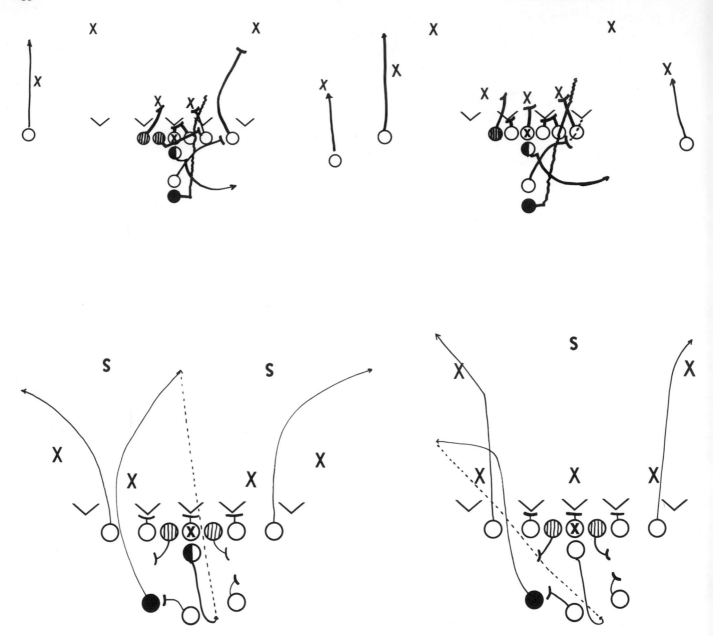

Figure 19. Automatic Plays

back calls out an even defense. In effect, there have been two plays designed, one for use against an odd defense and one for use against an even defense. The final call of the quarterback determines which of the plays will be executed. This automatic is used to avoid the mass confusion and inherent weakness of the called play, which was strong in arrangement against one particular defense but weak against another.

The second diagrammed play in Fig. 18 is a pass play that was designed originally for use against a four-two defensive backfield alignment, or any defensive alignment that did not utilize a single safety man. When this standard defensive alignment does occur, the play switches automatically to the alternate play as diagrammed.

Check Signals or Play Changes

As pointed out before, situations frequently arise during the course of a football game when it is desirable to change, at the line of scrimmage, the play originally called in the huddle. These check signals are different from the automatic plays in that they can be used at any time to change any play as desired by the quarterback. This is the audible system of signal changing. An example of a good time to change signals might be against an over-shift of the defensive alignment with excessive concentration at one defensive spot, the spot where the quarterback had decided to launch his attack. This arrangement should be available also to take care of the improper spacing of the defensive alignment, possibly due to personal carelessness. The quarterback should be in a position to take advantage of these situations.

There is a multitude of techniques for calling checks. One method is to have the quarterback simply call out "check" before the starting count is given. The quarterback then gives the team a new play. This is one reason why some coaches like to have all of their plays numbered. The check call can be of course a fictitious call, with the quarterback merely repeating the play he called in the huddle.

Another technique used to change a play is designed merely to change the spot on the line of scrimmage where the ball carrier will attack. An example of this method would be to have the quarterback call out "in one" or "out one." This would indicate to the team that the ball carrier was to carry the ball through one hole nearer or farther away from the center than originally planned.

Still another popular technique is the use of "key" colors. A certain color, let us say red, is selected by the coaches as the "key" color for a particular game. When the quarterback calls this color at the line of scrimmage, the next number or series of numbers indicates a new play. The "key" color simply cancels out the play given in the huddle. With red as our "key" color, the quarterback might say, prior to the starting count, "Red— 24," meaning that play number 24 will be run in place of the one given in the huddle. Any announced color other than the pre-selected "key" color acts only as a blind, and has no effect upon the originally called play.

Many techniques can be thought of to handle the play change possibility at the line of scrimmage. The important thing to realize is that a device of this type will afford considerable flexibility to your offensive attack.

The Quick Play

At times it is desirable to upset the defense by having the offensive team put the ball into play one second after they have arrived at the scrimmage line. When not used too often, this has the element of surprise, and frequently catches the defense out of balance. Thus the team that comes to the scrimmage line in one offensive alignment and then shifts into another could have the ball snapped on the call of "shift" occasionally to catch the defense unprepared.

There is a tendency on the part of many modern football coaches to utilize this technique on every play. This style has been variously termed, but it is most recently referred to as "race horse football." To develop this style of attack, the ball is always snapped on the first count after the mandatory one second stationary position at the scrimmage line.

The advantage of this type of play is that the team can run many more plays per game. True "race horse football" has the offensive players running back to their huddle the moment the official's whistle has declared the ball dead or the play completed. The play signal is given rapidly in the huddle and the team runs up to the scrimmage line. Obviously, the "boys" must be very well conditioned physically and highly trained mentally for this style of play, physically to decrease the possibility of sloppy play due to tiredness, and mentally to keep the offensive team from violating the mandatory one second stationary offensive position, prior to putting the ball into play. The players must have almost instantaneous play recall as the signal is given: there isn't much time to think over play assignments. (This is something to strive for irrespective of the style of attack strategy to be used, but something that really causes a headache to many coaches.)

Chapter 8

Popularly Used Offenses

A discussion of some of the major strengths and weaknesses of popularly used offenses may prove valuable as an aid to the final selection of the coach's team offense. There are many offensive variations and combinations used in modern football, almost all derived from a few standard offensive patterns. This section will preview some of the more popularly used standard offenses. Chapters 9 and 10 will give specific analyses of the total team offensive play.

SINGLE WING FORMATION

The single wing formation derives its name from the fact that one halfback is set in a flank or wing position. Prior to the rule change which allowed a pass to be made from any point up to the line of scrimmage, the single wing was the most popular formation. The single wing formation still is used by many outstanding teams. It has been modernized by adapting some of the T-formation explosive philosophy.

The primary strength of the single wing lies in the potential running power to the strong or wing side. It also affords excellent deception in its spinning attack possibilities. A strong short passing attack blends

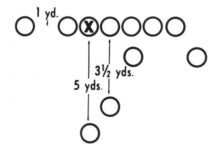

Unbalanced Single Wing

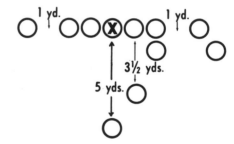

Balanced Single Wing

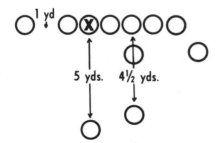

Unbalanced Box Single Wing

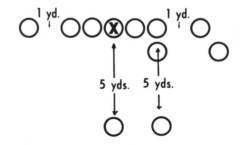

Balanced Box Single Wing

Figure 20.   Standard Single Wing Formations

itself very well with this offensive formation, due to the availability of four eligible receivers. Powerful two-on-one blocking techniques are frequently used in the running offense together with trap blocking. Fig. 20 shows standard single wing formations. This single wing formation is considered to be a possession type offense with short but consistent gains the rule in place of the long explosive runs.

A primary weakness of the single wing formation illustrated is that the weak side attack is very apt to be just that—weak. As a result, coaches have developed many alignment variations in attempts to strengthen the weak side attack. Unfortunately these variations tend to remove some of the potential strength of the strong side attack. Fig. 21 shows attempts made to increase the potentialities of the single wing formation.

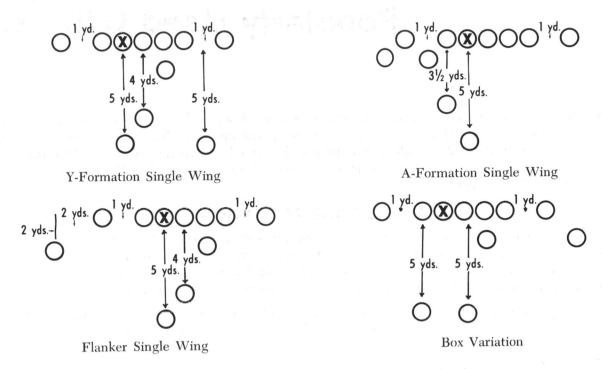

Figure 21. Single Wing Formation Variations

Backfield requirements are fairly rigid in the single wing formation. Two strong blockers are needed—one as the wing back, and the other as the quarterback, who is known as the blocking back. The fullback, or spinning back, must be a power runner for a successful inside attack. The tailback, or left halfback, must be extremely versatile since he has triple responsibilities—running speed for sweeps, passing ability, and punting ability. In actuality the key back in the successful operation of this attack is the tailback.

Line requirements also are fairly well defined. The center should be a big strong man who can center with accuracy to deep backs. He must be mobile, as he is in a relatively poor blocking stance. The guards need mobility and speed. They have the task of leading wide end run plays. The tackles must be big, and fast enough to fill the gaps left by the guards. The ends must be rugged individuals. Their primary task lies in their responsibility for blocking tackles alone, or in combination with the wing back.

Personnel requirements for the single wing are quite demanding if the standard single wing power offense is to be used; however, teams have adapted T-formation type man-for-man blocks to the single wing alignment. Quickness of movement now becomes the major line personnel requirement.

A major value of the single wing today is that it is not too frequently used, as compared with the T-formations. As a consequence, many teams do not know how to defend against its power. The contact resulting from the powerful traps and double teams is usually more severe than that of the T-formation. In addition, the fact that the interference leads the ball carrier, rather meets him downfield, makes this offense a rugged and difficult one against which to defend.

There are six basic series of plays in the single wing offense:

1. The ball is passed to the tailback, who drives directly into the line or sweeps the ends without any preliminary fake.

2. The ball is passed to the tailback who fakes or gives to the wingback. (A recent adaptation of the so-called "belly" or "drive" series has been used in the single wing offense by placing the tailback a step in front of the fullback and one step to his left. The tailback receives the ball from center and then "rides" the fullback. The fullback then either carries the ball into the line, or continues on his fake with the tailback carrying the ball off tackle or around the end.)

3. The ball is passed to the fullback, who hits the line in a power sequence or gives the ball to the quarterback on the "buck lateral" series.

4. The ball is passed to the fullback, who spins and fakes or gives to the tailback.

5. The ball is passed to the fullback, who fakes or gives to either the tailback or the wingback.

6. The ball is passed to the fullback, who fakes or gives to the wingback.

Key Running Plays—Unbalanced Single Wing

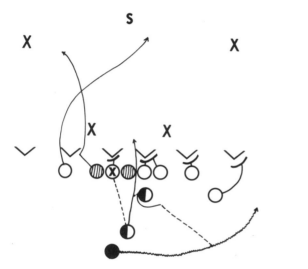
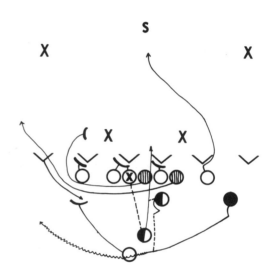

Figure 22. Buck Lateral

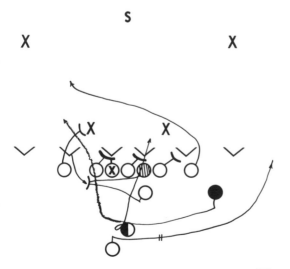
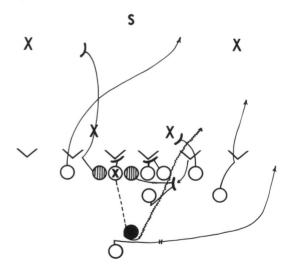

Figure 23. Fullback Spinner

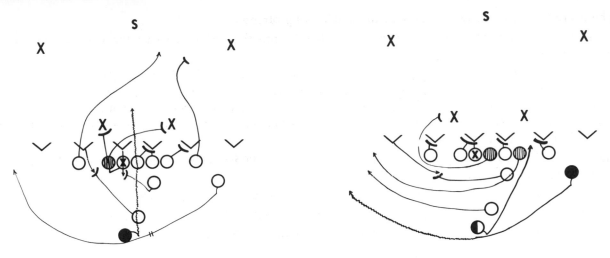

Figure 24. Tailback Spinner

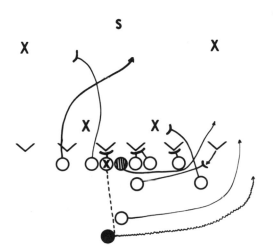

Figure 25. End Sweep

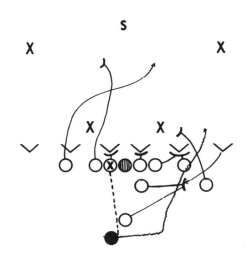

Figure 26. Cutback

Key Pass Plays—Unbalanced Single Wing

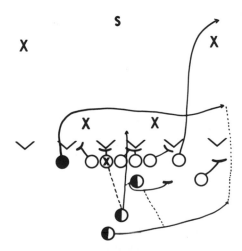

Figure 27. Buck Lateral Pass

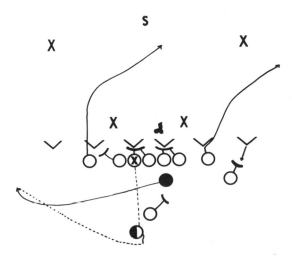

Figure 28. Flair Pass

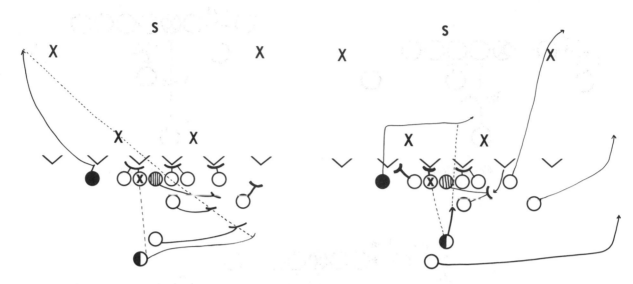

Figure 29.   Delayed Pass   Figure 30.   Buck Jump Pass

DOUBLE WING FORMATION

The double wing formation is really an attempt to improve upon the single wing formation. The credit for the origination of this style of offensive play goes to Glenn (Pop) Warner of coaching fame. Coach Andy Kerr increased the popularity of the double wing formation while at Colgate University.

Warner developed the double wing out of an effort to produce power to the short side. Most teams defended the unbalanced single wing by over-shifting to the strong side. Warner decided that by placing the tailback as a flanker to the left he could have his team hit with power in either direction.

The original double wing formation was the close formation called the "A" formation. This formation has a tight, unbalanced line, and the formation is compact. The "A" formation possesses much straight-ahead bucking power because the fullback is in relatively the same position as in the single wing. The basic play of the double wing is the reverse play, with the fullback giving the ball to either wing back. From the reverse plays as bases, spin plays or fake reverse plays are used. The forward passing attack from this formation is very deceptive, and features reverse passes and spin passes which carry the threat of a running play.

The "A" formation was expanded to the "B" and the "C" formations. In the "B" formation, the triple threat back was moved from the left wing position to a position about 5 yards behind the center. The quarterback took the left wing position. The left end was split about 1 yard to put him in position to get downfield on passes. The "C" formation was similar to the "B" formation except that both ends were split, and sometimes the wingbacks were widened. This was done until the formation actually became a spread formation as popularly used in the "deep south." (See Fig. 31)

Three distinct series of plays are used in the double wing. One series has the fullback either give the ball to the left wing, fake to him and keep the ball, or hand-off to the right wing. The second cycle involves the fullback's either faking to the right wing or giving the ball to him. The third sequence is based on straight bucks, and features lateral passes around the ends.

The success of the double wing running plays depends upon good deception by the fullback and wingbacks. They must all be good actors and fakers. Good ball handling is absolutely essential. It is evident that intelligent, sustained blocking is vital to the efficiency of these plays.

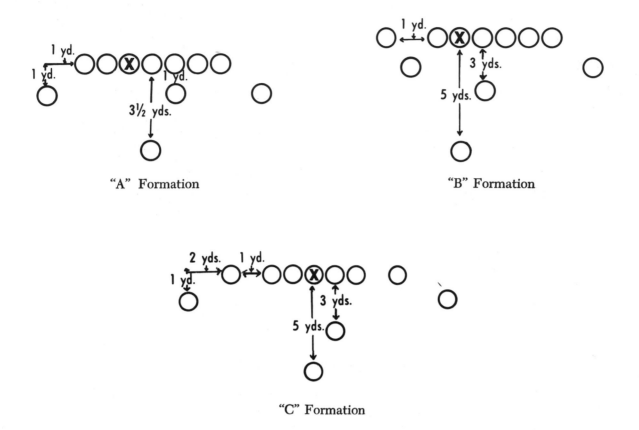

"A" Formation

"B" Formation

"C" Formation

Figure 31. Double Wing Formations

Key Running Plays—Double Wing Formation

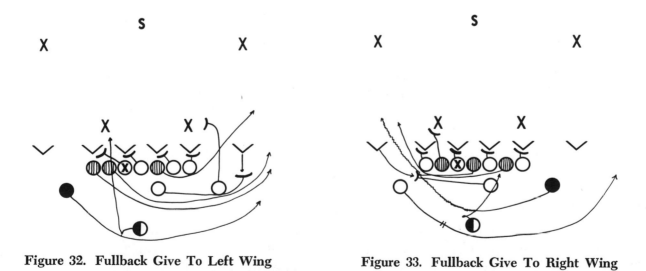

Figure 32. Fullback Give To Left Wing   Figure 33. Fullback Give To Right Wing

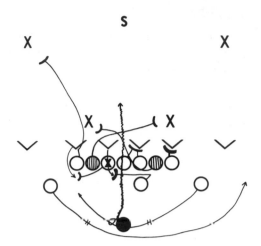

Figure 34.   Fullback Double Fake and Keep

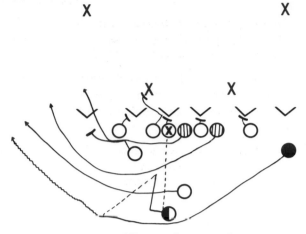

Figure 35.   Buck Lateral

Key Pass Plays—Double Wing Formation

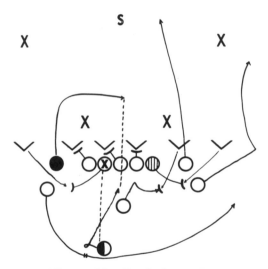

Figure 36.   Buck Jump Pass

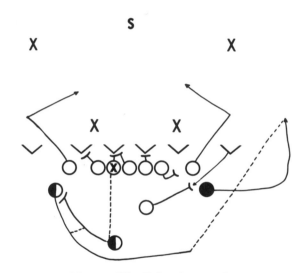

Figure 37.   Fake Sweep Pass

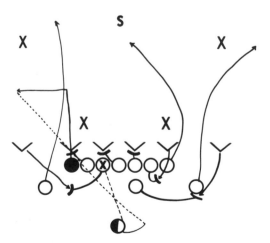

Figure 38.   Sideline Cut Pass

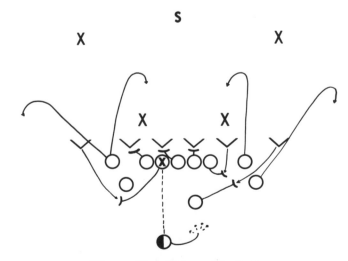

Figure 39.   Button Hook Pass

SHORT PUNT FORMATION

Another attempt to increase the weak side efficiency of the single wing formation was the short punt formation. The short punt derives its name from the fact that it is a modification of the deep punt formation. The deep punt formation is still used, but primarily as a regular punting formation.

The location of the backfield personnel makes the outside running attack relatively weak. The inside attack is, however, very strong and deceptive. It is an excellent passing and quick kick formation. The pass and punt protection are strong, and the pass receivers are located so as to be readily available for downfield maneuvers.

This formation, like the single wing, requires a triple threat tailback. The semi-wing backs must be very fast runners. The fullback must be a power runner. The tackles should be big and strong, as well as mobile, to carry out their heavy blocking assignments.

The primary plays develop from direct passes to the tailback or the fullback. The fullback also executes spinner type plays, giving or faking to the tailback and left wingback. (See Fig. 40)

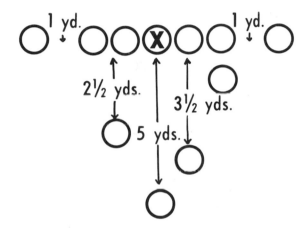

Figure 40. Short Punt Formation

Key Running Plays—Short Punt Formation

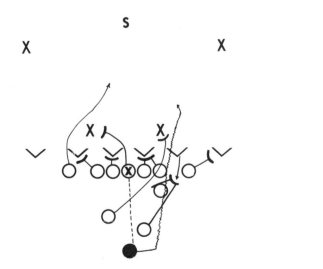

Figure 41. Tailback Inside Tackle

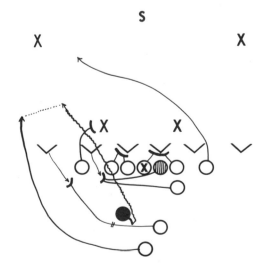

Figure 42. Quarterback Inside Tackle

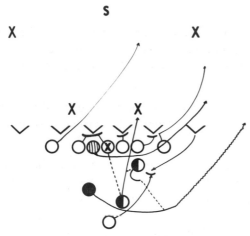

Figure 43. Buck Lateral

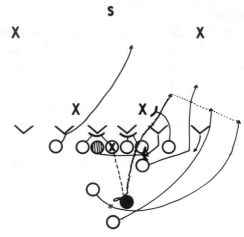

Figure 44. Fullback Inside Tackle

Key Pass Plays—Short Punt Formation

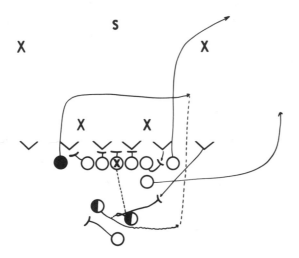

Figure 45. Running Pass

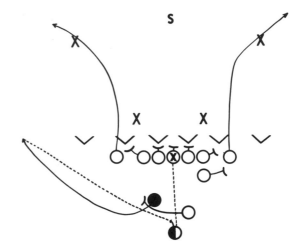

Figure 46. Flair Pass

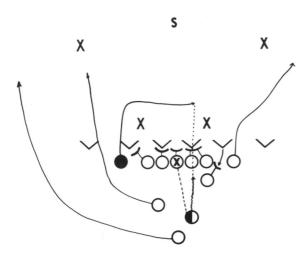

Figure 47. Buck Jump Pass

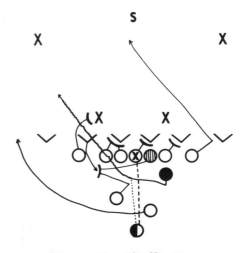

Figure 48. Shuffle Pass

T-Formation

In the early 1940's, a rule change was made for the passer in football. Prior to this change, the passer had to be at least 5 yards behind the line of scrimmage before he could pass legally. The new rule allowed the passer to be anywhere behind the line of scrimmage when executing his pass. This simple change caused a revolution in offensive football strategy.

In the early years of American style football, a T-formation was used. This play was generally discontinued when the power-packed single wing offense came into vogue. The original T-formation was handicapped seriously by the passing rule then in effect.

George Halas, Chicago Bears, and Clark Shaughnessy, Stanford University, were two of the first coaches to revert back to the old T-formation. The added threat of a quarterback who could pass from any point behind the line of scrimmage greatly increased the effectiveness of the offense. As a result of the use of the T-formation, Stanford moved into national prominence at the collegiate level, and the Chicago Bears set a new scoring record of 72-0 in the professional champion play-off game. Army added the last necessary push to full acceptance of this style of play with "Doc" Blanchard, Mr. Inside, and Glenn Davis, Mr. Outside. The T-fever swept the country at all levels of football competition.

Tight-T Formation

The tight-T formation uses a balanced line with the ends split about 1 yard from the tackles. The quarterback is up close to the center in a position to receive a direct hand pass from him. The fullback is lined up directly behind the quarterback, about 4½ yards from the scrimmage line. The two halfbacks are lined up parallel, arm's length from the fullback's extended hand, and about 4 yards from the scrimmage line. (See Fig. 49)

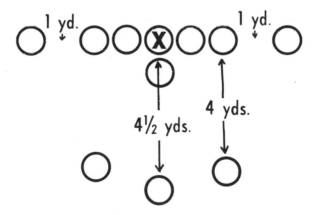

Figure 49.   Tight-T Formation

Major advantages of this tight-T formation are: (1) the center becomes a more effective blocker; (2) the passing game is faster in execution; (3) the running game is stronger because of the ball handling deception and the speed with which the attack takes place; and (4) man-for-man blocking is used because of the speed of the runnning attack. To increase the effectiveness of the offense, teams employed man-in-motion and flanker variations. The outside attack was greatly increased by placing these flanker men outside of the end they were to block.

Obvious disadvantages are that the quarterbacks must be an outstanding performer with good ball handling deception, running ability, and passing ability. In addition the linemen must be able to handle man-for-man blocking assignments. The three deep backs must be powerful inside runners and fast outside runners.

As pointed out in an earlier section, the T-offense, like all other offenses, depends for its success upon the sequence of inside and off-tackle power, together with end run speed. Not until the defensive maneuvers of opponents began stopping this sequence of plays were all the subsequent plays added. These three, together with the quarterback sneak, were, and still are, the"bread-and-butter" plays of this offense.

Key Running Plays—Tight-T Formation

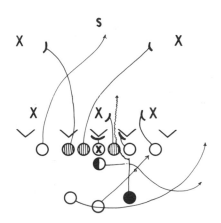

Figure 50.   Dive Right

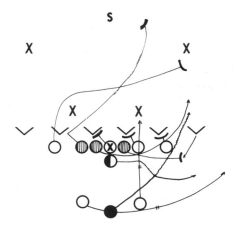

Figure 51.   Fullback Off-Tackle

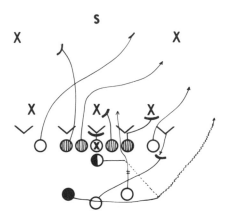

Figure 52.   Pitch-out Right

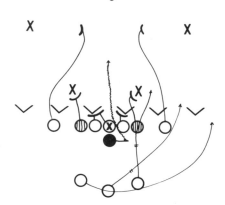

Figure 53.   Quarterback Sneak

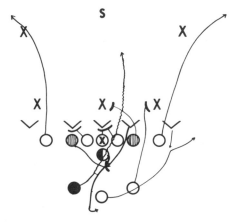

Figure 54.   Deep Trap Play

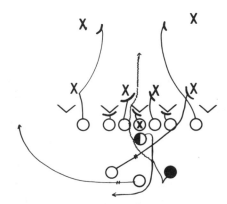

Figure 55.   Cross Buck

Key Pass Plays—Tight-T Formation

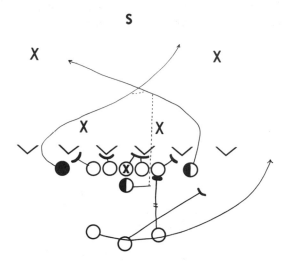

Figure 56.   Quick Pass to End

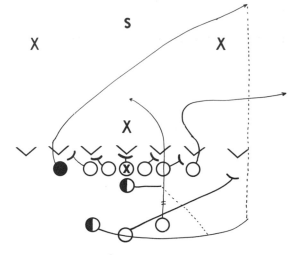

Figure 57.   Pitch-out Pass

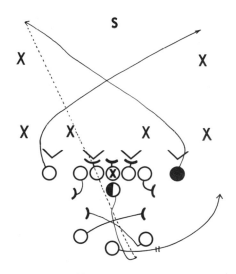

Figure 58.   Criss-cross Pass

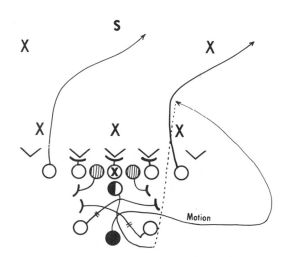

Figure 59.   Man-in-motion Pass

Winged-T Formation

The winged-T formation is an outgrowth of the standard tight-T formation. It is an effort to utilize single wing blocking in the T-offense without losing the effectiveness of the quick hitting T-attack. Actually, the winged-T was devised after the man-in-motion and flanker attack. Some coaches, wishing to use the man-in-motion concept in addition to single wing type blocking, decided that it would save practice time devoted to man-in-motion split timing by simply placing the man-in-motion in a set wing position. The wing man is employed in the same fashion as he was in the single wing offense. The winged-T formation thus is able to utilize single wing double team and trap blocking with the quick opening attack of the T.

Teams have used this variation of the T-formation profitably when man-for-man blocking was not successful. Another advantage lies in the fact that a third pass receiver is strategically located for rapid downfield maneuvering. The wing-T can be run with either a balanced or unbalanced line, and line splits can be adapted effectively to this attack. (See Fig. 60)

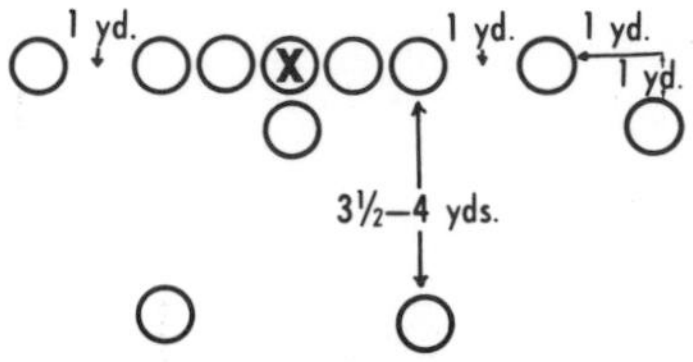

Balanced Winged-T 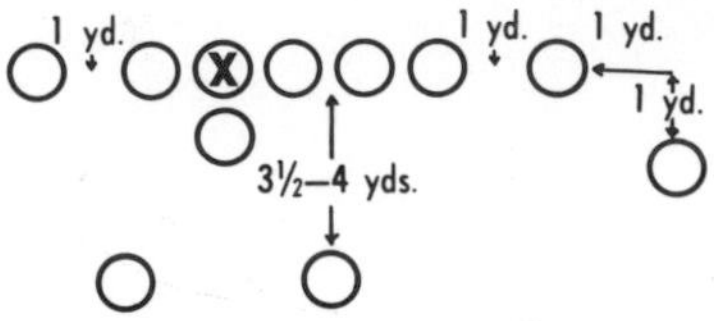   Unbalanced Winged-T

Figure 60. Winged-T Formation

Key Running Plays—Winged-T Formation

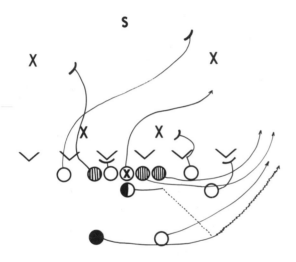

Figure 61. Pitch-out

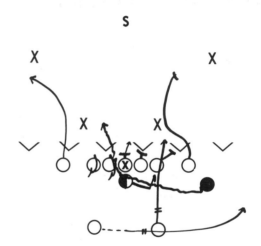

Figure 62. Scissor

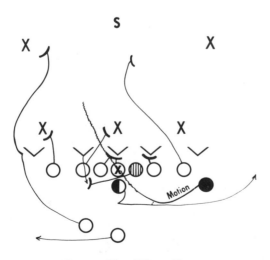

Figure 63. Wing Power

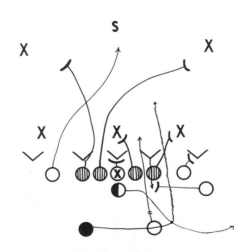

Figure 64. Wing Trap

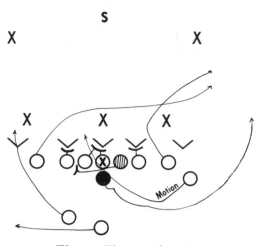

Figure 65. Bootleg Play

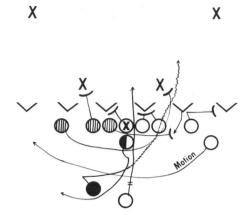

Figure 66. Counter Play

Key Pass Plays—Winged-T Formation

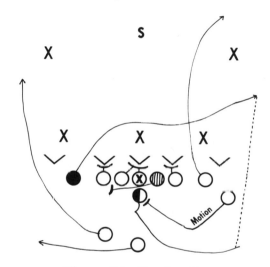

Figure 67. Bootleg Pass

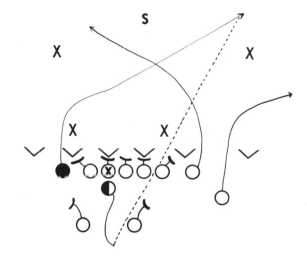

Figure 68. Criss-cross Pass

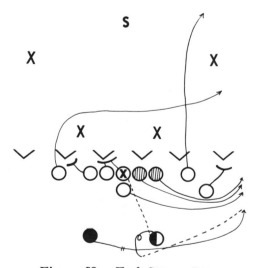

Figure 69. End Sweep Pass

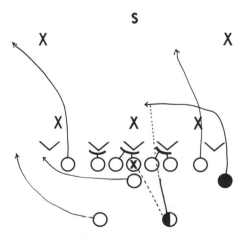

Figure 70. Buck Jump Pass

Slot-T Formation

A variation of the winged-T formation that uses split ends and a wing back is known as the Slot-T formation. Either or both ends split from their respective tackles a distance from 1 to 9 yards. The wing or slot man plays on either side between the end and the tackle and 1 yard off the scrimmage line. (See Fig. 71)

The advantages of this personnel placement results in extreme pressure on the defensive team. The basic concept of the winged-T attack is maintained, and, the ends are in strategic pass receiving positions. It becomes almost impossible to contain the ends at the scrimmage line. As a consequence, the defense will find it quite impractical to use a 9-man front defensive alignment. (See page 180) By splitting the ends an abnormal distance from the tackles, the defense must spread out their protective pattern. The effect of the pressure upon the defensive protective strategy will tend to increase the running potential of the slot-T offense. If the defense spreads to increase their pass protection, they automatically decrease in running defense efficiency and vice versa.

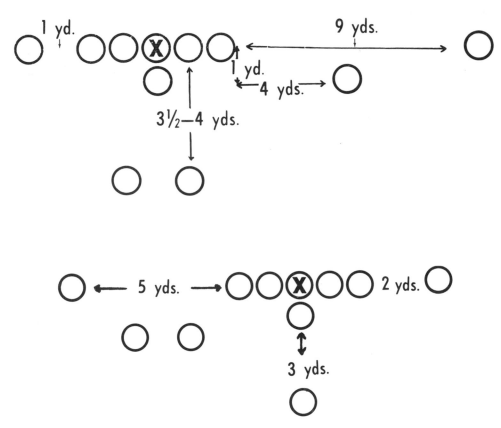

Figure 71. Slot-T Formation (Some variations)

Split-T Formation

Don Faurot at the University of Missouri first introduced the split-T formation in 1941. The success of this formation was immediate. The Missouri team led the nation in net rushing yards per game with an average of 307 yards. Faurot used this offense while coach of the Iowa Navy Pre-Flight team, and set a new rushing record of 324.4 yards per game. "Bud" Wilkinson, of Oklahoma University fame, and Jim Tatum, of Maryland University fame, continued to alert coaches to the tremendous running potential of this formation.

The original idea of the split-T offense was to compensate for the lack of a talented triple threat back. The T-formation was employed, using a split line and a running quarterback. The line split was varied according to the defensive alignment. The specific distances varied between 1 and 4 feet. By spreading the line, the defense had to widen. This increased the blocking angles for the offensive linemen and made their assignments easier to perform.

The success of this style of offensive play depends to a large extent upon the faking and running ability of the quarterback. The quarterback carries the ball on two of the four "bread-and-butter" plays: the quarterback sneak, and the off-tackle keep play. The basic difference in this offense is the path of the quarterback. The split-T quarterback operates up and down the line parallel to the line of scrimmage. He stays within 1 yard of the scrimmage line, which permits a faster hitting hand-off play than that of other T-formations. The pressure on the defense is strong, as they do not have time to diagnose more than one of the basic plays. The passing attack in the original split-T formation was very limited. The primary pass play was, and still is, the end run option pass.

To operate the split-T offense effectively, the linemen must be highly mobile and fast. Speed is essential in all 11 positions. The linemen must be able to handle man-for-man blocking against opponents who have considerable room to maneuver. The halfbacks need straight ahead drive power and outside running speed. The fullback is essentially a blocker who must be able to block the defensive ends in or out.

The primary advantage of the split-T lies in the simplicity of its play patterns. The formation alignment allows the same plays to be run in either direction, thus the number of plays is greatly reduced. A coach can concentrate on the three basic plays to each side and the quarterback sneak. This will allow adequate time to teach these plays against all possible defensive variations, and the team should be ready for any defense from the first game on. (See Fig. 72)

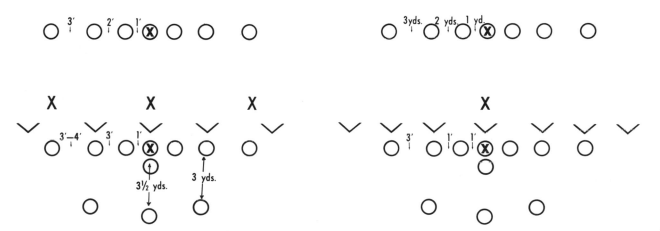

Figure 72. Split-T Formation Variations

Key Running Plays—Split-T Formation

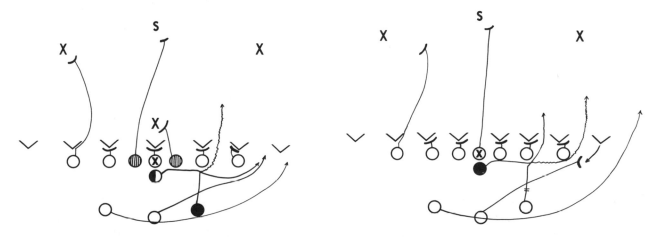

Figure 73. Dive Right Play   Figure 74. Quarterback Keep Play

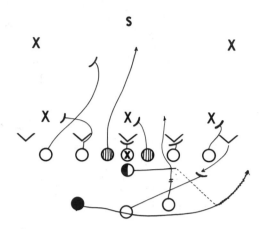

Figure 75.   End Run Play

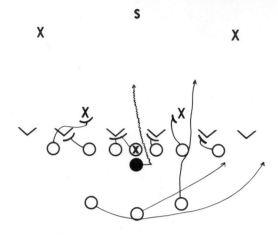

Figure 76.   Quarterback Sneak Play

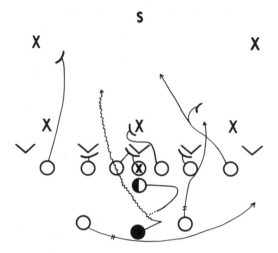

Figure 77.   Fullback Counter

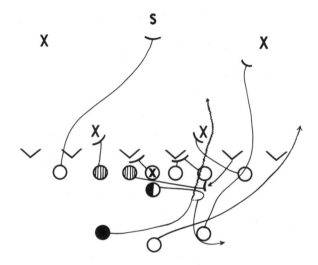

Figure 78.   Trap Play

Key Pass Plays—Split-T Formation

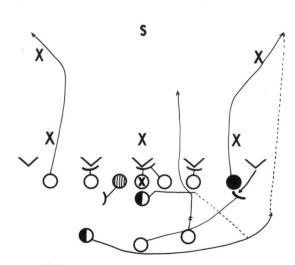

Figure 79.   Deep Running Pass

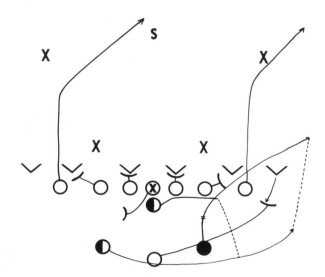

Figure 80. Flat Running Pass

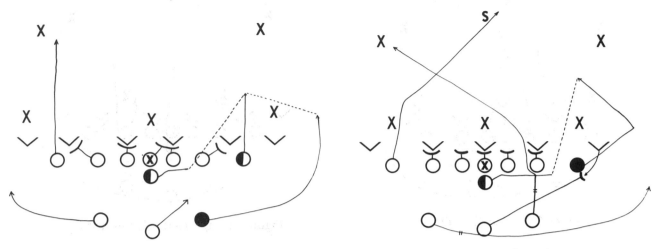

Figure 81. Quick Pass   Figure 82. Fake Dive Pass

Tandem-T Formation

The tandem-T formation is a combination of the quick hitting attack of the T-formation and the power of the single wing attack. The offense usually is run from a balanced line with normal single wing backfield alignment. The quarterback is aligned behind the center, but slightly to his left. The right halfback is aligned behind the outside leg of the right tackle and is facing toward the defensive left guard. The fullback is aligned in the regular single wing position, but he is facing directly at the center. The left halfback is in the standard single wing position. (See Fig 83)

The primary disadvantage of this attack is that the outside strength is weak to either side, and the weak side attack is not very strong. The inside attack can be explosive or delayed with double team and trap blocking. The passing potential from this formation is good. Three receivers can move immediately into the downfield territory and the pass protection is strong.

This offense has excellent possibilities, providing the personnel is suited to this style. The right halfback must be an excellent blocker and pass receiver. The fullback must be a single wing type power runner. The left halfback must have straight-ahead power and outside running speed. The quarterback must be a strong blocker and good passer. The ends must be able to handle heavy blocking assignments, as well as pass receiving duties.

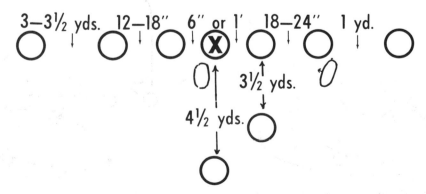

Figure 83. Tandem-T Formation

Key Running Plays—Tandem-T Formation

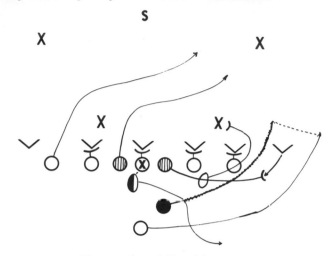

Figure 84. Off-tackle Power

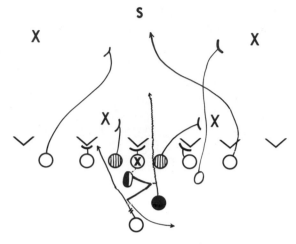

Figure 85. Fullback Quick Opener

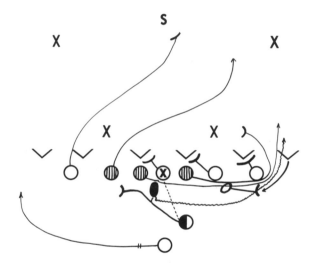

Figure 86. Quarterback Off-tackle

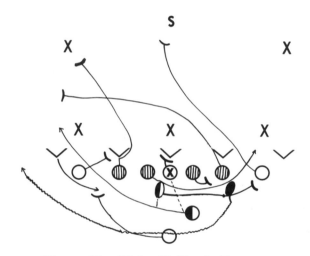

Figure 87. Right Halfback Reverse

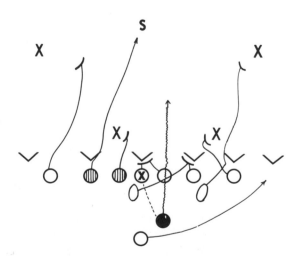

Figure 88. Fullback Power

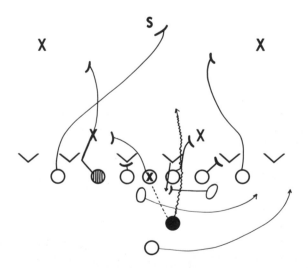

Figure 89. Wing Trap

Key Pass Plays—Tandem-T Formation

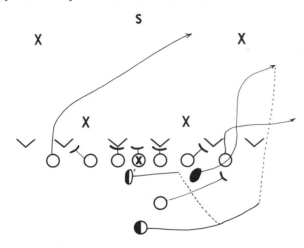

Figure 90. Running Pass

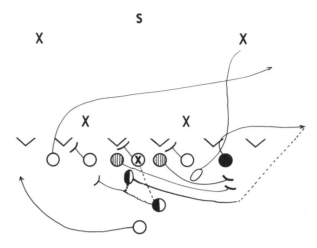

Figure 91. Running Pass

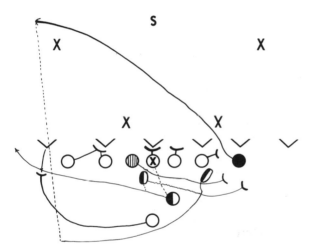

Figure 92. Reverse Pass

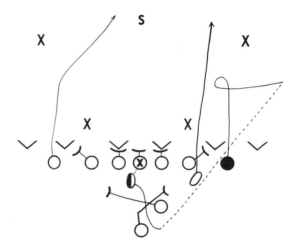

Figure 93. Sideline Cut Pass

Double Winged T

A recent concept of the T-formation is the combination of the T with the double wing formation. The ends can be split or tight. The backfield all can be in flanker positions or the fullback can be left behind the quarterback. The particular alignment used will depend upon the offensive strength desired.

The outside and off tackle attack is strengthened by the use of the man-in-motion. The inside attack is run with a fullback in the standard deep back position. To be highly effective, this offense demands the services of an excellent passer. The primary purpose of the flanked backfield is to increase the effectiveness of the passing attack. (See Fig. 94)

The double winged T (see the T.C.U. Spread also) was adjusted into a "shot-gun" formation by placing the quarterback into a deep single wing tailback position and moving the fullback into a slot position. This is a pass formation used when the defensive pass rush does not allow the passer ample time to "drop back" and an obvious passing situation prevails.

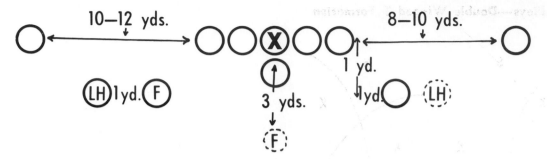

Figure 94. Double Winged T Formation

Key Running Plays—Double Winged T Formation

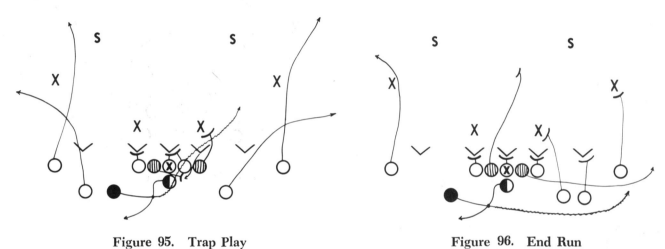

Figure 95. Trap Play

Figure 96. End Run

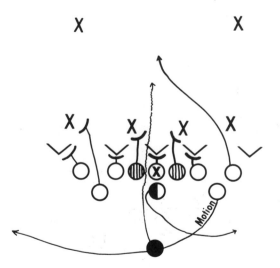

Figure 97. Fullback Power

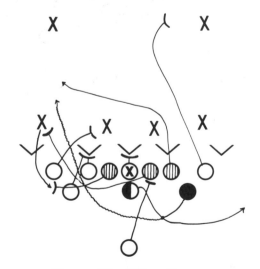

Figure 98. Wing Reverse

Key Pass Plays—Double Winged T Formation

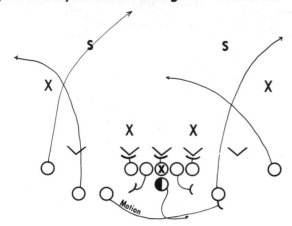

Figure 99. Four Out Pass

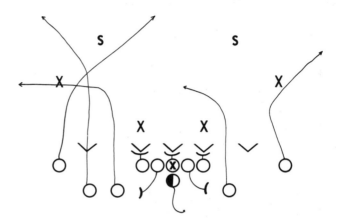

Figure 100. Five Out Pass

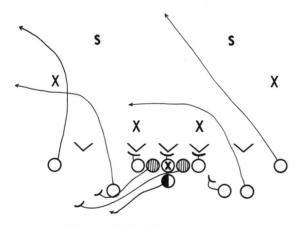

Figure 101. Running Pass

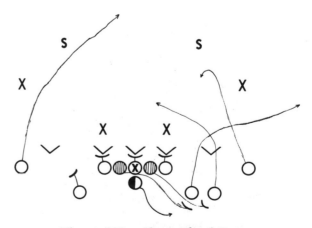

Figure 102. Short Flood Pass

I Formation

A variation of the T formation that incorporates the running power of the traditional T and the passing threat of the pro style of play was devised by John McCay at University of Southern California. A quality quarterback and powerful, fast fullback are needed to execute properly this USC offensive concept.

The deep back uses the upright stance while the up back is in the traditional three point position. The deep back is sent in motion (fly) often to put added pressure on the defense. This gives much of the effectiveness of the slot, winged, or flankered set positions without the defense knowing the immediate side the man is going to. Three standard backfield "sets" are used, with some variations made in peculiar instances or by particular coaches. (See Fig. 103)

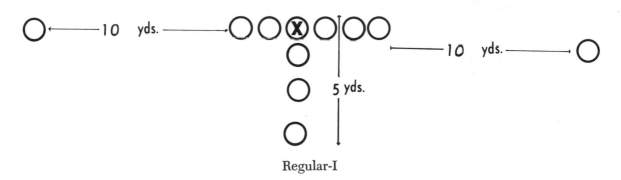

Regular-I

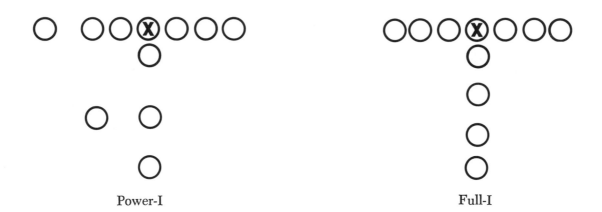

Power-I   Full-I

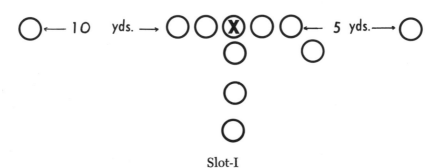

Slot-I

Figure 103. I Formation

Key Running Plays—I-Formation

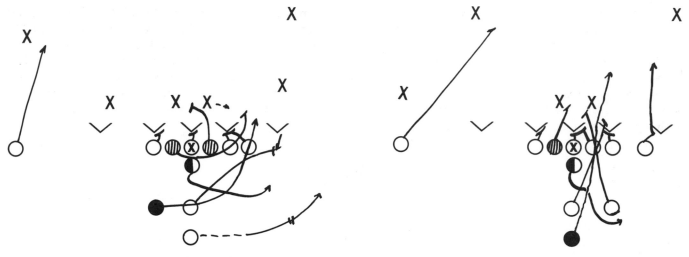

Figure 104. Off Tackle

Figure 105. Power

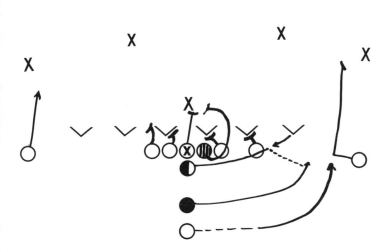

Figure 106. Option

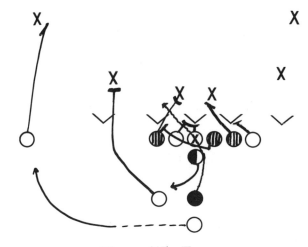

Figure 107. Trap

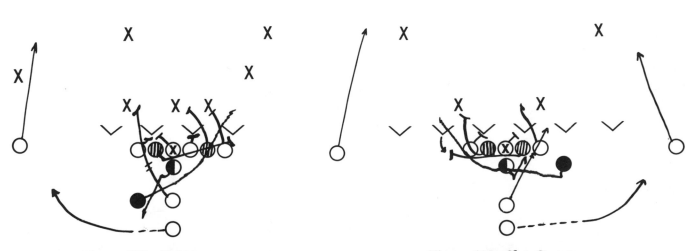

Figure 108. Counter

Figure 109. Slot Counter

Key Pass Plays—I-Formation

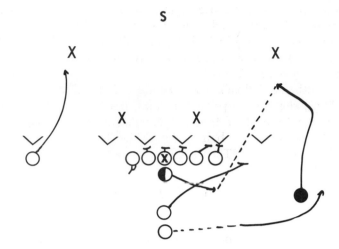

Figure 110. Option Pass

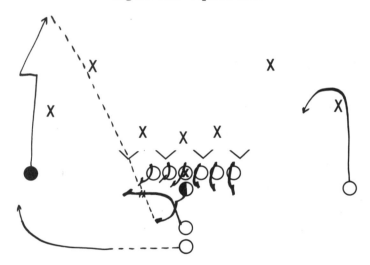

Figure 111. Deep Pass

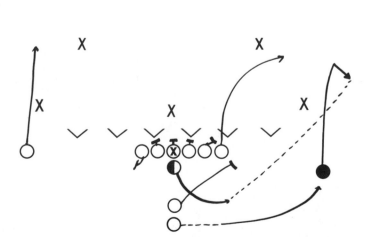

Figure 112. Overload Pass

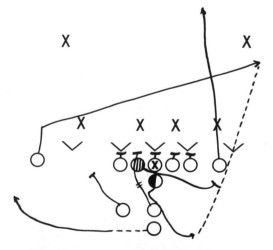

Figure 113. Waggle or Throwback

Y or Wishbone-T

A rather recent innovation in T type offense alignment has been made popular by Daryl Royal of Texas University. The offense alignment is particularly suited to a powerful, quick fullback. It is upon the ability of this man that most of the success of the attack depends, a factor that is characteristic of many offenses. By moving the fullback forward a couple of steps he is in a real quick hitting position, and he must be attended to by the defense at all times. (See Fig. 114)

It became apparent that with the fullback up-close the defensive tackle could be put under extreme duress by not blocking him. Thus, the triple option concept came about. (See Fig. 115) The quarterback has three choices (1) to give to the fullback if the first man inside the defensive end is not coming down-the-line, (2) fake to the fullback and keep the ball going inside the defensive end, or (3) fake the keep and lateral to the halfback on the sweep path. The triple option can operate from the following basic blocking rules:

FB—drive for outside leg of guard—be ready to receive ball at all times.

RH—block linebacker on outside or anyone in that area.

On end—take deep outside man.

On T—take first man to inside on or off the line of scrimmage.

On G—take first man on line of scrimmage inside offensive tackle.

C—man over or offside linebacker.

Off G—man over or off linebacker.

QB—step out looking at defensive tackle spot, then end.

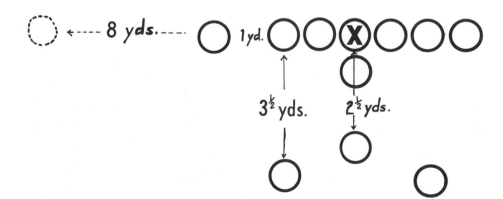

Figure 114. Y or Wishbone-T

Key Running Plays—Y or Wishbone-T

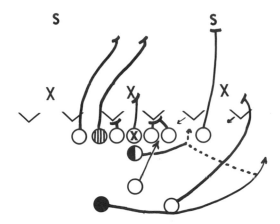

Figure 115. Triple Option

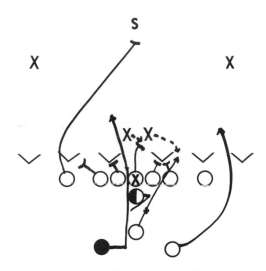

Figure 116. Handback

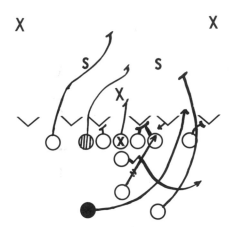

Figure 117. Off-Tackle Power

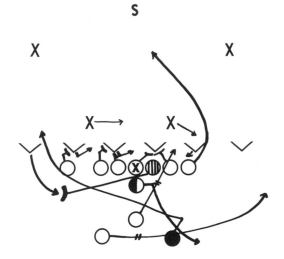

Figure 118. Counter

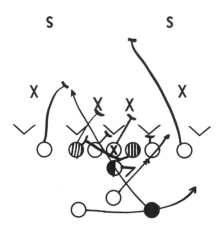

Figure 119. Cross-Back

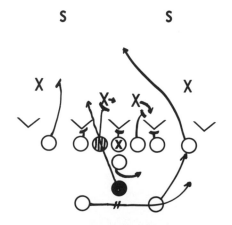

Figure 120. Dive

Key Pass Plays—Y or Wishbone-T

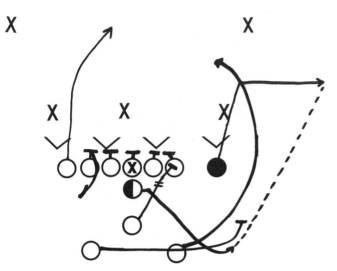

Figure 121. Triple Option Pass

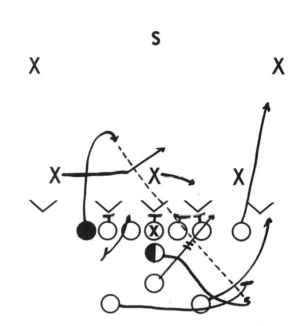

Figure 122. Throw Back

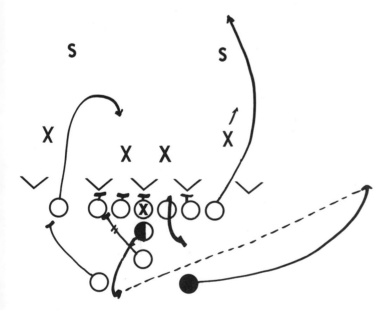

Figure 123. Throw Back Flare

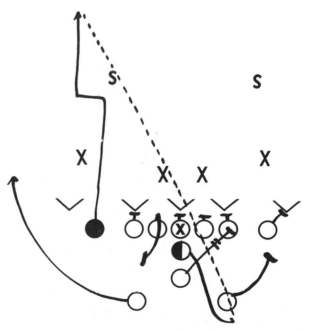

Figure 124. Deep Go

Supplements to the T Formation

Coaches frequently modify the aforementioned basic T formations by splitting their lines, putting a man in motion, and/or by the use of the wide split end and/or flanker. Each of these supplementary methods is designed to increase the efficiency of the offense and to take advantage of particular team personnel strengths.

The split line. With the advent of the split-T formation came the basic concept of the split line. The moving of offensive linemen away from each other is done to cause the defensive personnel to make a similar adjustment. This movement of the defense usually increases the blocking efficiency of the offensive line-men, because better blocking angles are available for cross blocks and traps. The spreading of the defense also makes the quick hitting dive type plays much more effective. With the defensive team spread apart, it becomes necessary for the offensive team to keep the defensive players in their originally spread positions. The offensive running hole is there before the play even starts. Straight man-for-man blocking to hold the defense momentarily in check is usually adequate for a quick hitting straight ahead attack.

The split line concept can be incorporated into any style of basic offensive alignment. Just about every style of offense is, or has been, used at some time with the split line. The primary essential for linemen in the split line offense is great speed of movement. This is also true of backfield personnel. The quicker the reaction of team personnel, the more effective the split line attack.

The man-in-motion. The man-in-motion idea has been used from the start of the modern T formation movement. The original idea was to move the man-in-motion from his regular backfield position to a flanker position. This man-in-motion usually had one of three primary tasks to perform: (1) block the end in on an outside play; (2) block the linebacker in on an off tackle play; or (3) cut in between the defensive line-backers to catch a quick jump pass. This man-in-motion was used also to catch deep and flair type passes.

The strategic advantage of moving one of the backfield men in motion toward the flank is its effect upon the defense. The defensive personnel must make a rapid adjustment to compensate for this sudden over-shift of offensive balance. If the movement is made to protect against this moving man, the defense against outside plays and passes is seriously handicapped. If the defense adjust to the outside for protection, the inside running plays become more effective. Particularly at the high school level, but true also at the college level, linemen and linebackers are very apt to "admire" this man's movements, rather than attend to their more specifically assigned defensive tasks.

Another way to use the man-in-motion attack is to place men in wing or flanker positions and have them move toward their own backfield. This is just the reverse of the original man-in-motion concept. It is a basic maneuver of the double winged T formation and the winged T. This type of maneuver is very similar to the single and double wing reverses. By putting the wing man in motion, he resumes a standard deep backfield position as the ball is centered. The advantage is that the man is already moving as the ball is centered, giving him more speed to the outside and off tackle. The defense must honor this moving man, thus causing a shifting of their defensive plans and making more effective the counter type of play.

The wide split end and/or flanker. The use of a wide split end became very popular during the 1958 football season, even though it had been used in previous seasons. Coach Earl Blaik of Army created great interest in this style of play with his so-called "Lonesome George" split end maneuver. The "lonesome" end never did come into the Army huddle and received his plays by foot and hand signals from the huddle. The rule book states that all 11 offensive men must be within 15 yards of the ball when the ball is declared "ready for play." Once the ball is declared "ready for play," the players may spread any distance they wish from the ball. By keeping the end out of the huddle and about 15 yards distance from the ball, the end could move to a very wide position without a great deal of extra running.

The professional style of offense usually uses combinations of wide split ends and flankers (backfield men split wide). It is a fairly common maneuver to split one end wide on one side and place a wide flanker on the other side.

The use of a wide split man is very effective, especially if this man has good running speed and pass catching ability. The defense must adjust to cope with this wide spread man. If the split man is good enough, the defense will find it almost impossible to cover this man defensively with one halfback. This means that the defense must at all times double cover this split man. It is obvious that the standard defensive pattern used by the team will be disrupted, as they now have two men busy watching one offensive man. What makes this a serious weakness for the defense is that the split man is so far removed from the remainder of the offensive team that the defensive men are usually completely out of the regular play area.

It is true that the split man can be covered singly. To do this effectively, the defensive team must, for its own security, appoint the best defensive halfback to this assignment. This seriously weakens the defensive strength of the opponent.

Before using the widely split man, the coach should carefully consider two points: (1) Is the split man fast enough and clever enough to be a serious threat to the opponent and (2) Can the offense afford to remove this man from its regular pattern of play—remember, this split man will be wasted, more than actually used, as a ball carrier.

The split end and/or flanker can be incorporated into practically any offensive alignment. Teams with an excellent passer should seriously consider this maneuver. The pass catching threat is what makes this alignment highly potent.

Spread Formation

Spread formations are not new to football. However, the more modern use is known as the "shot gun" formation. In this formation, the quarterback is in the deep back position. This gives him more time to execute his pass, particularly valuable against a hard rushing, blitzing defense.

The basic advantages of the spread formation are: (1) the defense must deploy to meet the threat; (2) angle blocking is made possible giving the blocker an advantage; (3) the passing game is greatly enhanced; and (4) the quick kick can be most effective. The basic disadvantage lies in the weakness of the running game; this part of the attack can be used from these styles of play, however.

Over the years, two spread formations have been tested and accepted: (1) the Texas Christian spread; and (2) the Southern Methodist spread. The SMU spread had two backs in normal position which increase the inside power potential. The Texas Christian spread used a balanced line and moves the ends out about 8 yards. The triple threat back is directly behind the center, 5-7 yard deep. (See Fig. 125, and Fig. 126)

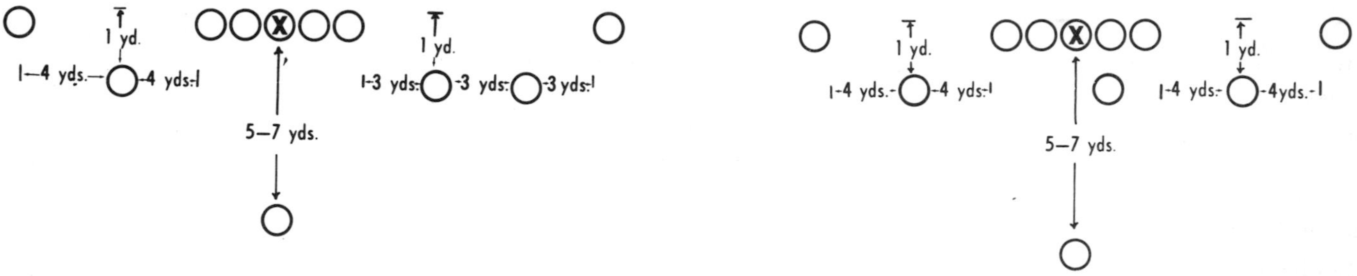

Figure 125. Texas Christian Spread Formations

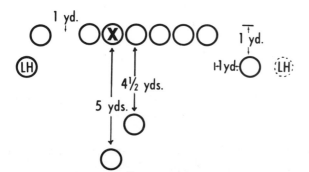

Figure 126. Southern Methodist Spread Formation

Many spread formation variations can be used advantageously. The diagram shown in Fig. 127 illustrates another popular spread formation variation.

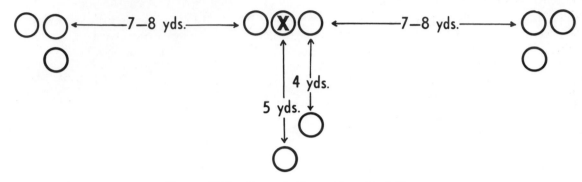

Figure 127.   Spread Formation Variation

Key Running Plays—Spread Formation

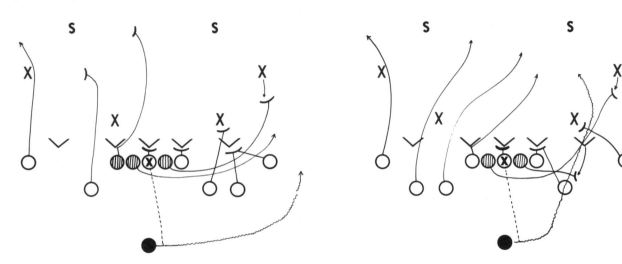

Figure 128.   End Sweep

Figure 129.   Off Tackle

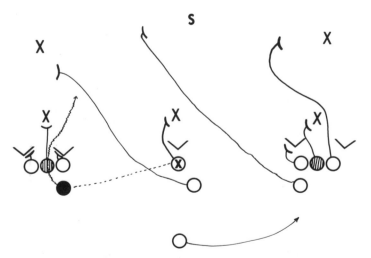

Figure 130.   Halfback Quickie

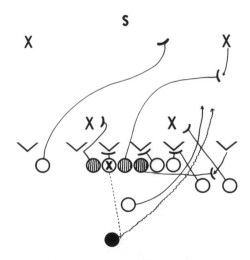

Figure 131.   Off Tackle

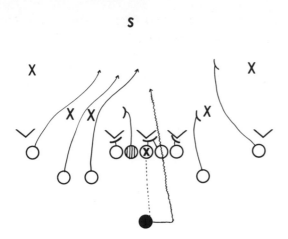

Figure 132. Buck Play

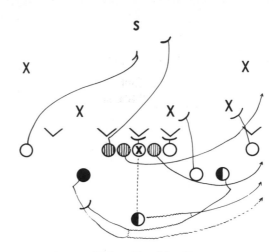

Figure 133. Double Reverse

Key Pass Plays—Spread Formations

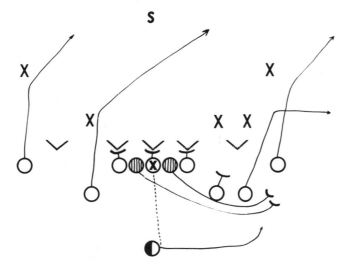

Figure 134. Running Pass

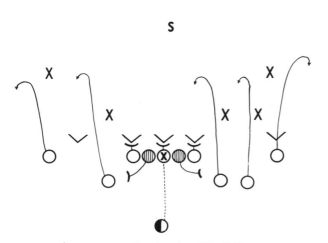

Figure 135. Button Hook Pass

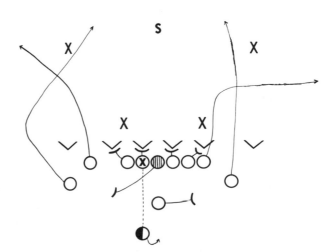

Figure 136. Four Deep Pass

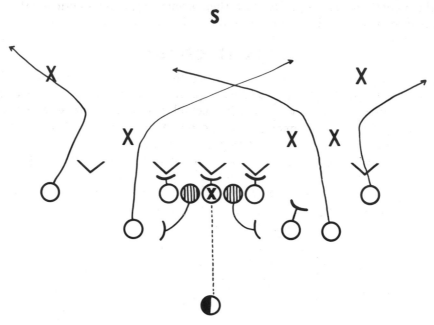

Figure 137.   Halfback Cross Pass

MULTIPLE OFFENSE

Multiple type offenses have been used by football coaches for many years. The addition of the Notre Dame Box, the New York Giant's A-formation, and the Double Wing to the Single Wing constitute a multiple offense. Single wing coaches have frequently varied their basic formation by shifting both left and right, adding flankers, and running from both the balanced and unbalanced line. The theory of multiple type offenses is to combine player alignment variations to befuddle the defense. All multiple offenses have consisted of variations of standard formations, or specially selected "key" plays from two or more formations.

Clarence "Biggie" Munn, former outstanding coach of Michigan State, popularized the term multiple offense. He is, no doubt, the most successful exponent of the idea of using a variety of formation alignments. He did not simply select standard "key" plays from other offenses; rather, he adapted the theoretical advantages of these separate offenses into his particular style of play. Munn thus was able to attack one particular spot in the defensive line from 14 offensive formation variations. This was done without any effect upon the primary blocking responsibilities of the key linemen.

In practically all instances of multiple offenses, the primary causation was successful defenses employed by the opposition. Michigan State coaches experimented with various formation changes and play patterns to compensate for defensive successes of opponents. In some instances, personnel changes of team members made variations of standard offenses desirable.

The major advantage of multiple offenses lies in the defense problems for the opposition. It becomes essential to prepare several defenses to meet the numerous offense combinations. Michigan State experiments with varied offenses early in the contest. Once defensive weaknesses are uncovered, there is concentration on that particular offensive pattern.

Practically any offense can be used successfully. This is true when your team personnel is equal to, or better than, the opposition. A notable example of this can be demonstrated by citing Oklahoma University and "Bud" Wilkinson. The split-T offense, with only very limited variations, had kept the Oklahoma teams on top or near the top in national ranking for several years. The time comes eventually, however, when the defense catches up to the offense. At that time the smart coach starts to vary his set offense by supplementing it with formation changes and variations. The style of play then swings into the multiple offense category. The experienced coach who does not use the multiple concept, in part at least, is rare.

VARIABLE OFFENSE

The term variable offense refers to a particular offense that uses many variations in backfield alignments. While this is a rather new terminology, the basic concept is by no means new. The single wing offense has been used as a variable offense for many years. The actual variability was achieved by moving backfield men closer or farther away from the scrimmage line, or by moving backs out to wide flank positions. The concept of variability has been incorporated into the modern T formation.

The professional teams use various backfield "sets" to give them some advantage, at least tentatively, at the point of attack. These variable patterns are arrived at quickly from a standard position, traditional straight T or I sets, by a team shift. The defense is now pressed to make a rapid alignment adjustment or suffer a positioning weakness. The college teams usually move into their selected sets directly from the huddle. This eliminates the probability of an illegal procedure on occasion.

Chapter 9

Team Offensive Play (The Running Game)

The offense in modern football is highly specialized and extremely complicated. There are a great many offensive patterns used with considerable success; however, all offenses are developed from a few basic formations or combinations of formations. The manipulation of players from each basic formation varies considerably according to the particular coach; however, each formation adapts itself to certain basic patterns of movements. The complexity of defenses, plus the tremendous variation in team personnel, cause constant additions to and/or variations of these fundamental offense patterns. If a coach understands basic formations and "key" plays, and if he knows the theory fundamental to team offense, however, the addition and variation of plays is much less confusing. This section will deal with the theory behind the running game.

BASIC LINE MANEUVERS

The team running offense is made up of a group of plays designed to move the ball through or around the opposing players. Each individual play is developed for some specific reason. Some plays are calculated to be used individually with no particular relation to other plays. Some plays are designed in series, meaning that several plays all will start with an identical pattern of movement. The variation will be in the end result of the play—the person who carries the ball, and the specific point of attack. The obvious advantage of series of plays is that the defense has no way of knowing exactly where the attack is to be made until the very last moment; thus the pressure is placed upon the defense to protect itself against any variation from the series. The defense cannot safely concentrate its attack against one specific point, but must be ready for all the eventualities of the series being run.

Other running plays are designed to be used against only certain teams for certain specific reasons. These plays usually result from scouting reports on the opponents. Each play is designed to take advantage of some specific defensive play or player weakness.

A final style of play is calculated to surprise the opposition completely. The Statue of Liberty and the Naked Reverse are plays of this kind. When these special plays are used at psychologically favorable moments, they usually catch the defense "asleep," and generally result in long gains or scores.

The offensive running game is built upon four basic line maneuvers calculated to open holes in the defense: (1) double team blocking; (2) trap blocking; (3) man-for-man blocking; and (4) cross blocking.

Double team blocking. Before the T-formation, the power in football was applied by double team blocking. This style of blocking was the primary strength of the single wing attack, and is still a favorite type of line play for many coaches. In this kind of blocking, it is said that it actually takes two offensive men to effectively block one of the defensive men. In reality this is often the case, though many coaches will not face it! Double team blocking is effective only when the two offensive linemen can properly perform this coordinated blocking. This type of blocking means also that at least three men are needed to open a hole. Ac-

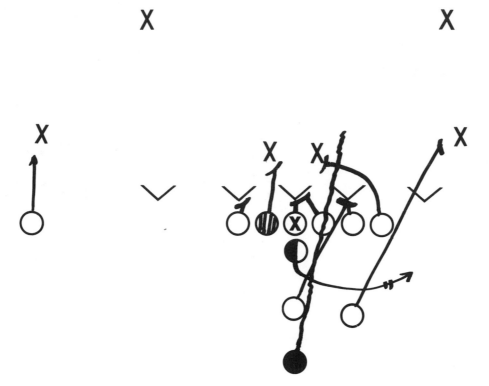

Figure 138. Power-I   Double Team Blocking

tually the coach is thinking more of short consistent gains rather than of the explosive types that result from some other styles of blocking. Ball carriers should remember that they always run close to the double team block when hitting the line. The double team block should move the defensive opponent out of his original position. (See Fig. 138) The mechanics of the double team block have been explained in a previous chapter. (See page 72)

Trap blocking. Trap blocking normally consists of a double team block on one defensive man and a man-for-man block on the other. The man-for-man block is considered a surprise type block, with the block-er coming from some position removed from the immediate scene of action. (See Fig. 139) The theory behind the trap block is to slow down an overly-aggressive defensive lineman. This type of block is frequently used also against some defensive lineman who has just made a spectacular play. It is a means of taking advantage of the immediate enthusiasm of the particular man.

It is always hoped in a trap block that the defensive man is penetrating into the offensive backfield. Mod-ern football offenses have rapidly gone back to the trap style of play. The popularity of the trap continues despite the fact that the modern concept of defense is one of containment without deep penetration. As a consequence, it becomes obvious that the trap is not doomed to failure if the man does not penetrate. It does mean that the man delegated to perform the trap must fully expect that the opponent will not charge. (For mechanics of the trap block, see page 70.)

Man-for-man blocking. A modern movement in football has been to assign one offensive lineman the task of blocking one defensive lineman. This idea became very popular with the adaptation of the modern T-forma-tion.

Man-for-man blocking can be incorporated into any style of team alignment; however the spread or split line increases the effectiveness of this kind of play. The dispersion of offensive linemen causes a compensat-

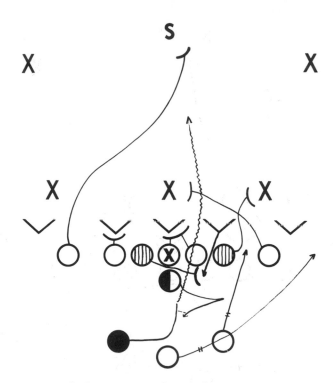

Figure 139.   Trap Blocking From the Tight-T Against a 5-3-2-1 Defense

ing spread of the defensive linemen, consequently the hole is already open. The task of the offensive lineman is simply to keep the hole open.

An obvious advantage of man-for-man blocking is that more players become available for downfield blocking. As a result there should be longer gains.

No offensive blocking system exists that does not have some very strong disadvantages. It is when the coach ignores these disadvantages that he runs into much difficulty. Total consideration must be given when fitting an offense to a particular team.

The first question is whether or not the particular defensive man is more alert, stronger, and more aggressive than the offensive man. If he is, the man-for-man style of offense is doomed to failure. If the men are relatively equal in ability, then it becomes a question of whether or not the offensive man can effectively block a defensive man who is playing directly in front of him, or to the hole side of him. (See page 47 for proper blocking mechanics) If the offensive man cannot handle his opponent under these circumstances, then the man-for-man style of play should be discontinued or supplemented. (See Fig. 140)

Cross blocking.   Cross blocking is actually the exchange of assignments from the man-for-man system. This style of block has the definite advantage of increasing the blocking angle for the lineman. By increasing the angle from no angle, head-on, to an inside-out angle, the difficulty of the block is greatly reduced. Cross blocking is most popular with relatively tight offensive line alignments, but can be used effectively with any team alignment. A disadvantage of this style of play is the slight reduction in the explosiveness of the offensive attack. A more serious disadvantage of cross blocking is that an alert defensive man can move across the line of scrimmage before the cross block takes place. If this happens in the case of either of the two defensive men concerned, the offensive play will not succeed. (See Fig. 141) The coach must realize the limitations of his team personnel in relation to the opposition he will meet. (For blocking mechanics, see page 72)

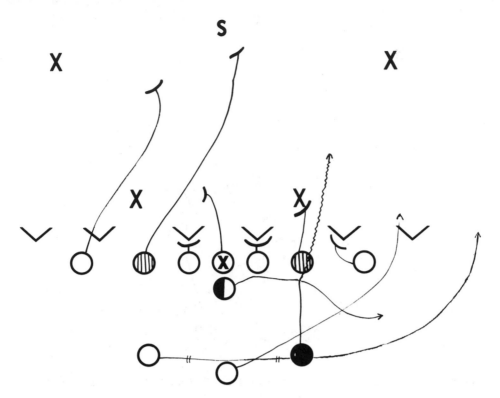

Figure 140. Man-for-man Blocking From the Split-T Against a 6-2-2-1 Defense

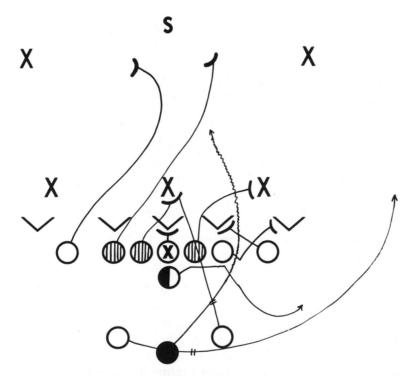

Figure 141. Cross Blocking From the Tight-T Against a 5-3-2-1 Defense

Variations and combinations. Almost all types of blocks other than the four basic ones mentioned are variations and/or combinations of these fundamental blocks. Some examples are given for variations and combinations of the aforementioned classifications of blocks. (See Fig. 142)

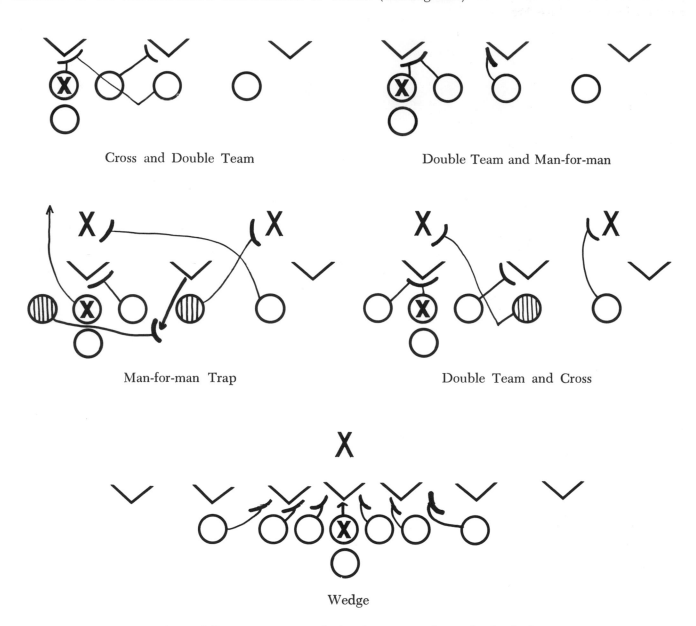

Figure 142.   Variations and Combinations of Standard Blocks

Basic Play Patterns

The football offense consists of a great variety of play patterns. There are three basic maneuvers that are the "bread-and-butter" plays of practically all offenses, however, regardless of the fundamental team formation used. This pattern consists of a straight ahead play, an off tackle play, and an end run. These three plays in sequence form the nucleus of the entire T-attack. In addition this pattern of maneuvers, coupled with the reverse, is the heart of the single wing attack, and is frequently used as the "buck lateral" sequence. All the additional plays are usually supplementary to these three "bread-and-butter" plays.

The straight ahead play. In the T- vernacular, this particular play is known as the dive play. Most coaches consider this play the primary play of the T- offense. It is this straight ahead power that makes possible the two outside plays. The dive play should have enough effectiveness to hold the defensive men in constant fear of it. (See Fig. 143)

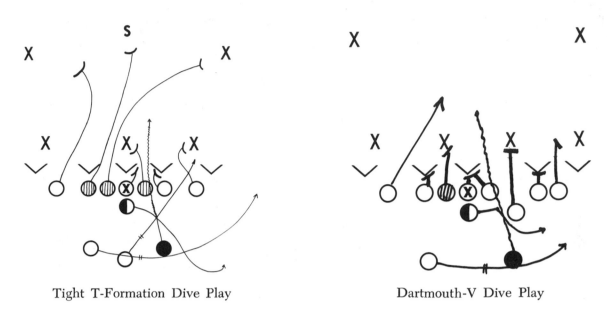

Tight T-Formation Dive Play   Dartmouth-V Dive Play

Figure 143. The Straight Ahead Play

The off tackle play. The off tackle play is a semi-inside play. It is run between the defensive end and tackle. The dive play holds the defense stationary, or pulls the defensive linemen into the inside. The off tackle play takes advantage of this movement by faking the dive play and running the ball off tackle. (See Fig. 144)

The end run. The end run is the final play of the "bread-and-butter" sequence. The defensive guards and linebackers are held in position by the threat of the dive play. The tackle and end are held in check by the threat of the off tackle play. The ball is faked to the men entering both of these play holes and then given to a man going wide around the end. (See Fig. 145)

Actually, the threat of any one of these plays makes their counterpart effective. If a defense is arranged so as to strongly protect against the outside running speed, the inside or explosive attack becomes highly effective. If the defense is concerned mainly with the inside attack, the outside play will usually be successful.

Supplementary Play Patterns

The three basic plays mentioned above are supplemented by cross-bucks, traps, reverses, counters, sweeps, quarterback sneaks, bootlegs, draw plays, and special plays.

Cross-buck. The cross-buck depends upon deception for its success. The offensive men are manipulated so as to confuse the defense. When the play is properly executed, it is impossible to be certain who has the ball. Cross-buck plays are of three general types, each of which will be considered briefly.

One procedure is to have one of the backs cross in front of another back. In the play diagrammed in Fig. 146, player number 3 moves forward immediately upon the snap signal. Player number 4 delays one half count, usually by taking a drop step (kick step) with his right foot, and then drives into the line as indicated. The quarterback fakes the ball to the number 3 man and gives to the number 4 man.

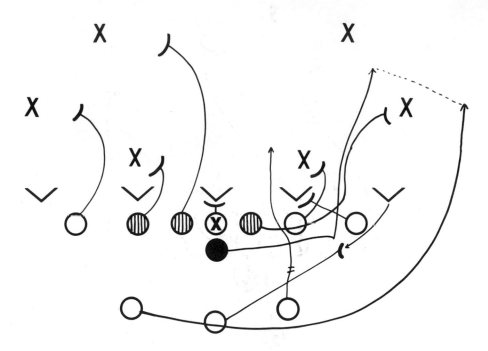

Split-T Quarterback Keep

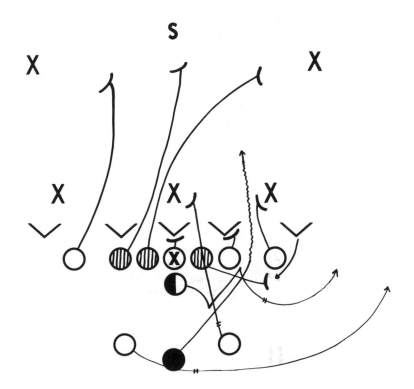

Outside Belly Play

Figure 144. The Off Tackle Play

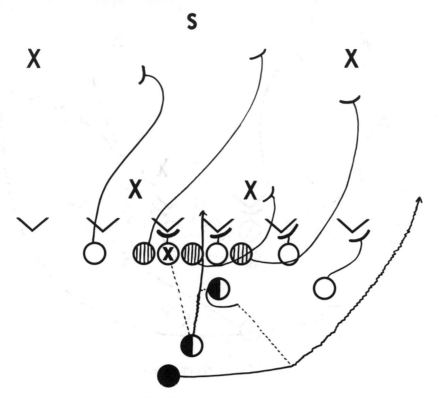

Single Wing Buck Lateral

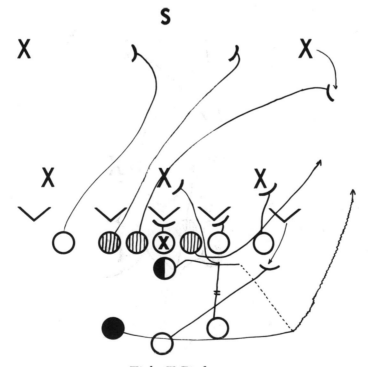

Tight-T Pitch-out

Figure 145. The End Run Play

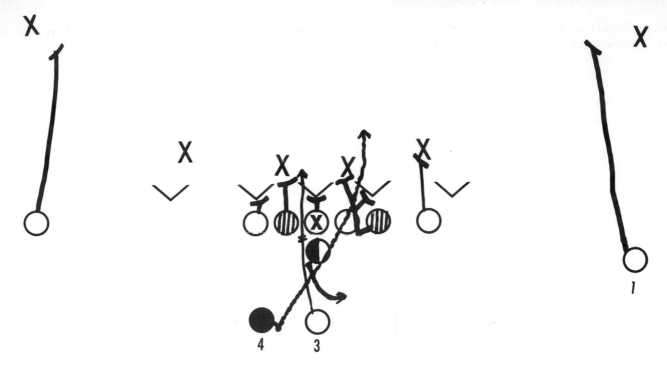

Figure 146. Power-T Cross-Buck

Another way of maneuvering on a so-called cross-buck series is given in Fig. 147. In this sequence, the first player to move does not move across in front of the second player. The second player, however, does

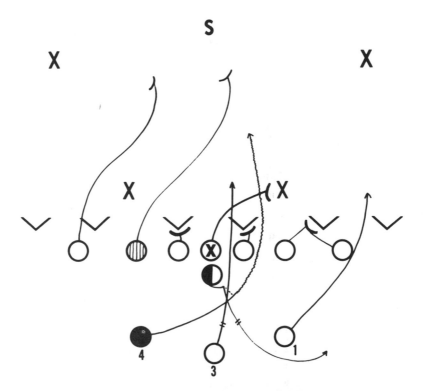

Figure 147. Split-T Cross-Buck

move across the path followed by the first player. Player number 3 drives straight into the line. Player number 4 takes a lateral step with his right foot, and then moves on into the line on a diagonal path. The quarterback can fake or give to either man.

The third popular method of running this cross-buck pattern is to have the backs run on parallel paths. While not a true cross-buck, the deception of the cross-buck pattern is not lost. In the play diagrammed in Fig. 148, the quarterback reverses out from the center, gives to player number 1, and fakes to player number 3.

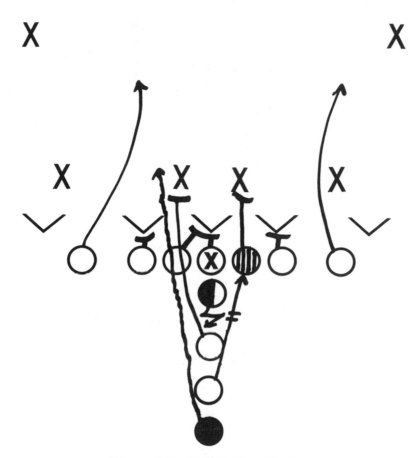

Figure 148. Full-I Cross-Buck

It must be remembered in all of the cross-bucks that the actual holes hit by the backs can be moved up or down along the scrimmage line. The paths shown in the examples are not the only available ones.

Trap plays. It may be recalled from the previous discussion of trap blocking that, even though the defensive opponent does not penetrate, the trap can still be fairly effective.

The trap is designed to make the overly-aggressive lineman move more cautiously, thus making him more susceptible to standard blocks. In the coaching vernacular, the trap play "keeps the defense honest." Traps can be executed by either linemen or backs. (See Fig. 149)

Reverses. The reverse play is designed to make the defense react to the pull of the play in one direction while the ball is actually carried in the opposite direction. This style of play is highly successful against teams that attempt to over-shift against the strong basic attack. It is valuable also against linemen and linebackers who tend to drift with the movement of the backfield. Reverses are an essential part of the single wing spinning attack. The fullback usually makes the hand-off; however, the reverse can be achieved by having the tail back hand-off the ball to the reversing wing back. (See Fig. 150)

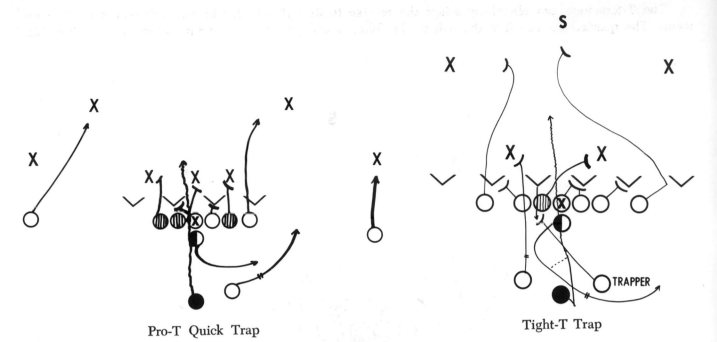

Pro-T Quick Trap   Tight-T Trap

Figure 149. Trap Plays

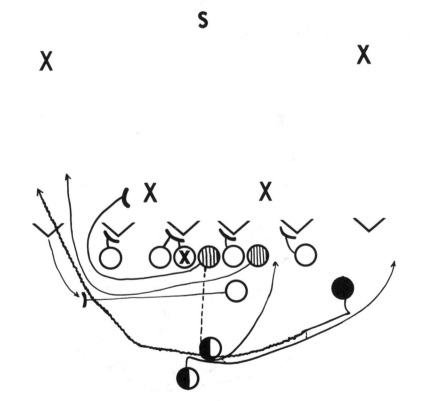

Figure 150. Single Wing Reverse

The T-formation can effectively adapt the reverse to its style of play by two different basic T movements. The quarterback can fake the ball to the fullback and give to the reversing halfback. (See Fig. 151)

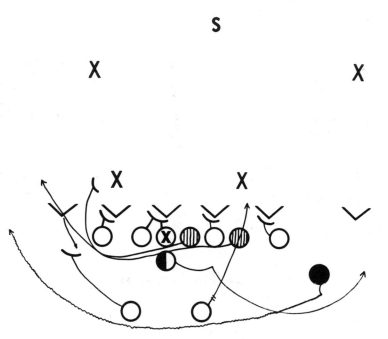

Figure 151. Winged-T Reverse

A second method is to have the quarterback give the ball to one halfback who hands-off to the opposite halfback. (See Fig. 152)

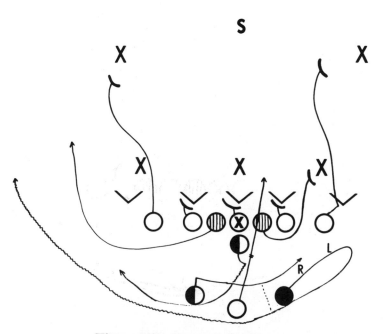

Figure 152. Power-I Counter

Counters. In theory and effect, the counter play is quite similar to the reverse play. The effectiveness of the play results from the fact that the pull of the play is in one direction, whereas the ball is actually carried in the opposite direction. This style of maneuver can be run from all offensive sets. (See Fig. 152 and 153)

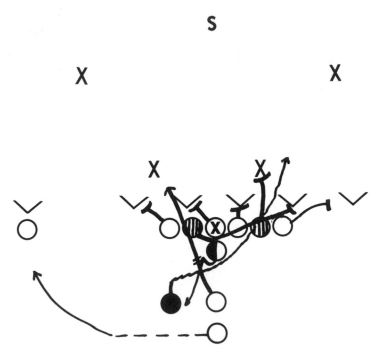

Figure 152a. Power-I Counter

Counters are probably slightly more effective from the T-formation. The reasons for this are the position of the running backs, and the fact that the defense is generally concentrated at the strong point of the T attack. (See Fig. 131)

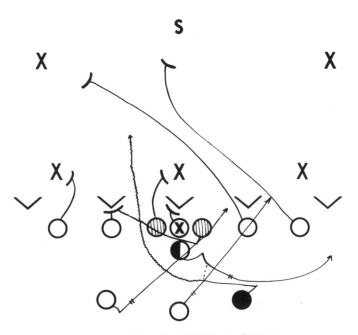

Figure 153. Semi-Split-T Counter

Sweeps. The sweep play is an attempt to overpower the outside of the defensive line. It has the advantage over the pitch-out type of play in that more blockers are available in front of the ball carrier, as no backfield men are used as fakers. Usually the running guards and/or tackles lead the ball carrier along with the remaining backs. (See Fig. 154)

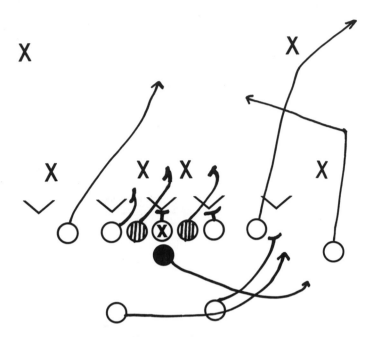

Figure 154. Flanker-T Power Sweep

The T-formation generally does not pull the linemen; however the onside guard can effectively pull to help lead the play. The major blocking assignments in sweeps fall upon the backs. The sweep is a power-packed offensive maneuver. (See Fig. 155)

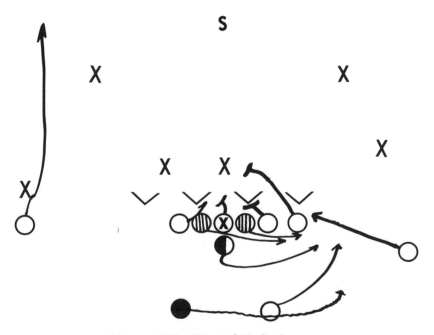

Figure 155. Winged-T Sprint-out

To assure the success of sweeps, the blockers must fully understand their blocking assignments. The play is planned to move outside the defensive end. If the end should drift, however, the assigned blocker takes his out, and the other blockers lead the ball carrier past the inside of the drifting end.

Quarterback sneak. The quarterback sneak is almost a basic play of the T-formation. This play is essential in holding the middle of the defensive line in position. Without a quarterback sneak, the defense need not be concerned about quick-hitting plays over the middle. The quarteback sneak with power and wedge blocking can be employed successfully for that necessary yard or two situation. With wedge blocking, the quarterback merely drop steps in order to allow the wedge to form. Then the quarterback follows the wedge. (See Fig. 156)

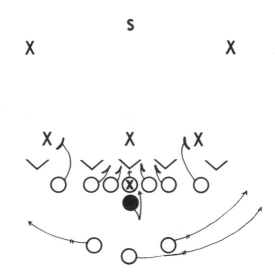

Figure 156. Tight-T Quarterback Sneak

The other style of quarterback sneak has the quarterback take a fake step to one side, and then drive over the middle. This lateral step is used so that the defensive linemen will move laterally, thus making the line blocking assignments less difficult. (See Fig. 157)

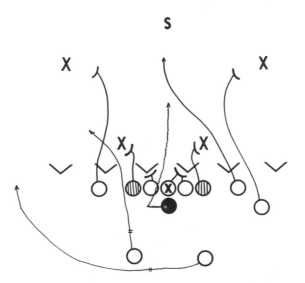

Figure 157. Winged-T Quarterback Sneak

Bootlegs. The bootleg play is actually a naked reverse play in which the quarterback keeps the ball, usually held on his away hip, after faking to his backfield. The path of the quarterback is directly opposite the direction of the fakes. The success of this play depends upon the expert handling of the ball by the quarterback and the complete deceit of the defense. The defense must be fooled into expecting the play to move in the obvious direction. Bootleg plays are used only after the defense has been detected over-shifting in the direction of the offense. The bootleg play generally is quite successful against teams that tend to "gang" tackle. It is a surprise play and can be used successfully only when the defense is caught completely off guard. (See Fig. 158)

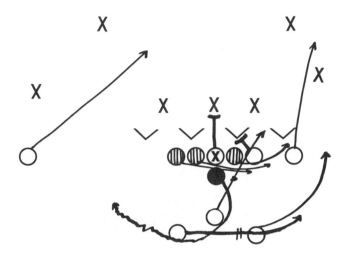

Figure 158. Wishbone-T Bootleg

Draw plays. The draw play is used in modern football to keep the defensive team from swarming in on the quarterback. The play is usually successful when an obvious pass play is called. The movements of the backfield and ends indicate a pass play. The quarterback fakes as though to execute a pass, but instead of passing he hands the ball off to one of the blocking backs. This is usually the task of the fullback, but can be done by any back. The draw play is used effectively by teams that employ man-for-man pass protection. In this type of defense, the blockers usually move the defensive men on past the quarterback, thus opening up the center of the line. The fullback is instructed to advance toward the first "daylight" that he sees. (See Fig. 159)

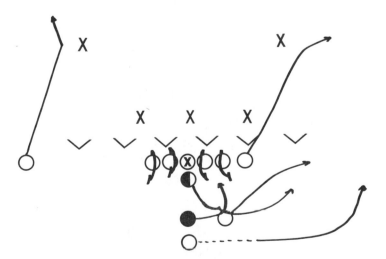

Figure 159. Sprint-out Draw

The quarterback draw play is basically the same as the fullback draw in Fig. 137. The fundamental difference is that the quarterback does not retreat more than two or three steps, and then carries the ball through the middle of the defensive line.

Special plays. Special plays are used to completely surprise the opposition. To be successful, these plays must be called at just the right moment. Probably they can be used but once a game, unless the opposition shows no sign of team flexibility.

Sally Rand or Naked Reverse. This play depends upon the pull of the offensive faking for its success. The play starts in one direction and ends up going in the opposite direction. It can be classified as a deep reverse play. In the play diagrammed in Fig. 160, the pull of the play is to the right. The left end, guard, and tackle execute shoulder check blocks, then allow their opponents to penetrate. The end and tackle loop around behind their opponents to be in a position to execute a screen or cut-off block.

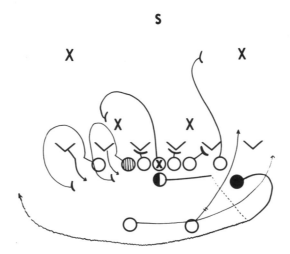

Figure 160.   Winged-T Sally Rand

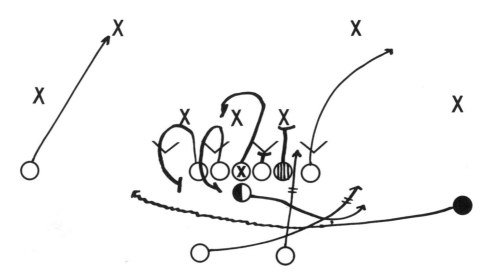

Figure 161.   Pro-T Flanker Reverse

End-around play. The end-around play can be executed either as a reverse or as a completion to the normal direction of the faking. It must be remembered that, to insure the legality of this play, the end must face his own goal line before he is eligible to take the ball on a hand-off. (See Figs. 162 and 163)

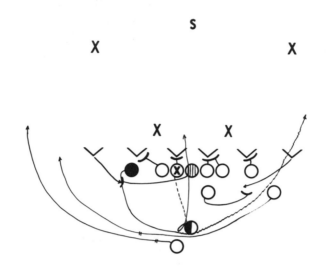

Figure 162. Single Wing End-Around

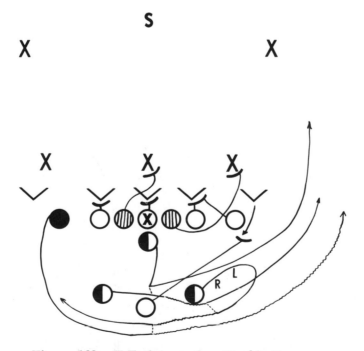

Figure 163. T-End Around or Double Reverse

Statue of Liberty play. The Statue of Liberty play works on the same principle as the draw play. The play is designed to appear to be a pass play. The intent of the play is to cause the defensive backs to retreat for pass protection, and to have the weak side end attempt to tackle the passer. Perfect timing of the play is essential for its success. The hand-off should be made at the moment the end is about to tackle the passer. (See Fig. 163a)

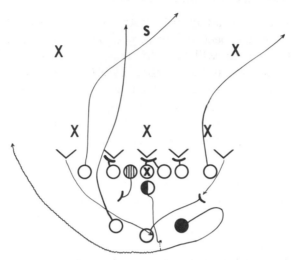

Figure 163a. T- Statue of Liberty

The Statue of Liberty play can be run effectively as a fake punt. The deception of the play comes from the punter. He must go through with all the actions of a real punt in order to deceive the opponents. (See Fig. 164)

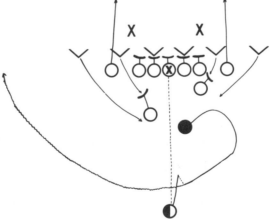

Figure 164. Fake Deep Punt Statue of Liberty

Rule Blocking

A proverbial problem of the modern football coach is deciding how he will have his team combat the ever-changing opponent defenses. The problem is one not only of meeting a different defense with each opponent, but it is also highly probable that each opponent will present several defense variations. Football defense has been revolutionized from one or two standard maneuvers to a myriad of complexities. It is a pathetic team that is always one week behind in its blocking assignments. There is nothing more frustrating to a coach, or to a team, then to be prepared for a certain few defenses, only to have the Saturday opponent use completely new defenses. The following week is spent teaching the team how to combat these new defenses. The next Saturday an entirely new defense confronts the team. This can continue on throughout the season, and the team never is really ready for a Saturday encounter. The reverse of this can be true also. The defense can always be one week behind the offense.

To prepare the team adequately, the season should not start without full preparation for any defensive eventuality. This preparation can become a difficult problem to overcome in the limited weeks of pre-season practice. To combat ever-changing defenses, and to fully prepare for the opening game, the up-to-date coach uses rule blocking. There are at least four concepts of rule blocking: (1) defense alignment technique; (2) number system; (3) zones or area play; and (4) player options.

Defensive alignment techniques. To adapt this system to his offense, the coach must determine first of all what defensive alignments he can expect the opponents to use against his offense. He then decides upon the play blocking assignment variations he will have his team use against each of the selected defenses. The offensive line and backfield are then taught the specific blocking assignments against each of the selected defenses. The defenses selected usually are categorized as "even" or "odd" defenses. The even defenses are the 4-, 6-, and 8-man lines. In each case, against a balanced line, opponents will be directly opposite the offensive guards. The odd defenses are the 5-, 7-, over-shifted 6-, and 9- man line. In each case, against a balanced line, opponents will not be "head-on" the guards, but a man will be "head-on" the center.

To put this technique into effect, the quarterback first calls a particular play in the huddle. When the offensive team is lined up on the scrimmage line, the quarterback calls out the defensive alignment. The call of 44 would indicate a 4-4-2-1 defense, 54 would mean a 5-4-2 defense and so on. This call would then put into effect all the blocking assignments of the offensive team. The coach who adapts this style of play will attempt to arrange his blocking assignments so that relatively few assignment changes will be necessary.

This system is usable for a relatively small number of offensive plays. The greater the number of offensive plays, the greater the probability that everyone will not remember his assignments. The primary disadvantage of this technique lies in the fact that many defensive teams are trained to change their defensive alignments as the quarterback makes his call. In addition, even though the team may be lining up in a certain defense, it may actually be attacking with an entirely different defense. An example would be the four man line that always shifts into a 5-, 6-, 7-, 8-, or 9-man-line just prior to or as the ball is snapped from center.

Number system. The number system is put into effect by a procedure similar to that of the defensive alignment technique. The basic difference is that the coach must first diagram the specific defensive alignments he may expect to face. He then assigns numbers to the defensive positions diagrammed, numbers which must be consistent from diagram to diagram. After the numbers have been assigned, the coach diagrams each play he wishes to use against all the predetermined defenses. As in the defensive alignment technique, the coach attempts to devise his play blocking assignments so that a particular player is always blocking the same number. The number does not change, but the positioning of that particular player may change.

As is noted, this technique is almost identical to the one first mentioned. It tends to simplify the learning of blocking assignments for the offensive team, however. Once the players fully comprehend the location of the various numbers according to different defensive alignments, the learning of assignments becomes a matter of remembering one, or at the most two, numbers for each play. The technique will be of aid in eliminating the confusion that frequently exists as to who you mean when you say, "Block the end." Players tend to think of the end as a particular person rather than as a particular position. The major disadvantage of this system is that the offensive players will not remember immediately, for example, where the number 3 man is in a particular defense. Confusion over defensive numbers can occur readily. (See Fig. 165)

For the examples given in Fig. 165, the rules for this dive right play are as follows:

Left end—6 man

Left tackle—5 man

Left guard—offside 1 man, or 7 man

Center—0 or 7 man

Right guard—onside 1 man

Right tackle—onside 2 man

Right end—onside 3 man

Zone or area play. One of the more popular systems of rule blocking is the zone method. To use this technique, the coach draws up the desired blocking assignments for a particular play against each of the selected defenses. The next step is to write exactly what the players are to do. To use this system, the players must learn a terminology that can simplify a rule into a few words. The following terms are generally used:

Over. The defensive man is "over" the offensive man when a directly forward charge by the offensive man would take him into contact with any part of the defensive man.

Inside. This term indicates the defensive man who is in the "gap" between two offensive players. "Inside" means to the offensive player's inside or towards the center.

Outside. "Outside" indicates a player in the "gap" outside or away from the center side of the offensive player.

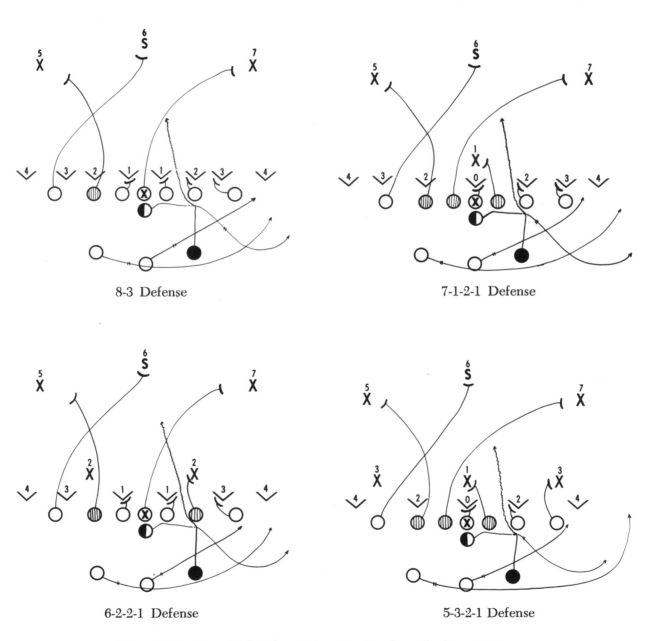

Figure 165. Dive Right Play Using the Number Blocking System

Linebacker your side. This indicates a linebacker on the same side as the assigned player.

Off Linebacker. This means the linebacker who is on the other side of the center.

Middle Linebacker. This is the linebacker who is directly behind the center or two guards.

A man. This could indicate the safety man, or some other designation could be used.

B man. This would indicate the strong or play side halfback.

C man. This would mean the weak or away from the play side halfback.

Linebacker as wide as you. This would indicate a linebacker over or outside the end.

These are a few of the popularly used terms. Any similar simplified terminology can be used. The diagrams in Fig. 166 show how this zone type of rule blocking would be used for a specific play.

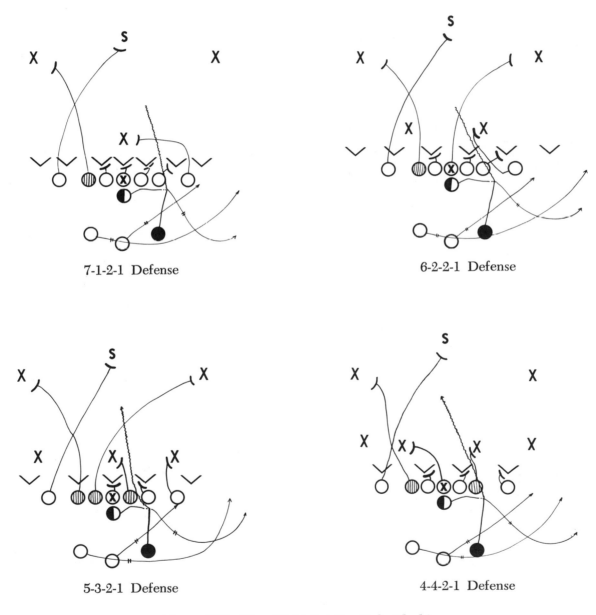

7-1-2-1 Defense

6-2-2-1 Defense

5-3-2-1 Defense

4-4-2-1 Defense

Figure 166. Dive Right Set For Rule Blocking

Rules for Dive Right Play

RE—LB your side, man over   RT—Over, outside, MLB

RG—Over, MLB   C—Over, B unless offside MLB

LG—Over, B   LT—C

LE—A

The major advantage of this system is that the offensive men are not concerned directly with the particular defensive alignment. They are concerned basically with the position of the man in their particular area. As a result, the shifting, changing, or new defense will not seriously affect the play blocking assignments. The team that masters this system should be ready for any defense.

Michigan State Rule Blocking. The Michigan State rule blocking principles are designed to simplify the play learning assignments for the offensive team, especially the linemen. The basic concept utilized in this system is lane blocking. Michigan State believes firmly in the power of the unbalanced line and uses the following numbering system:

To shift to an unbalanced line left, players number 4 and 6 merely change positions. The rules for line blocking assignments do not change with the shift of the strength from one side to the other.

The entire blocking system breaks down into four component parts: (1) lane rules; (2) dive rules; (3) sweep rules; and (4) trap rules.

Lane rules. The primary rule here is that your lane consists of from head on you to head up on the next offensive man away from the play. With no one in the lane, you block the nearest dangerous linebacker. This type of blocking is used for power plays, with the nearest halfback blocking the first man off the lane called.

Dive rules. Dive plays in the Michigan State system are usually run with a 1 yard split down the line. Everybody lane blocks on each dive play except the "call" man. This man area blocks—covers two lanes. The ball carrier follows the head of the "call" man who makes the key block. If the defense is a gap defense, the "call" man calls "gap" and everyone blocks in and the play is run as a veer.

Cross blocking can be employed by having the quarterback call two numbers in the huddle. For example right half at 45 would mean that the 4 and 5 men cross block their lanes. The man with no one against him (the free man) goes first.

Sweep rules. The near halfback attacks the first man outside the end man on the offensive scrimmage line in or out. The even linemen block man on, or first man to the inside on, the scrimmage line. The odd linemen pull, step deep, swing end, and block in downfield. The fullback leads the play. The offside end runs an in and out pass pattern.

Trap rules. There are seven different trap rules in this system.

Two trap

a. 2 man—take men head on, if free take first man to inside
b. 3 man—block man on you, now LB your side
c. 4 man—block first man to your inside
d. 5 man—block first man out at the hole
e. 6 man—block man on, now first man to your left
f. 7 man—block through the 2 hole
g. 8 man—take safety

Three trap

a. 2 man—block man on three man, none, false block man over you, allow WB to clear then block first man on
    secondary to outside.
b. 3 man—post man over you, none, block first man to your inside
c. 4 man—block the first man to your inside
d. 5 man—pull and block first man past our 3 man
e. 6 man—set up man over you and block first man to your left
f. 7 man—pull and block through the hole
g. 8 man—go for safety

Four trap

a. 2 man—if free, take first LB to inside; if covered, false block man over you, and go for first man in second-
    ary to outside
b. 3 man—if free, take first LB to inside; if covered, false block man over you and go for first LB to outside
c. 4 man—block man over 5 man; none, false block man over you and go for first LB to outside
d. 5 man—post man over you; none, first man to inside
e. 6 man—block first man to left
f. 7 man—pull and block across the hole
g. 8 man—safety man

Five trap

a. 2 man—cut off first lineman outside of 3 man
b. 3 man—pull and block first man across the 5 hole
c. 4 man—post man over you; none, block first man to right
d. 5 man—if covered, pull and block first opponent to your left; otherwise, take first man to your right
e. 6 man—talk to 7
    drop step and take position on first LB to your left
f. 7 man—block first LB to your right; man over you, allow 6 man to clear first

Six trap

a. 2 man—take defensive safety
b. 3 man—check man on you or first man to your outside
c. 4 man—pull and block the first man out at the hole
d. 5 man—post man on; now first man to your right
e. 6 man—block man on or first man to your right
f. 7 man—46—pull and block end out
    RH at 6—block the man over center; none, pull and block out at end
g. 8 man—46—block the LB your side
    RH at 6—block the first LB to your inside

Eight trap

a. 2 man—check first man outside of 3 and then take the cut off
b. 3 man—pull through the hole and block to your inside
c. 4 man—block man on you or first man to your right
d. 5 man—pull, block first man out at the hole
e. 6 man—block man on you or first man to your right
f. 7 man—block man on you or on outside shoulder, none, block first man to right
g. 8 man—block man on or first man to your inside

Nine trap

a. 2 man—safety man
b. 3 man—pull around end and seal inside
c. 4 man—block man head on; none, first man to right
d. 5 man—pull and hook end in
e. 6 man—block man head on; none, first man to right
f. 7 man—have responsibility for second man in and LB
g. 8 man—have responsibility for second man in and LB

Player options. The player option system can be used alone or in conjunction with the afore mentioned systems. When used alone, the quarterback gives a play in the huddle. This play tells the backfield what to do and the spot on the line where the ball carrier will go. The team, after lining up on the scrimmage line, determines the particular blocking that will take place, usually by having either the guards, center, and tackles, or the ends and guards, call numbers or letters. The call of the man nearest the point of attack becomes the "key" call. The particular number or letter will tell the men at the point of attack what type of blocks to use. The following list indicates some of the more popular play blocking designations and what they mean:

A- X- or "me": these signals indicate that the straight man-for-man blocking assignments will be used.

B- Y- or "you": these signals indicate that the cross blocking technique will be used.

C- Z- or "us": these signals indicate that trap blocking will be used.

To keep the defense from deciphering the code, the designated players call these signals whether or not the play is coming to their side. The plays diagrammed in Fig. 167 are examples of this system in operation.

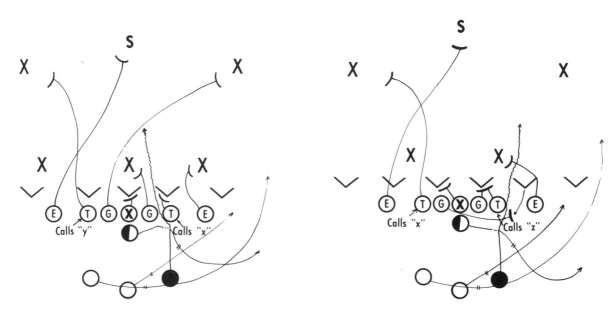

Fig. 167 Dive Right Showing Two Player Options

As was mentioned, player options are used frequently in conjunction with specifically planned plays. The coach teaches his players definite blocking assignments for each play. The players are then given the option of changing their blocking assignments, if the defensive alignment or particular defensive player strength so dictates. The diagram in Fig. 168 show four methods of opening the inside dive hole. In these plays, the right tackle calls the blocks by the designated letters. Any designations can be used; the more the player appeal of these designations the better.

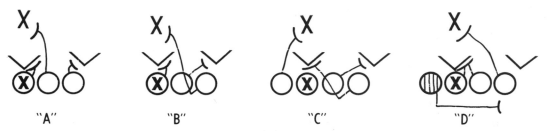

Figure 168. Player Options For The Dive Play

Chapter 10

Team Offensive Play (The Passing Game)

PASSING CONCEPTS

Since the rule change, which allows a passer to execute his pass anywhere behind the line of scrimmage, the passing attack has become a vital aspect of the total team offense. There are four theories relative to the passing attack in modern football. The concept selected by the particular coach will depend almost entirely upon the player material available.

One idea considers the passing attack as a complement to the running game. The pass is part and parcel of the total team offense. When this idea is utilized, the pass is used frequently as a short and intermediate yard gainer, the same as in the running game. A series of plays thus may include the pass as well as the run, with only an occasional "all the way" pass attempt. This is probably the most acceptable theory used today. This causes the defense to be ready for everything. It is quite probable that the defensive team that must prepare to stop both a strong running attack and a strong passing attack will not be entirely ready for either because of limited defensive practice time.

A second theory has the pass as a basic weapon. It is the fundamental part of the total team offense. The running game simply supplements the passing game. Intricate pass patterns become the concern of the coach. The running game is used to "keep the defense honest." Some professional and college teams employ this idea of the pass. It is obvious that the team must have an exceptionally talented passer and quick, fast, sure-fingered ends, together with a line that can give the passer adequate time to make his pass.

The third concept has the passing game as a supplement to the running game. The belief is that the running game is really the important part of the offense. This is the idea that possession is nine-tenths of the game. The pass is used only to "loosen up" the defense, or to fit a certain defensive weakness that may appear. The split-T offense is built on this particular concept. The quarterback is not necessarily a good passer, but must be an excellent faker and runner. The halfbacks do most of the limited passing on "option" end run plays.

The fourth belief considers the pass as a "last resort" type of weapon. The relationship between the pass play and running plays, if present at all, is purely coincidental. This is the pass on third down idea. "Old timers" refer to this technique as the "pass and a prayer" system.

Pass Protection

Before investigating various pass patterns, a discussion of pass protection for the passer is important. The plan of protection to be used for the passer will depend, in part, upon the theory behind the pass play. If the pass is a part of the running offense, no special pass protection will be needed other than to keep linemen, ends excluded, from going beyond the line of scrimmage. This idea will be expanded in the section on specific pass patterns as a part of the descriptions of popular offense plays.

If the pass is separate and distinct from a series of running plays, some special consideration must be given to the method of keeping the defense from molesting the passer. To be certain the pass is an effective weapon, the receivers need time to maneuver, and the passer needs time to locate the receivers without concern for the defensive linemen. Two types of pass protection plans are being used successfully by modern football coaches: (1) cup blocking and (2) man-for-man individual blocking.

Cup blocking. In this system, the center and guards remain in their original places, or they may hit any opponent directly in front of them with a quick step charge and screen block. This is followed by an immediate retreat to the original position, which operates to counteract the momentum of the defensive player. The defensive man has to readjust before striking again. The tackles drop back about 2 yards, and the two backfield men are assigned to the zones just outside the tackles. The cup defense has the advantage of being standardized for any type of defensive alignment. The passer must stay within the confines of the formed cup.

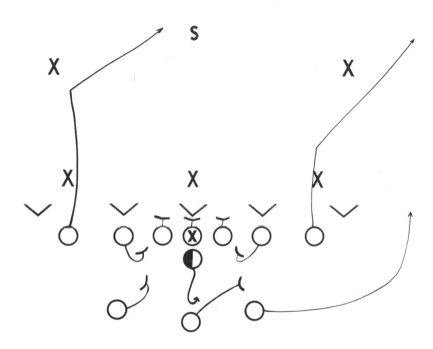

Figure 169. Split-T Pass With Cup Blocking

A major disadvantage of this system is that the offensive linemen often obliterate the quarterback's downfield view of the field. In addition, if no receiver is open, there is little chance for the quarterback to escape the defenders. The quarterback has no running room and frequently finds it necessary to "eat the ball." (See Fig. 169)

Individual blocking. This type of blocking can be either passive or aggressive. The style to use is determined by the ability of the offensive linemen.

Passive blocking. If the technique is to be a passive one, the linemen take a short drop step with their outside feet as the ball is snapped. This step is carried out by a pivot on the inside foot, followed by a drop step with the pivot foot. The blockers must maintain a low, crouched position and wait for the opponent to indicate his intended path of approach. If the opponent is coming on a path to the blocker's outside, the blocker drives into him with a shoulder block allowing forward progress, but on a path that will move the rusher on past the passer. The blocker keeps his head between his opponent and the passer.

The step and pivot action of the pass protectors invites the opponents to penetrate on an outside lane. This opens the middle for the possible escape of the passer. Should the opponent select an inside path, or change from an outside to an inside path, however, the blocker uses an aggressive shoulder block to drive the opponent into the center.

Another method of using the passive blocking procedure is a reverse of the foregoing technique. The pass protectors take a pivot and then drop step on their outside feet. This maneuver invites the opponents to penetrate on an inside path. The ends are persuaded to take an inside course by the action of the passer, who stays close to the line of scrimmage for a couple of counts. Now the passer can move out from the scrimmage line and swing wide to either side of the field, giving him an excellent view of the pass pattern and providing him with the option of running down the sideline, if the defenders have all retreated with the pass receivers.

Passive blocking does not mean relaxation on the part of the protectors. *Remember, never allow a rusher to proceed along a path that leads straight to the passer.*

Aggressive blocking. Another method of protecting the passer is one very similar to the cup technique. The same theory applies as for individual passive blocking, with the blockers' being immediately aggressive rather than passive. The blockers drive hard into their opponents at the snap signal. Contact is immediately severed, as the blocker reacts to the initial charge by drop stepping as described for passive blocking mentioned before. On short passes, the protectors need not bother with the drop step, but simply continue the aggressive block.

In this individual style of blocking, the general rule used is to block a man who is in your immediate territory. If no man is in this immediate area, drop back a step or two and help where help seems needed. *Always be alert for penetrating linebackers.*

An advantage of the individual blocking technique is that each man has a specific rule to follow and knows who he is to block. The passive technique drives the defensive linemen away from the passer also, making it possible for him to run with the ball when all receivers are covered. Another major advantage of

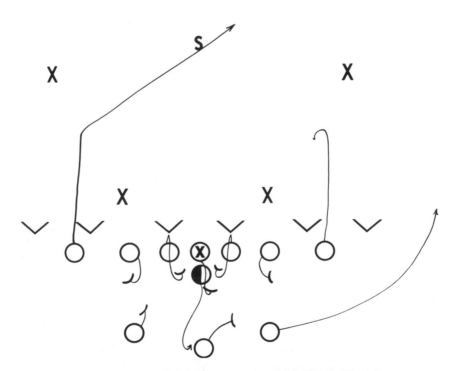

Figure 170. Split-T Pass With Individual Blocking

the individual technique is that it adapts itself well to "draw" type plays that are so popular today. The major disadvantage is that the defender must be as good or better than the rusher. A slow-thinking protector is sure to be out-maneuvered by a smart rusher. The pass protection used actually is only as good as the individual men who are to perform it.

The Running Pass

The running pass should be a part of any coach's schedule of offensive plays. The running pass takes advantage of defensive shifts and maneuvers calculated to stop the running offense. The running pass threat will make the defense "keep honest." It will result in the defensive halfbacks' staying back in normal position, rather than being allowed to move up closer to the scrimmage line. This type of passing attack should keep the defense out of 8- and 9-man-lines, which are devised to stop the running attack. Frequently the running pass will result in touchdowns, if the defense fully believes that a running play is coming at them. Several of the running pass possibilities will be given following.

Optional pass. The optional pass is now a major threat to end run plays. The end run is so devised as to allow the runner the option of continuing his run or passing downfield. This style of play is used popularly with both single wing and T formation offenses. The pressure put on the defensive backfield is tremendous. They have no way of knowing whether to come up to stop the runner or to stay back and cover the receiver. The pressure is unbearable if the outside linebacker and end have been blocked out of the play. (See Fig. 171)

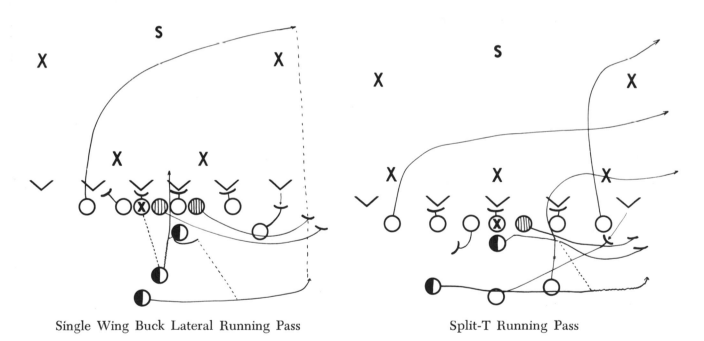

Single Wing Buck Lateral Running Pass   Split-T Running Pass

Figure 171. Optional Pass

Button hook passes. The running fake button hook pass is used to keep the defensive linebackers from concentrating solely on the running game. It is also an effective weapon to use against stunting type defenses. The threat of this pass will tend to cause the defense to use more standard types of maneuvers, which should give the running game a better chance to operate successfully. (See Fig. 172)

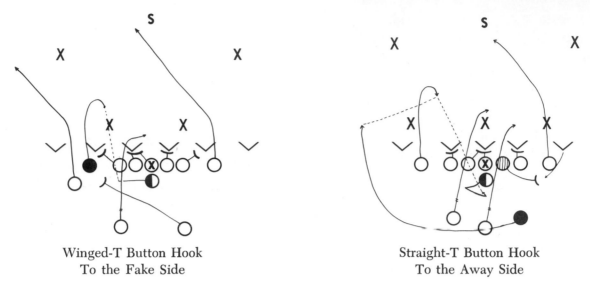

Winged-T Button Hook
To the Fake Side

Straight-T Button Hook
To the Away Side

Figure 172. Button Hook Passes

Screen passes. The screen pass can be used effectively after a fake run by throwing the pass to the side away from the fake run. The pull of the play will cause the defensive backfield to rotate toward the run, leaving the weak or offside relatively defenseless.

The success of the screen run fake pass lies, as in all running passes, in the deception of the fake. The play must be performed so as to convince the defense that the intent is to run the ball. It is essential that all fakes be carried out well beyond the scrimmage line. (See Fig. 173) As in all pass plays, linemen other than ends are not allowed downfield until the ball is in the air.

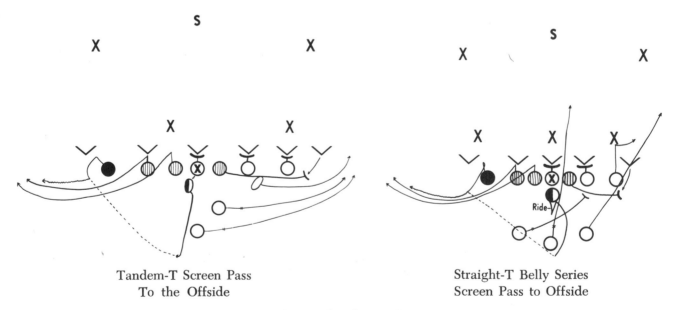

Tandem-T Screen Pass
To the Offside

Straight-T Belly Series
Screen Pass to Offside

Figure 173. Screen Passes

Quick passes. Quick passes are quite similar to button hook passes. The basic difference is that the receivers do not stop. The theory is identical to that of the button hook running passes: draw in the defense and pass over them. Some quick passes are executed without any preliminary, fake, others are thrown after fake runs. (See Fig. 174)

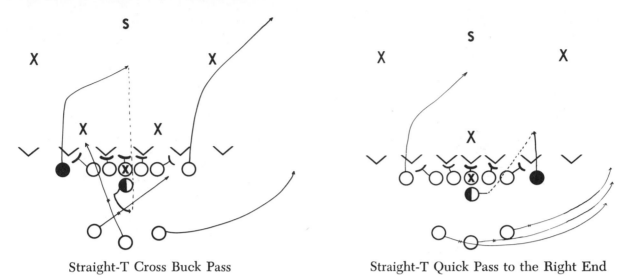

Straight-T Cross Buck Pass   Straight-T Quick Pass to the Right End

Figure 174. Quick Passes

Straight Passes

The straight pass may or may not start with a fake run. This pass is usually thrown from the deep (5 yards from the line of scrimmage) position. The line uses either cup or individual pass protection. This can be considered the standard pass offensive pattern.

V-out pattern. The V-out pattern gets its name from the movement of the ends on this particular play. Both ends start straight down the field, and each man moves on an arc toward the sidelines. The passer attempts to "hit" the receiver just before the receiver goes out of bounds. The pass is usually thrown with considerable height so that the end can run under the ball to make the catch. (See Fig. 175)

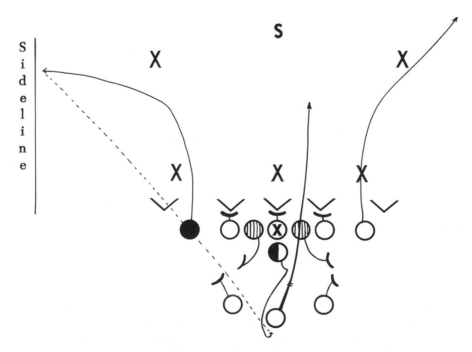

Figure 175. V-out Pattern

Flag and post passes. Two pass routes are known commonly as the flag path and the post path. Specifically, a *flag* route directs the receiver at the "coffin corner" or goal line marker. This pattern results usually from a vertical path down the field as a preliminary followed by a cut directly at the corner flag. The *post* pattern is similar but the final direction is into the middle of the field directly at the near goal post. (The two terms are used often in relation to a variety of pass plays to give easy directions to the receivers.) (See Fig. 176)

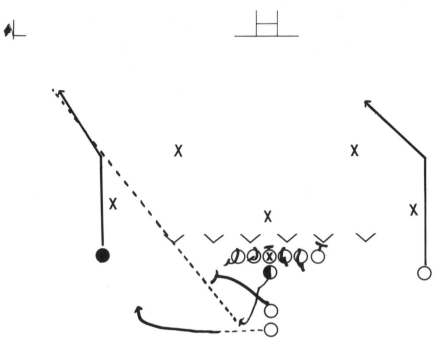

Figure 176. Flag and Post Passes

Sideline cut. The sideline cut pass is similar to the V-out. The basic difference is that the receiver heads straight downfield and then cuts sharply toward the sideline. This pass is used against a defensive halfback who is staying back from the end to prevent a pass completion behind him. It can also be used effectively after the completion of the V-out pattern, which was used against a close-guarding defensive man. (See Fig. 177)

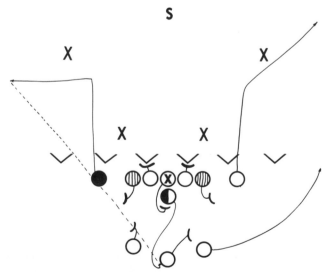

Figure 177. Sideline Cut Pass

Out-and-in or in-and-out passes. The out-and-in pass is effective against a defensive man who is overly cautious about his outside territory. The defensive man moves rapidly on the out maneuver to maintain a position slightly ahead of the offensive man. This pattern also takes the end away from the safety man, who is covering the middle territory. The return cut to the inside should put the receiver in the clear, apart from both the guarding halfback and the safety man. The in-and-out pass is the reverse of the foregoing. It is used against a halfback who tends to go with the inside fake, and cannot react rapidly to his outside. (See Fig. 178)

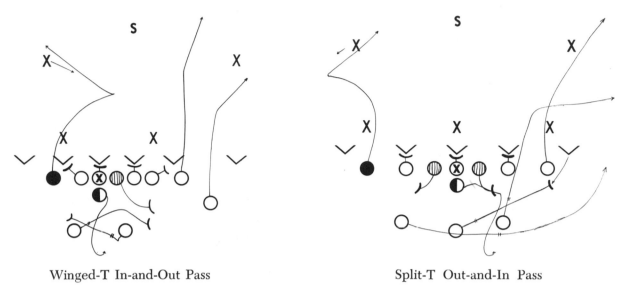

Winged-T In-and-Out Pass   Split-T Out-and-In Pass

Figure 178. Out-and-In or In-and-Out Passes

Button hook passes. There are several variations of the button hook pass. This style of pass is used against teams that retreat rapidly on a pass play. In addition it can be used with a drop-off variation in which one man pulls a defensive man out of position. The second, or drop-off, man, stops in the vacated defensive territory. The pass is usually thrown with speed and little arc. Lateral passes can be easily added, of course, to the button hook pass. (See Fig. 179)

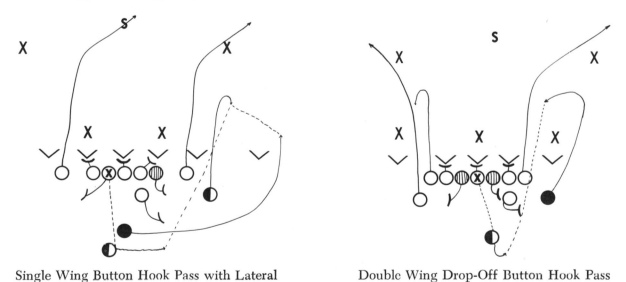

Single Wing Button Hook Pass with Lateral   Double Wing Drop-Off Button Hook Pass

Figure 179. Button Hook Passes

Zone flooding. The zone flooding pass maneuver is used primarily against teams that employ the zone defense technique against passes. The attempt is made to send two or three men into one zone. This should make it impossible for one man to cover all the receivers. (See Fig. 180)

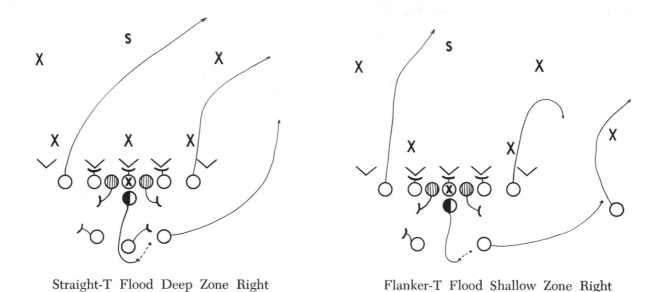

Straight-T Flood Deep Zone Right   Flanker-T Flood Shallow Zone Right

Figure 180. Zone Flooding

Cross passes. The cross pass is used to confuse and befuddle the straight man-for-man pass defense. The cross can be made with the ends, the end and a halfback, or any other combination. (See Fig. 181)

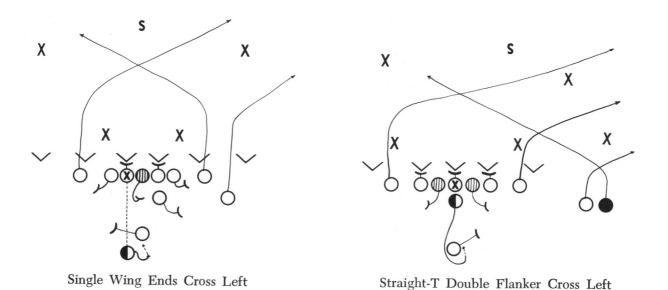

Single Wing Ends Cross Left   Straight-T Double Flanker Cross Left

Figure 181. Cross Passes

Flair passes. This pass is usually intended for a halfback. The name comes from the path followed by the halfback. The receiver flairs wide into the flat before turning on an arc downfield. A decoy deep receiver is sent out first to draw the defense with him. This is a valuable pass pattern to use against man-for-man defensive teams that try to cover the flat with linebackers. A fake buck temporarily detains the linebacker, giving the halfback ample time to move far to his outside. The flair pattern can be run by an end from the **winged**, flanker, or man-in-motion attack. (See Fig. 182)

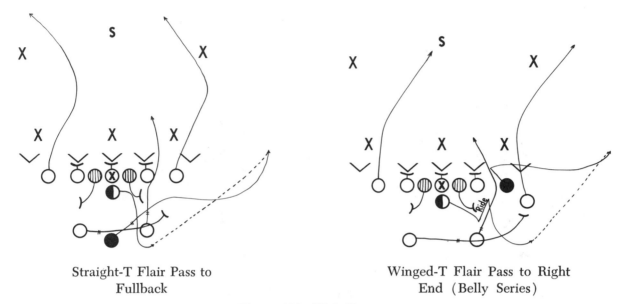

Straight-T Flair Pass to
Fullback

Winged-T Flair Pass to Right
End (Belly Series)

Figure 182. Flair Passes

Screen passes. The screen pass is a highly effective offensive weapon and should be a part of all offensive attacks. It is a surprise type of maneuver that takes advantage of careless defensive linemen. The trickery consists of passively blocking one side, or all of the defensive line. The linemen then are allowed to pursue the passer. The offensive linemen, who have released defensive men, now stand ready to lead the receiver downfield, or to move toward a sideline to form their blocking wall. Excellent line deception and split timing are necessary for the proper execution of this play, and the linemen must know downfield blocking procedures. Otherwise the linemen might overlook a defensive halfback. Linemen cannot cross the scrimmage line until the pass has been completed. It is advisable to have the pass receiver call out "go," so that the linemen will know when to proceed downfield. (See Fig. 183)

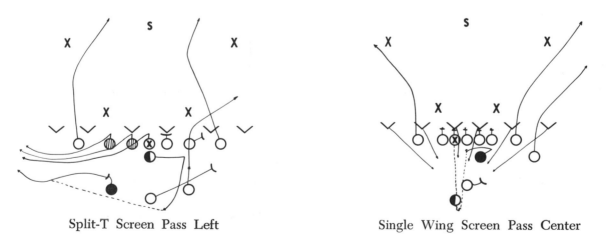

Split-T Screen Pass Left

Single Wing Screen Pass Center

Figure 183. Screen Passes

Trailer or check-out passes. The trailer pass is similar to the screen in that it is completed at or behind the scrimmage line. The primary difference between the trailer and the screen lies in the fact that the linemen do not provide a wall of interference. The linemen carry out regular pass protection assignments. The trailer pass is used against teams whose defensive backfield men are aware of deep passes. The rapid retreat of the defensive backs leaves a wide gap between them and the scrimmage line. The pass is intended to take advantage of this particular gap. It should be noted that the pass receiver makes a temporary block before proceeding out for the pass. (See Fig 184)

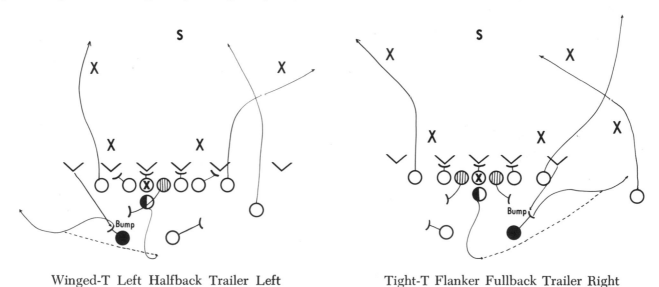

Winged-T Left Halfback Trailer Left   Tight-T Flanker Fullback Trailer Right

Figure 184. Trailer Passes or Check-out Passes

Over-loading the deep territory. Fairly long thrown touchdown passes can be arranged against the deep man-for-man pass defenders. This style of pass is very effective against the box type defense; however, it can be used successfully against any relatively slow charging defensive team that plays a man-for-man defense. (See Fig. 185)

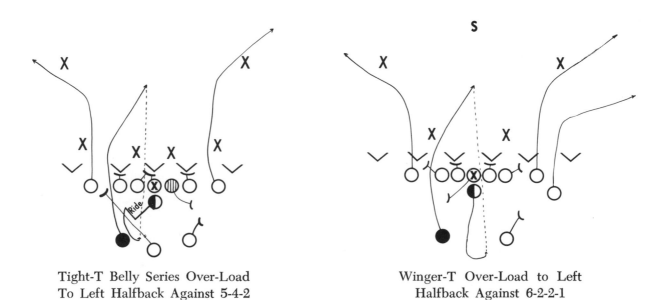

Tight-T Belly Series Over-Load   Winger-T Over-Load to Left
To Left Halfback Against 5-4-2   Halfback Against 6-2-2-1

Figure 185. Over-Loading The Deep Territory

Straight deep pass. (*Fly*). The split end and/or flanker attack goes well with the straight deep pass. In this style of attack, the split offensive man attempts to out-run the defensive halfback. If the offensive man is quite a bit faster than the defensive man, the chances are very good that he will get into the clear behind the defensive man. In the past, this type of pass was referred to as "a pass and a prayer." (See Fig. 186)

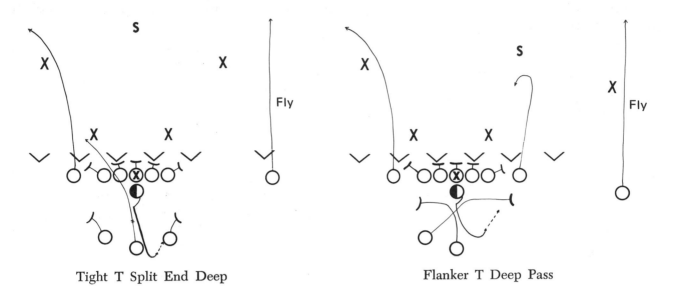

Tight T Split End Deep   Flanker T Deep Pass

Figure 186. Straight Deep Passes

Look-in pass. The look-in pass is an excellent complement to the straight deep pass from the split end or wide flanker alignment. The look-in pass can be used to set up the straight deep pass by drawing the defensive halfback in close to protect against the short pass. The straight deep pass can be used also to set up the look-in pass. The pass receiver in this pattern cuts diagonally across the field from the side to the middle in front of the defensive halfback. This is an effective short gainer pass. (See Fig. 187)

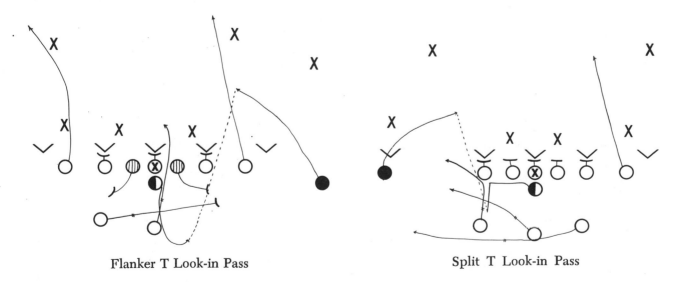

Flanker T Look-in Pass   Split T Look-in Pass

Figure 187. Look-in Passes

Delay pass. Team defenses that drop rapidly their linebackers and/or secondary leave gaps between the scrimmage line and the pass defenders. Offensive pass receivers can be delayed in their positions momentarily (count 1001, 1002) and then sent into these openings. Also, a defensive team that "crowds" the scrimmage line on a "sure" running situation can be surprised occasionally by the use of a delayed pass. (See Fig. 188 and 189)

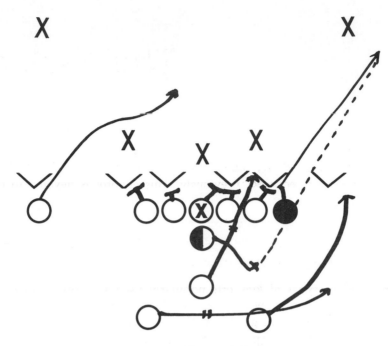

Figure 188. End Delay

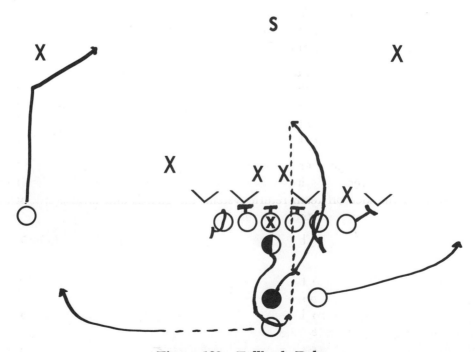

Figure 189. Fullback Delay

Chapter 11

The Kicking Game

The kicking game consists of kick-offs, punts, extra points, and field goals. The individual parts of these particular kicking skills have been covered previously. This chapter is devoted to the team offense and defense phases of the kicking game.

The Kick Off

The kick off should be considered from two distinct angles: kicking off and returning the kick off.

Kicking off. There are three types of kick offs popularly used in football. One type kicks the ball deep into the opponents' territory. This is the most widely-used kick off technique. The second method is to kick the ball in such a way that the chances are good that the opponents will handle the ball poorly. The third method is the onside kick, in which the hope is that the kicking team will recover the ball.

Kick off alignment. It is important that the team which is to kick off has its personnel in the correct positions on the field. The two fastest men on the team should be placed at the outside end positions on the kick off line, or as the second men in at each end. If these speedsters are placed at the outside positions, they should be given no outside responsibility. Their task is to proceed to the kick off receiver by the shortest and quickest route possible. The ends, who in this case are the second men in from the side lines, veer out and have the outside responsibility. This technique is used to disrupt the opponents' blocking strategy.

The other key personnel in the kick off alignment are the safety men. Some teams use one safety man, others employ two safety men. If one safety man is used, he usually is placed next to the kick off man. If two safety men are used, they usually are placed as the third men in from each sideline position. These safety men trail the first wave of attack down the field and literally are assigned the duty of safety men. They have the task of preventing touchdown runbacks. Obviously these safety men need to be "sure" tacklers.

The guards are placed in inside positions, one on the side of the kick off man and one on the side of the safety man. The tackles assume the next inside position alongside the guards. If indications are that the opponent uses a numbering of the kick off team return system, the guards and tackles criss-cross as they proceed downfield, each assuming the other's original assignment.

The kick off man is told to follow the ball downfield as fast as possible. This man frequently makes the kick off tackle.

The aforementioned alignment of the team personnel will provide power and strength down the middle and speed and maneuverability on the outside. It is desirable to have everyone except the kicker line up on the 35-yard line. Some coaches prefer to have the men all face to the inside; others like to have their men face downfield from a three point stance. The important point is to teach the men not to move until the kicker is even with them on his approach. As a result of watching the kicker kick the ball, the team personnel should never be off-side. (See Fig. 190 & 191)

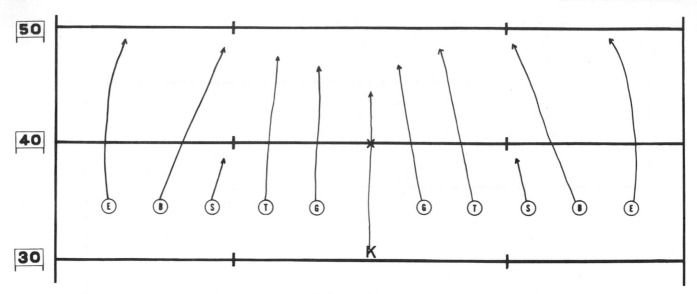

Figure 190. Straight Double Safety Kick Off

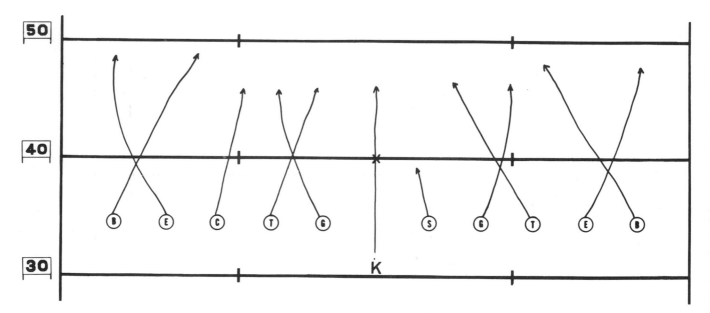

Figure 191. Cross Single Safety Kick Off

Returning the kick off. The primary objective of returning the kick off is to score a touchdown. If this is not feasible, the returning team must return the ball to at least their own 30 or 35 yard line. This puts the team in an advantageous position for the full exploitation of their offensive attack. Even if no gain is made from this spot, a kicking advantage is gained for the receiving team. The kicker can force the opponents deep into their own territory with a fairly good kick.

Alignment for receiving the kickoff. The kick off receiving rule states that five men of the receiving team must maintain positions between their own 40 and 45 yard lines. Usually, the coach places his linemen—center, guards, and tackles—in this forward position. The coach can place the remainder of his team personnel wherever he desires. Standard procedure, that will assure adequate coverage for any type of a kick off, is to place the ends at about the 25 yard line and on the hash marks. The halfbacks are placed on the 10 yard line and also on the hash marks. The fullback assumes a position in the middle of the field on the 20 yard line. The safety man is also in the middle of the field, but on the goal line.

If the kick off man is an exceptionally long distance kicker, the ends should be moved back to about the 18 yard line, the fullback to the 15 yard line, and the two halfbacks to the 5 yard line. If the kicker is a weak kicker, the defensive personnel are moved 5 or more yards closer to the kick off man. These positions will be shown in the diagrams of the various types of kick off returns.

Middle return.   There are two types of middle returns popularly used by the kick off receiving team. The most standard procedure is forming a wedge to lead the ball receiver up the middle of the field. This type of return generally is used when the kick off is a short one, or when the kicking off team uses a flat or rolling kick. The wedge is formed by having the receiving forward wall drop back to about 15 yards from the receiver. These men then turn and form the wedge, together with the remaining members of the team. The blocking rule is to block the first man in your path, usually with a cross body block. (See Fig. 192)

The other type of middle return uses cross type blocking. The cross is made by the forward line. The center or middle man has the responsibility of blocking the kicker. The men on either side of the center, usually the tackles, drop back and then cross block. The right tackle blocks the man to the right of the kicker, and the left tackle blocks the man to the left of the kicker. The guards can block the men on their side of the kicker or cross block by changing their assigned men, as done by the tackles. This must be decided beforehand by the coach.

The rest of the team personnel block straight as they did in the wedge return. The ball carrier stays within the alley formed by the blockers as long as possible. *Remember, the key man is the man who kicks the ball.* It is wise to assign both the center and the fullback to this man. Some coaches like to have the center charge directly at the kicker without any preliminary retreat, believing this procedure will catch the kicker in a very vulnerable position, as he will have just completed his kick. In addition, the kicker will be more concerned with this charging man than with kicking the ball the next time he has to kick off. (See Fig. 193)

Side line return.   Side line returns are usually very effective against teams that kick the ball high and deep. The key men to be blocked are the end man and the first man to his inside, on the side where the ball is to be returned. This can be effected by one of two methods.

In the first method, the outside man in the front line and the end on the same side are assigned to block the second man. The fullback and halfback, or safety man, are assigned the task of double teaming the outside man. If a cross takes place between the two defensive men, the offensive men switch their assignments. (See Fig. 194)

The second method of double team blocking is slightly different. In this technique, the outside man in the front line and the end double team the outside defensive man. The second and third front linemen double team the number two or second man in the defensive alignment. The fourth man in the front line and the fullback double team the third defensive man. The advantage of this style of kick off return blocking is that any of the four backs can return the ball without weakening the double team blocking. (See Fig. 195)

In either style of double team blocking return, the rest of the team personnel form a wall along the side lines, spaced about 5 yards apart. The wall formed is not parallel to the side line; it is slanted from the middle of the field to the second double team block. The rule for the wall blockers is that they will block any opponent who tries to penetrate the wall between them and the opponents' goal. *Remember, don't go out of the wall after the defensive men; let them come to you.*

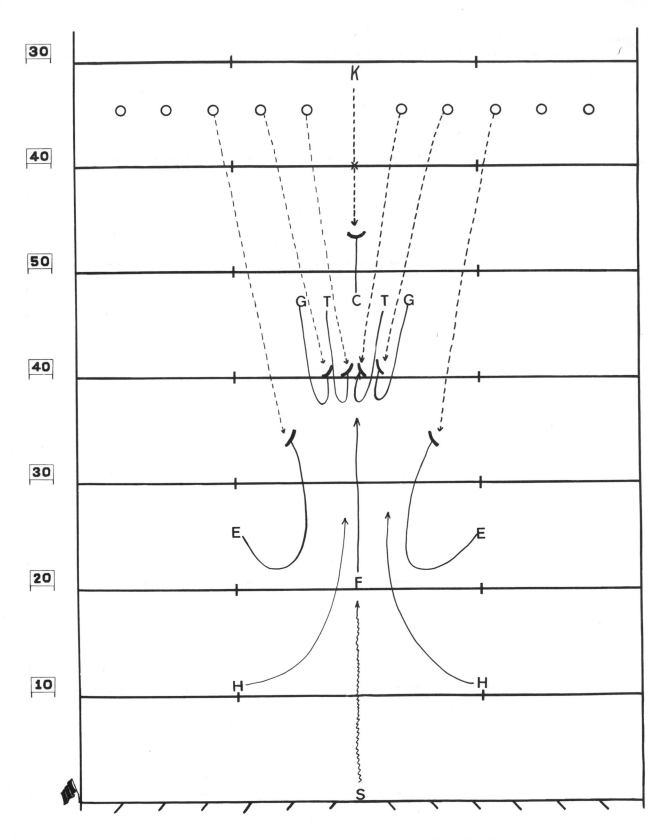

Figure 192. Middle Kick Off Return Wedge Blocking

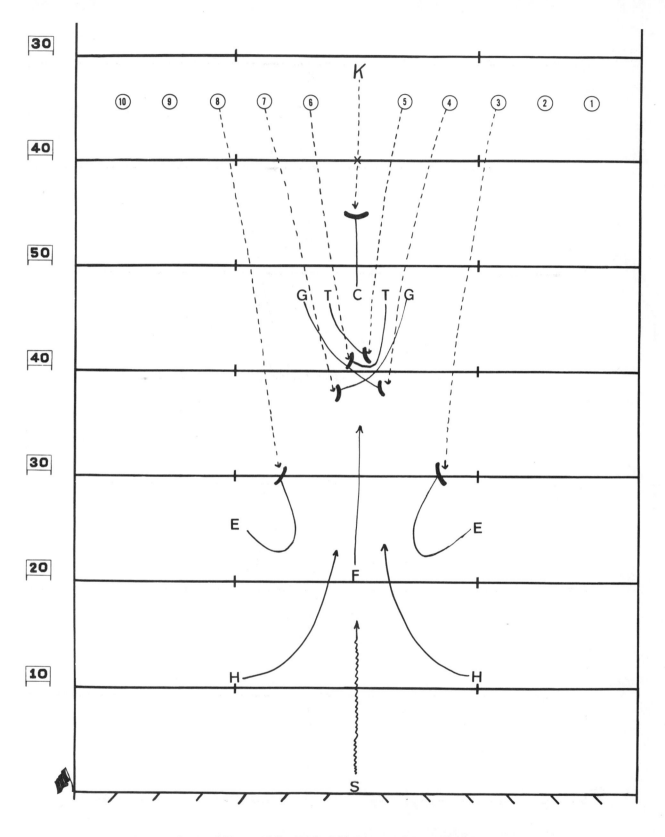

Figure 193. Middle Kick Off Return Cross Blocking

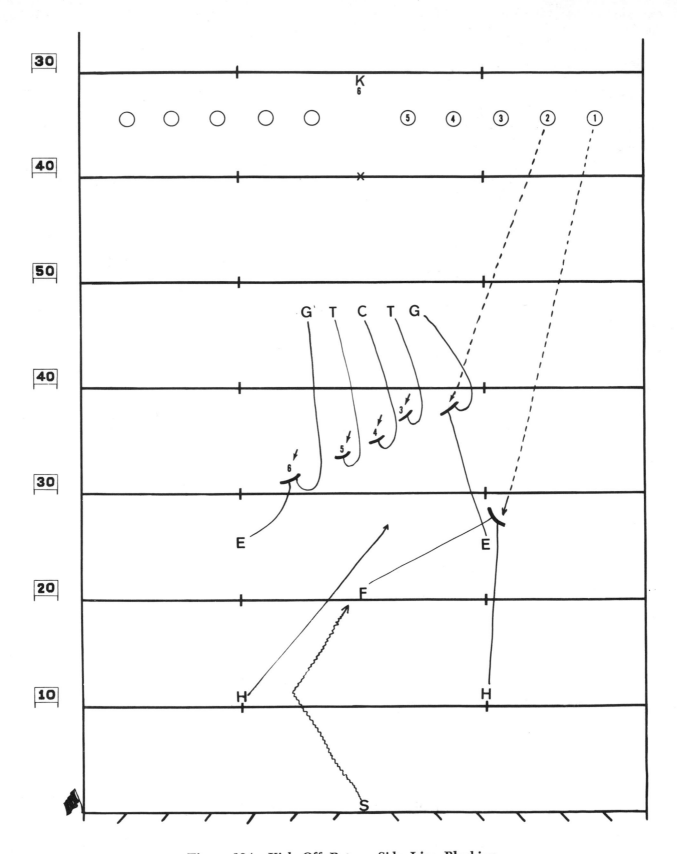

Figure 194. Kick Off Return Side Line Blocking

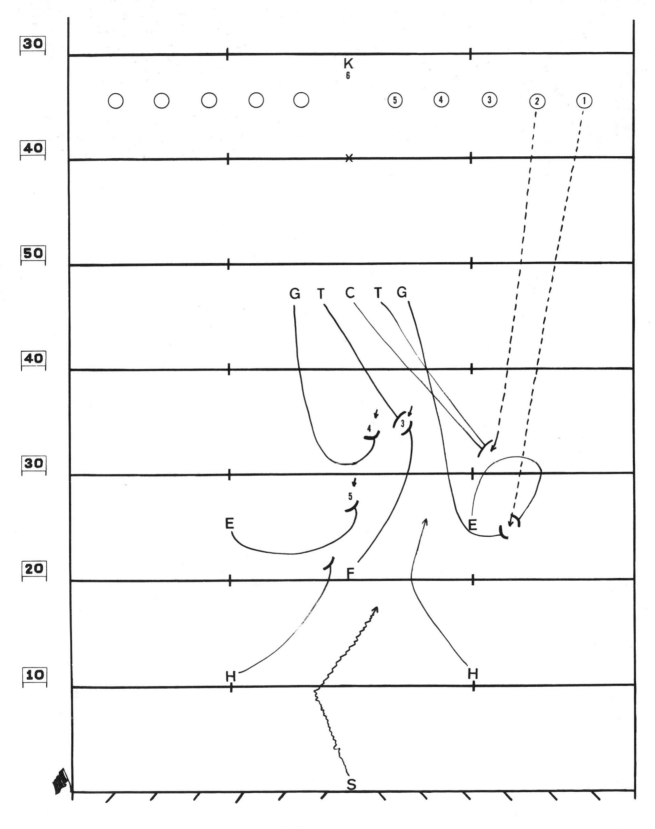

Figure 195. Kick Off Return Wall Right

The Punt

The punt play consists of offensive maneuvers to protect the punter and cover the receiver, and defensive maneuvers to block the punt and/or return the punt.

Punt protection. Punts are of two types: the quick kick and the regular deep punt formation kick. The protection used depends upon the style of kick employed.

Quick kick. The quick kick is much less popular than the regular punt formation kick. Its days of popularity are almost past, with few teams still employing it. The "wide open" variation of modern football, and the desire to control the ball as long as possible, have resulted in discontinuance of the use of the quick kick. The quick kick can be an effective team weapon, however, with its success dependent upon the surprise element. The defensive team must be fooled into thinking that a run is imminent, and the quick kick is made from the offensive formation being used. It is usually employed on second or third down. The idea is to punt the ball over the head of the safety man in the hopes that it will roll deep into the opponents' territory. (See page 27 for mechanics)

Regular kick. The regular punt formation is of two general types. The most widely used alignment has a tight balanced line with the ends split about 5 yards. Two backs protect the kicking side of the kicker, and one back protects the offside. The punter lines up 10-12 yards from the center. (See Fig. 196)

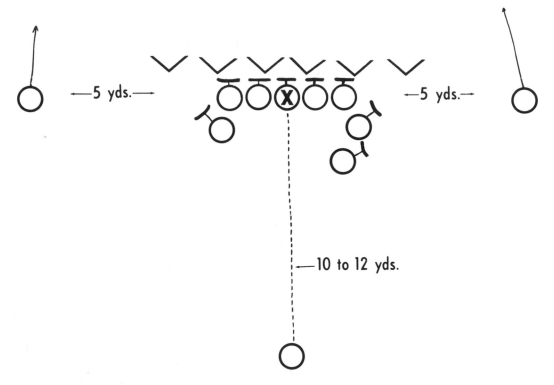

Figure 196. Standard Deep Punt Formation

The second and more modern version of punt protection is the spread protection. The primary value of this type of protection is that it tends to spread the defending team, making their block threat less serious. This formation also allows the offensive line time to move downfield much faster.

There is one primary concern to be considered before the team can use this punt protection technique. The center must be able to snap the ball at least 13 yards with some degree of accuracy. If the center cannot handle this assignment, the spread protection will be discarded in favor of the tight protection.

There are two generally accepted concepts of backfield placement in the spread protection. One idea is to place a close back on the kicker's offside about 1 yard behind the scrimmage line and between the guard and center. This man steps forward on his outside foot with the snap of the ball, then blocks across the center position to his own right. The onside up back is about 1½ yards deep between his center and guard. He steps forward on his outside foot with the snap of the ball and blocks across behind the opposite close back. The other back, usually the fullback, is 6-7 yards from the scrimmage line. He never steps backwards, but blocks the most dangerous onrushing opponent. (See Fig. 197)

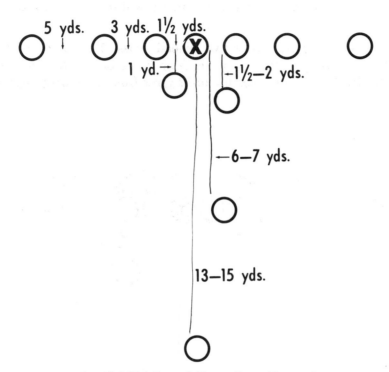

Figure 197. Spread Deep Punt Formation

The second theory of backfield alignment places all three backs in a line about 5-6 yards deep and parallel to the scrimmage line. Two of the backs are placed on the kicker's kicking side, and the other is spaced a yard or two to the left. These men maintain their original positions at all times, never allowing any opponent to penetrate through them. Some teams have used linemen in these backfield positions for added strength or protection and for added speed downfield. (See Fig. 198) The three deep backfield can be used with the tight line as well.

Blocking the punt. Many teams devote a great deal of time to punt blocking tricks. This punt blocking is undertaken usually by teams that have strong defenses, which cause the opponents to kick frequently. It is wise for all coaches to devise some punt blocking techniques. A blocked and recovered punt is a great morale builder for any team, and can frequently result in a touchdown.

Two general procedures are used to block punts. One method is to overload the defending halfbacks. This is usually done on the kicker's offside, with the tackle and end working together. One of them attempts to draw the back out of position, while the other pursues a path "up the alley." (See Fig. 199)

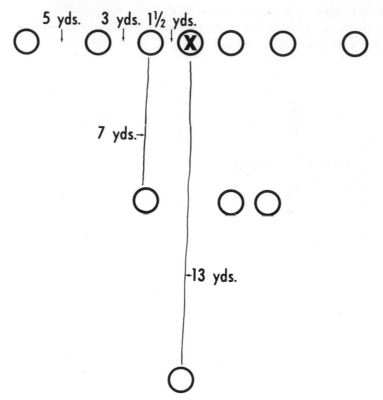

Figure 198. Spread Deep Punt Formation

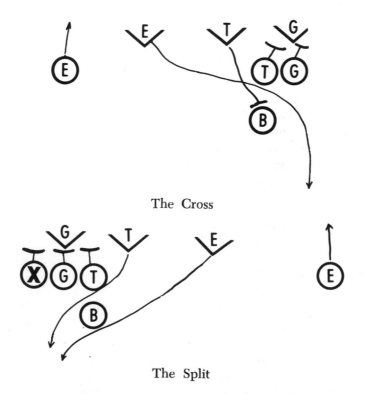

The Cross

The Split

Figure 199. Punt Blocking From The Side

The second technique of punt blocking is to drive directly "up the alley" either by overloading or by moving the center out of the way. The center is moved by the roll out procedure, in which one man grabs and pulls the center out of position, while the second man proceeds on to block the punt. (See Fig. 200)

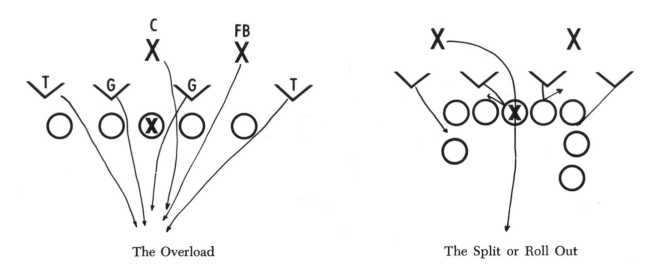

The Overload   The Split or Roll Out

Figure 200. Punt Blocking Over The Middle

Returning the punt. The principle behind the punt return is to go "all the way," meaning that the punt receiver must know how to handle the ball, and the blockers must know when and how to block. There are two patterns of punt returns used in modern football. One technique is to return the ball up the middle of the field; the other method is to return the ball up the sideline.

Middle return. The middle return generally is used when the kick is a poor one, and also to "keep the punting team honest," so that the sideline return will be more effective. To adapt the middle return, the receiving team lines up with a man head-on the guards and tackles of the punting team. The ends line up head-on the offensive ends, unless they play exceptionally wide. The defensive linemen block the offensive linemen to keep them from going downfield. The offensive men are released and the defensive men retreat rapidly. The guards take the first two men downfield in the middle. They can play the man on their side or use crossing tactics. The tackles hold, release, and sprint downfield as fast as possible. In turn, they assume a position somewhat shorter than the guards and block the first man on their side. The two halfbacks "dog" or trail the end on their side, keeping to their outside. This maneuver will cause the end to stay wide, as he expects to be blocked in by the back. The center and fullback, unless a double safety is being used, drop back rapidly and form a vanguard for the ball carrier, blocking anyone in the way. (See Figs. 201 & 202)

Sideline return. The defensive alignment for the sideline return is the same as that for the middle return. The initial reaction of the linemen is identical, in fact, in that they hold in the offensive linemen as long as is legally possible. The major difference now occurs. The linemen release their opponents and sprint for the sideline on a path parallel to the scrimmage line, following this course until they are about 10 yards from the sidelines. Then they turn downfield and form their wall. The linemen space themselves out about 7-8 yards apart. The onside end will be the first man in the formed wall, and the offside end will be the last man. The key block is the one made on the onside offensive end. This block is first made by the onside halfback. If he has not finished off the end, the onside linebacker will complete the job. It is absolutely essential that this man be taken out of the play. His removal allows the ball carrier to pursue a course up the sideline. The key blockers can be greatly assisted if the safety man heads up the middle of the field before finally heading for the sideline. Another technique is the use of twin safety men who criss-cross, faking or keeping the ball. (See Figs. 203 & 204)

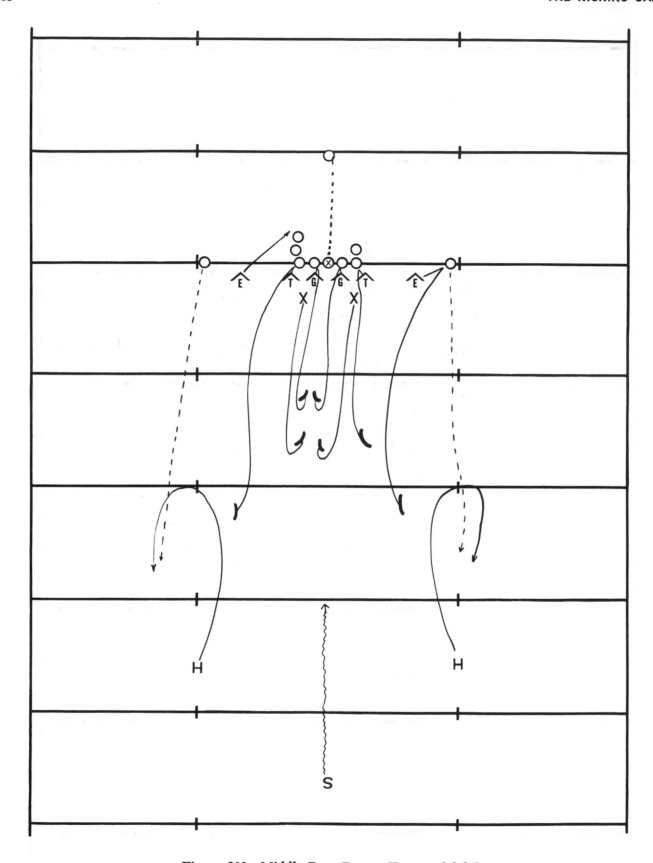

Figure 201. Middle Punt Return From a 6-2-2-1

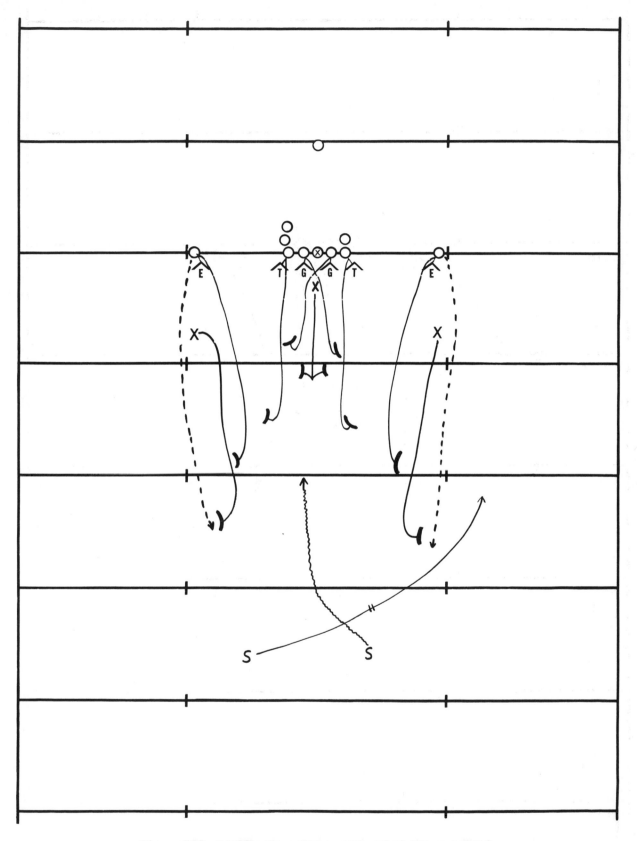

Figure 202. Middle Punt Return (Crossing) From a 6-3-2

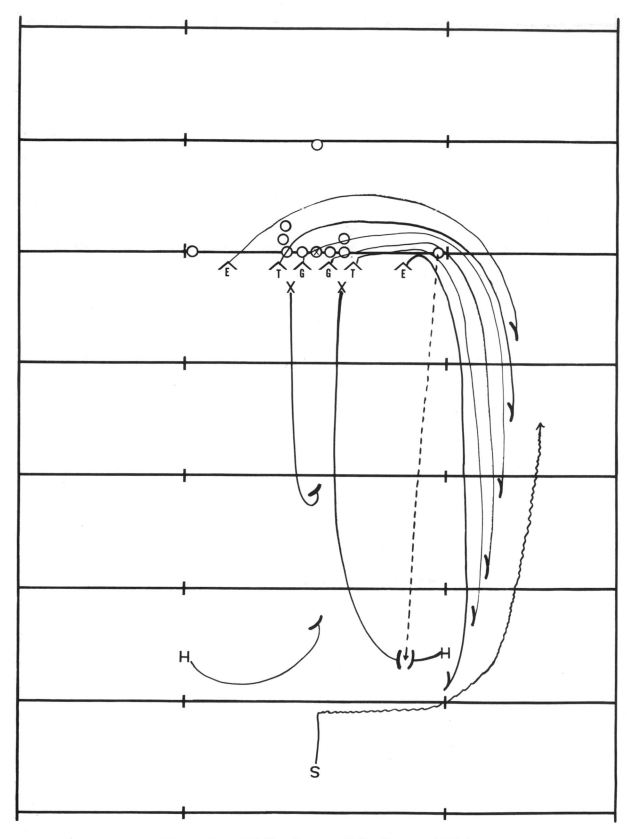

Figure 203. Sideline Return Right From a 6-2-2-1

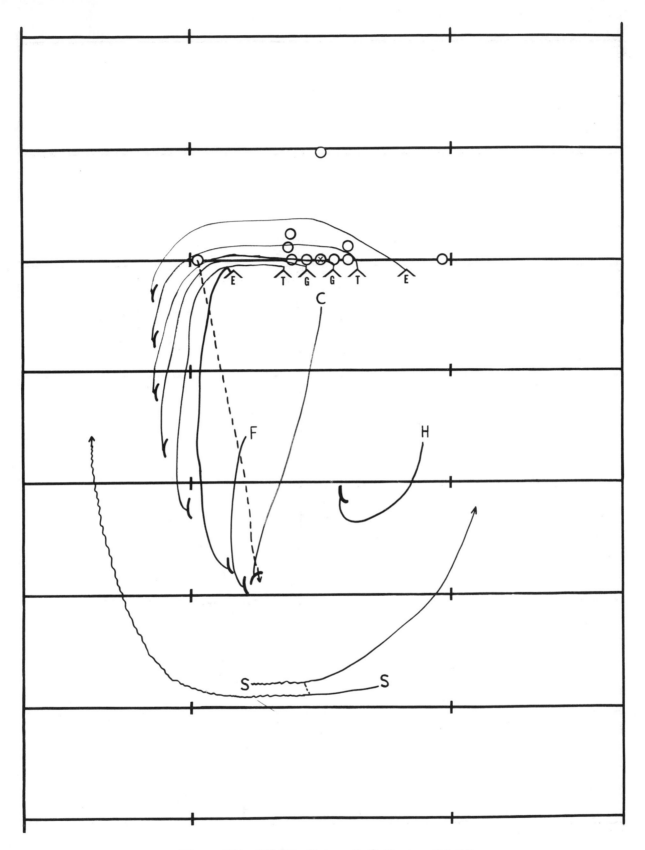

Figure 204. Sideline Return Left From a 6-1-2-2

Punt return practice offers an excellent opportunity to provide sprinting practice for the team personnel. It will tend to increase the running endurance of the linemen and enhance their physical fitness. It is necessary to spend a considerable time on sideline punt returns if you wish to have them "pay off" in long gains and touchdowns. A punt returned "down the throats" of the punting team is an excellent method of shattering the opponents' morale.

Field Goal and Extra Point Kick

Field goal and extra point protection. The team protection used in the field goal and extra point kick is identical. The one accepted technique is to have the kicking team line up in tight line from end to end. These linemen have inside protection responsibilities. A backfield man lines up tight to, and within a hand's forward reach of, each end. Their responsibility is to bump anyone going to their outside, while being concerned primarily with inside protection. The holder lines up 7-8 yards behind the center. (See Fig. 205)

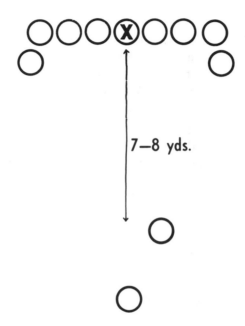

Figure 205. Field Goal and Extra Point Protection

Blocking the field goal or extra point. The usual procedure in attempting to block these special kicks is to use an 8-man rushing line. As in blocking the punt, pulling and overloading stunts are used. (See page 163) A team does not have to kick the ball because it has assumed a kicking position. The three backs must be alert therefore to pass and run attempts from a fake kick.

Chapter 12

Team Defense

The modern emphasis in football is definitely on team offense. Unfortunately, strong defensive football is often neglected. This change from defensive to offensive play is due, in part, to the fact that explosive, wide-open football has replaced the possession type play of the past. Most coaches are now out for the touchdown on every play. A general theory seems to be that it is easier to defeat your opponent by out-scoring him than by keeping him from scoring.

The recent rule change which abolished the utilization of the platoon system at the college level is responsible, in part, for the swing to offensive football. The college coach is now faced with the problem of developing his offense and, at the same time, developing the offensive men into defensive men. This task is complicated by the fact that high schools still utilize the platoon system. Something had to give—logically, the defense suffered.

It is true that a high scoring team can quickly demoralize its opponent. Anxiety, frustration, and desperation are certain to set in, however, when the scoring potential of this team is throttled. It is often impossible, or at least extremely difficult, to out-score your high flying opponent. This task is greatly reduced, however, when the opponents' offense is thrown off balance by a strong and stubborn defense.

DEFENSIVE THEORY

A good defense will usually exist when the desire to stop the opponent is great. Included as a part of this "desire" must be a sound grooming in fundamentals, properly placed defensive personnel, and variations of defensive maneuvers.

Desire to stop the opponent. A primary responsibility of a coach is the development and maintenance of a high level of team morale. The cliché, "A team that won't be beaten can't be beaten," is true to a certain degree. "Desire" has been described by words such as determination, spirit, will-to-win, intestinal fortitude, and just plain "guts." The concept of team desire is fundamental to both team offense and team defense. One "gun shy" tackler can completely disrupt the defensive success of a team. Football is a game for "men." It is a contact game in which physical jars, bruises, aches and pains are commonplace. The true football "desire" of a player, or team, can readily be seen by the type of defensive football played, wherein lies the yardstick of courage, manliness, and "heart." The successful coach is the one who has developed a high level of "desire" in his team.

Fundamentals. Individual defensive fundamentals have been covered previously. The "smart" coach is the one who does not neglect these basic defensive fundamentals. A player with tremendous "desire" but poor fundamentals will be as effective as a double-barrel shot gun with only one shell. Constant practice of individual defensive fundamentals should be stressed throughout the football season. This defensive concentration is as vital to team success as is offensive blocking practice.

Properly placed defensive personnel. There is a multitude of defensive alignments popularly used in modern football. These patterns usually originate at the college level and pass on down to the high school level by means of magazine articles, books, and coaching clinics. There are many ingenious high school coaches who devise their own defensive patterns, which seems complicated, but is not a difficult task. The satisfaction it brings to the coach makes the effort highly worthwhile.

The theory behind defensive strategy is to arrange the team personnel so as to make the opponents' offense impotent. There are two generally different concepts of how to achieve this end. One idea is to stop the opponent from making any gains, or even penetrating into the opponents' backfield, causing losses to occur. The slogan of this defensive theory is "Give them nothing."

The second idea is based on the realization that it is quite impossible to completely throttle the opponents' offense, thus the strategy is one of containment. The defensive team seldom penetrates into the opponents' backfield. The strategy is to meet and control the opponents' charge and then play the ball. The general idea is to cause the opponent to have to punt on third down. The team allows no more than 3 yards per down, normally making it a fourth down and one situation. Should a pass be attempted and incompleted, the defense may find themselves in a situation where they can allow the opponent as much as 6 or 7 yards without giving them a first down. In these instances the slogan becomes "Give them 6, and so on . . ."

To stop the opponents' offense, it is necessary to place the defensive personnel in set defensive positions. As the ball is put into play, the defense either will be played straight as originally aligned or will be "stunted."

The straight defense.   The straight defense is almost identical to the original starting position. The players are assigned to protect certain predetermined territories, by either maintaining the original position on the scrimmage line or by penetrating a yard or two across the scrimmage line. The latter concept is really an attempt to move the defensive line across the scrimmage line without loss of original relative positions. As can be seen, one successful block that will move an opponent from his original defensive position jeopardizes the entire defensive strategy. This break in the defensive attack must be compensated for at once by teammates in the immediate area. If this is not done, the offense automatically gains "running room" and the advantage.

The stunting defense.   The stunting method of defensive strategy is to place the personnel in one alignment prior to the snap of the ball. As the ball is snapped, the defense shifts from their original positions into another alignment. The stunting type of defensive movement is more confusing to the offensive blockers and frequently befuddles them. The difficulty with the stunting defense is that some one of the defensive players may become a "lost soul," thus greatly weakening the defensive wall. Stunting defenses are usually successful only when all the defensive personnel carry out their assigned tasks, as is so true of all types of defensive play.

Selecting the Defense

The partciular defense to be used will depend upon your relative team strength and the offensive pattern of your opponent. If your team is over all superior to the opposition, probably almost any standard defense will be suitable. If your team is equal to your opponent, a carefully selected pattern of defensive play, geared to stop your opponents' strength, is desirable. If your team is inferior to your opponent, it is necessary that you utilize specially selected defensive patterns with the addition of stunts. An unexpected or unusual defense frequently catches an opponent unprepared, and will tend to demoralize them and render their offense impotent. *A combination of strategic defenses, plus a super-charged team determination, cause most of the upsets in football.*

To select the proper defense, it is important to know the strong points of your opponents' attack. This information usually is gathered through scouting reports. By knowing the opponents' strength, the defense can be arranged so as to have extra player concentration at the strong point. This concentration should be employed only when a serious weakness is not left open for the exploitation of an alert offensive team.

To concentrate at one or two points will inevitably weaken your defense at other points. The theory behind this maneuver, however, is to stifle the opponents' "pet" plays. The effect, again, is to demoralize the opposition. Nothing seems to disturb the average team more than to have its favorite plays stopped "cold." Because of the weakened defense at other points, it is desirable to have some of your standard defenses available. A mixing in of standard defenses will provide a change from one set style of play, which will help prevent the opponents from eventually taking advantage of your unavoidable defensive weaknesses. (Remember, some teams never do attempt to exploit these weaknesses, making a change unnecessary.) This idea should probably be stated as a defensive axiom: *Do not play the same defense all of the time—variety causes consternation and anxiety.*

Teaching the Defense

After the defense has been selected, there are four general steps that can be followed to teach it to the players. These steps are as follows: (a 6-3-2 defensive alignment is used in the examples)

(1) *Individual breakdowns.* Individual players are placed in their proper defensive positions one at a time. The individual is then shown the specific responsibilities and appropriate defensive maneuvers. The player is exposed to every conceivable block that he may eventually experience. This is done until each individual player has a good appreciation of the various offensive blocking techniques, together with an understanding of proper defensive counter-actions.

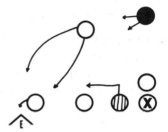 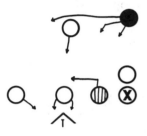

(2) *Half line breakdowns.* The procedure used here is to group three, four, or five defensive men at one time in their respective positions. Offensive players then repeatedly run all possible plays at these particular defensive men. This method avoids having one side of the line waiting for a play to be run at them, while the other side of the line is in action.

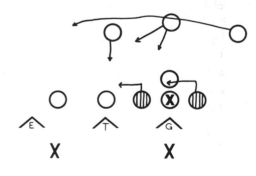 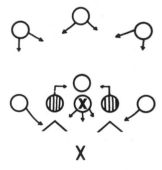

(3) *Full line drill.* This drill includes all the players on the defensive team except the deep backs. Running plays are stressed with an emphasis on pursuit and all-around defensive play.

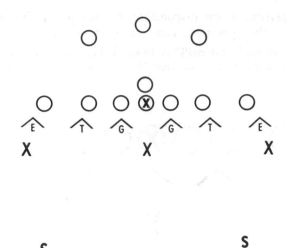

(4) *Full team drill.* This is the final step in teaching the defense, and has the full defensive team playing in a controlled scrimmage situation. The defensive quarterback is given various game condition situations and is called upon to select the appropriate defensive strategy intelligently.

Defensive Huddle

The defensive huddle is used for two primary purposes: to quickly inform the defensive team as to the defensive strategy to be employed without informing the opponents, and to help develop and/or maintain team "esprit de corps" or morale. Normally the defensive huddle is employed only by teams that utilize a variety of defensive maneuvers involving all 11 defensive men. If the defense "deep" backs are not involved in position and movement changes, they are not required to join the defensive huddle. Some coaches believe that the extra physical effort needed by the defensive backs to run up into the huddle after each play is too demanding, and therefore their inclusion is not required.

The defensive signal caller usually lines up facing his teammates at the spot where the ball is located by the officials. This defensive quarterback is not allowed to stand in the neutral zone while giving his signals. The defensive team members cluster around the defensive quarterback to receive the defensive signals. No arbitrary arrangment of personnel is used for this huddle such as that employed in the offensive huddle. The defensive quarterback relays his signals either by the use of words or by the use of fingers to indicate numbers.

Pass Defense

It has frequently been said that the most effective pass defense is a hard charging defensive line. This is very true. A hard driving defensive line will frequently tackle the quarterback or other passer before he can execute his pass. The hard charging line causes the passer to hurry his throw. This will often cause the passer to misjudge his receivers, and, quite often, will result in intercepted passes. Finally, by rushing the pass the offensive receivers do not have very much time to elude the defensive halfbacks. *Remember, the "perfect" pass is almost impossible to stop.*

Many coaches feel that it takes at least 7 men to adequately rush the passer. This means that, from the 6-man line, all six linemen and at least one linebacker should put on the rush. In the 5-man line, all five linemen, plus at least two linebackers, should be used in the rush. To allow the pass to be thrown with an attempt at an interception or incompletion, the reverse of the above principle should prevail, meaning that at least seven men should be on pass defense. The general rule is four men rush, seven men back; seven men rush, four men back; or, three men rush, eight men back; and, eight men rush, three men back.

Pass defense falls into three categories: zone, man-for-man, and combination zone and man-for-man.

Zone defense. As in basketball, the zone defense is devised to protect the entire playing area, by placing men at strategic positions and giving them specific territory assignments. The diagram in Fig. 206 indicates the areas for which the defensive personnel are responsible. An obvious weakness of the zone defense, a weakness similar to basketball zones, is that the opponents can over-load or "flood" one of the areas. When this occurs, the defensive man must protect against the deepest man. When the ball is thrown, the defensive man goes to the ball. *Remember, it is always better to sacrifice the completion of the short pass rather than the completion of the long pass.*

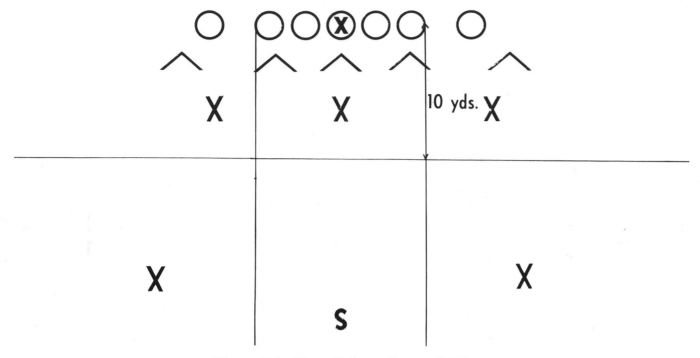

Figure 206. Zone Defense Responsibilities

Man-for-man defense. The man-for-man defense eliminates the problem of "flooded" zones; however, it increases the danger of leaving part of the field unprotected. As basketball coaches have discovered, one way

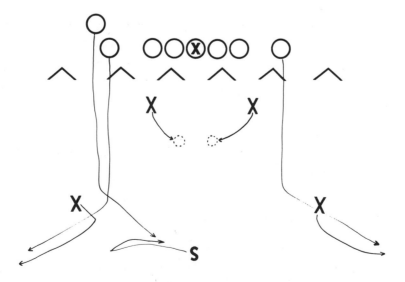

Figure 207. Man-for-man Pass Defense

to "shake loose" a pass receiver is to utilize screens. This technique consists of crossing ends or dropping men off. (See Chapter 10 Team Offensive Play (The Passing Game)) The defensive maneuver calculated to avoid screens is the planning of switches. As can be seen in Fig. 207, the left halfback switches his man to the safety man and, in turn, picks-up the man who was being covered by the safety man. The linebackers are responsible for covering delayed men out of the offensive backfield, by dropping straight back 5 or 10 yards and keeping their eyes on the blocking backs. When one leaves the blocking position, the linebacker on that side covers him. This technique also should give protection against screen passes.

Combination pass defense. Probably the most generally successful pass defense utilizes a combination of zone, man-for-man, and ball following defense. This defense gives the most adequate total protection of any defenses used. (See Fig. 208) It is necessary to establish a few general rules for this type of defense.

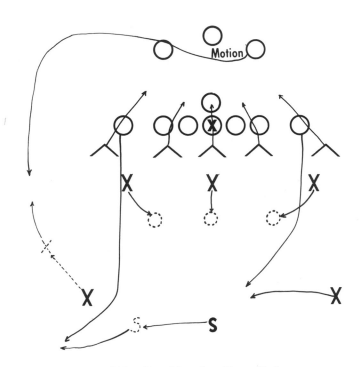

Figure 208. Combination Pass Defense

General Rules

1. Play head-on the offensive man coming at you. Halfbacks can play on the outside shoulder of the on coming end if only two men are coming downfield. This trick will not weaken the inside protection, as the safety man will be there to help.

2. Halfbacks play the end man-for-man while he is in their zone. If the man leaves the zone, go with him unless the safety man can pick him up, or unless you can switch your man with the man covered by the safety man.

3. Your primary responsibility is your zone. If no one is coming your way, drift to the center of the field.

4. When two men come downfield from one side, the halfback covers the outside man and the safety covers the inside man. If both men go down and out, the safety covers the deepest man. If both men go down and in, the safety covers the inside man.

5. A flanker or man-in-motion is covered by the halfback. (Some coaches prefer to have the end move out with a flanker.) When the offensive end and flanker, or man-in-motion head downfield, rule No. 4 prevails.

6. Linebackers back up 5 to 10 yards and move in until you can touch hands when arms are widespread. If the halfbacks call "button hook left (or right)," move laterally in the direction called, but do not take your eyes off the passer.

7. Linebackers cover man-for-man any delayed backfield man or end your side. Watch for screen passes and/or desperation runs by the passer.

8. All defensive backs and linebackers leave your position and go in the direction of the ball when the pass is finally executed. Be alert to assist in the tackle, interception, and/or run back.

Standard Defenses

As has been mentioned, there are many varieties of defensive maneuvers, almost all of which start from a few so-called standard positions. These positions fall into two general categories: the 8- and 9-man front or the odd or even alignment.

The eight- and nine-man front. If the total number of defensive linemen and linebackers combined is eight, the defense is considered to be composed of an 8-man front. These defenses are the: 4-4-2-1; 5-3-2-1; 6-2-2-1; 7-1-2-1; and the 8-3. While good against the running attack, these defenses are especially strong against the passing attack. The reason for this strength is the deep coverage afforded by the two halfbacks and one safety man. These defenses generally are used as primary defenses against any winged, flanker, or man-in-motion offense.

If the total number of defensive linemen and linebackers combined is nine, the defense is considered to be composed of a 9-man front. These defenses are the: 4-5-2; 5-4-2; 6-3-2; 7-2-2; and the 9-2. These defenses, just the opposite of the 8-man front defenses, are very strong against the runing attack, but inferior to the 8-man front against the passing attack. Additional strength is afforded against the running attack by the additional lineman or linebacker. The pass defense is weakened, particularly in the deep territory, because only two defensive halfbacks are available without a true safety man. These defenses usually are used against offenses that do not have winged, flanker, or man-in-motion alignments: the Split-T, the Tight-T, and the Short punt. They also are used when the offensive team is obviously going to attempt a running play: the goal line stands, short yardage third or fourth down situations, or other such plays.

The odd and even defenses. The defense is considered an odd defense if a defender is lined up in front of the middle offensive lineman. The other defenses are considered the even defenses and have defensive men lined up against the men immediately next to either side of the center man. The odd defenses are the: 5-man line defenses, 7-man line defenses, and the 9-man line defenses. The even defenses are the: 4-man line defenses, 6-man line defenses, and the 8-man line defenses.

A particular defense thus is regarded as an odd or even defense with an 8-man or 9-man front.

The monster or rover defensive man. Some coaches prefer to have their most capable (all-around ability) and aggressive linebacker always on the strong or wide side of the field. As a general rule it is more difficult to protect the wide portion of the field as offensive players have more space to manuever in. Some of this field advantage is nullified by placing the rover to that defensive side of the field. Another advantage is that but one man, the monster, needs to be trained in proper open field linebacker play.

Backfield rotation. It may be profitable now to consider general principles of backfield rotation against various types of running plays. A few moments devoted to that point might aid in a clearer understanding of defensive maneuvers from the standard positions. The first worry of the backfield is pass defense. Once a running play is obvious, the backfield rotation occurs.

On end runs. The usual procedure followed by the backfield against the end run is to have the onside halfback go up to meet the play at or behind the scrimmage line when in an 8-man front. He is assisted by the onside linebackers, who takes inside responsibility. The key for the onside halfback is the onside offensive end. The safety man moves to the onside halfback's position and becomes the second wave of attack, together with the middle or offside linebacker. If these men make the tackle, a short gain will have been made. The true safety man is really the offside halfback. His task becomes one of preventing a touchdown or defending against the running pass. This man moves cautiously, watching for a possible reverse play. (See Fig. 209)

The 9-man front defense changes slightly from the 8-man front maneuvers. The cornermen, or outside linebackers, key off the near halfback and usually take outside responsibilities, as did the onside halfback above.

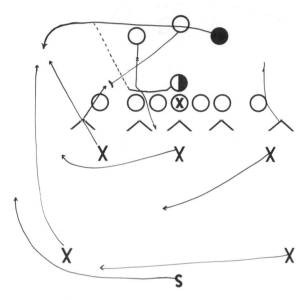

Figure 209. Backfield Rotation (Eight man front) Against End Runs

The onside safety advances more cautiously on the end run, as his position is similar to that of the middle safety man in the three deep defense. (See Fig. 210) The safety men key the end their side. The cornerman on the offside also keys the near halfback. If this man flows away, or sets up to block for a pass, the corner man moves back to cover the deep outside, releasing the safety man his side to the deep inside. On an end run away from the cornerman. he becomes the true safety man.

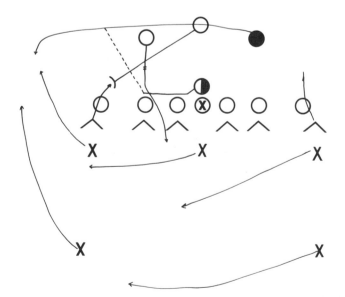

Figure 210. Backfield Rotation (Nine man front) Against End Runs

On off tackle runs. The movement of the defensive backfield against an inside the end run is quite similar to the end run maneuver. The cornerman, or the onside halfback in case of the 8-man front, takes outside responsibility. The linebacker nearest then takes the inside responsibility. The offside cornerman, or the offside halfback in case of an 8-man front, prevents cut-back maneuvers by the ball carrier. (See Fig. 211)

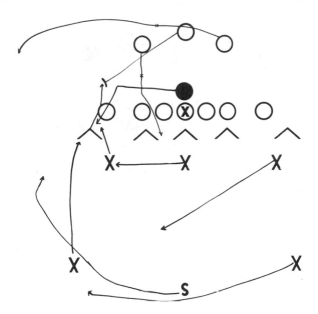

Figure 211. Backfield Rotation On Off Tackle Runs

On over the middle runs. The defensive backfield follows a funnel pattern against the over the middle runs. The linebackers converge sharply at the hole and should make the tackle. The safety man moves straight down the middle, and the halfbacks converge to the middle. If the halfbacks or safety man make the tackle, a gain will have been made. (See Fig. 212)

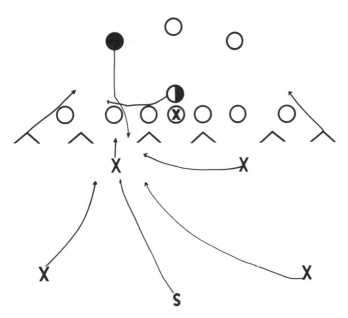

Figure 212. Backfield Rotation on Over the Middle Runs

Defensing the split end(s) and/or wide flanker(s). Modern football offenses tend to use a wide split end(s), wide split flanker(s), or combinations of split ends and wide flankers. These are used to spread the defensive alignment, allowing for more effective running and passing attacks. These offensive maneuvers present problems to the defending team, in that the traditional alignments must be modified to cope with these variations.

Three deep or 8-man fronts. The problem of the split offense is not too serious for the 8-man front defenses. The generally used defensive principle in the 8-man front is to have the defensive end split with the offensive end unless a slot back exists. In this case, the defensive end splits head on the slot back. In a 5-3-2-1 defense or 4-4-2-1 defense, the outside linebacker moves out to the position occupied by the end in the other 8-man fronts. The onside halfback moves out with the widest offensive man. The safety man plays head on the next inside eligible pass receiver. (See Fig. 213)

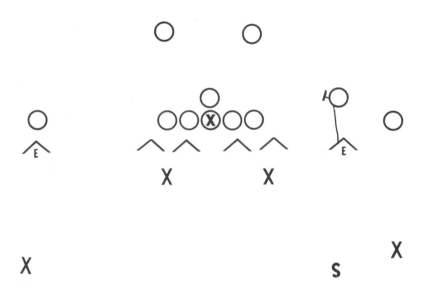

Figure 213. Eight Man Front—Defense Against Split End(s) and/or Wide Flanker(s)

Two deep or 9-man fronts. These defenses were devised to gain added strength against the running offenses. They were designed primarily for use against regular balanced T offenses; i.e., the split-T; however, they can be used effectively against any variation of the T offense, provided adequate maneuvers are taken to guard against the extra passing strength of the T variations. The defensive attempt made is to adjust to the potential passing threat of the changed offense without losing the potency of the 9-man front alignment against the running offense. Some of the more commonly used defensive adjustments follow.

Split ends (balanced backfield). Split ends can be single or double covered. In the single coverage, the cornerman or outside linebacker moves back about 7 yards deep and on the outside shoulder of the split end. The key for this backfield man is the end his side. Should the end release downfield, the halfback takes the deep outside pass territory responsibility. The safety on the side of the split end moves up to about 3 yards off the scrimmage line and 2 yards outside of the near offensive halfback. The key for the safety is the nearside halfback. If this man moves to the defensive man's right, the safety moves to the flat right for defensive purposes. If this offensive back moves to the defensive man's left, or sets up to block for a pass, the safety man covers the deep inside pass territory. (See Fig. 214)

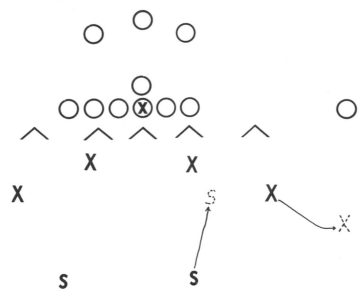

**Figure 214. Nine Man Front Defense Single Cover Against
Split End (Balanced Backfield)**

To double cover the split end, the defensive end man of the line moves out to the inside shoulder of the split end. This man forces the offensive end to the outside and covers the flat or flare territory. The cornerman uses the same procedure as when single covering the end. The safety plays the up position as before, but now has shallow inside pass territory. The total pass defense has changed to a strict zone defense. (See Fig. 215)

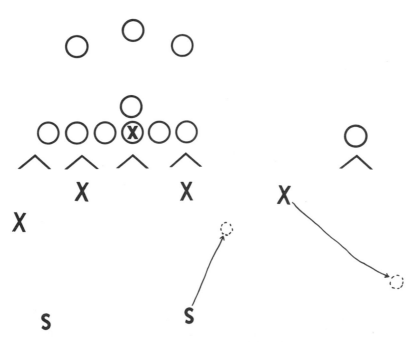

**Figure 215. Nine Man Front Double Cover Against
Split End (Balanced Backfield)**

Weakside flanker (regular ends). This type of offensive maneuver is usually covered by a semi-rotation of the defensive backfield. The cornerman and safety away from the safety play their normal positions. They both key the near halfback. The cornerman to the side of the flanker plays on the outside shoulder of the flanker and 5 to 7 yards deep. The onside safety splits the difference betwen the flanker and the end and stays 5 to 7 yards deep. The offside safety plays normal covering either inside deep, should the near halfback set up for pass protection or move to the right, or outside deep, if the halfback dives or flows to the defensive left. The cornerman plays normal. The cornerman to the flanker side keys the flanker. If the flanker runs a short pattern, the cornerman stays with him. If the flanker runs a deep pattern, the cornerman stays with him until released by the safety. The flanker side safety keys the end. If the end blocks, he is a free man in a zone. If the end releases and runs any type of short pattern, the safety goes immediately to deep outside position. If the end runs a deep pattern, the safety stays within his zone. (See Fig. 216)

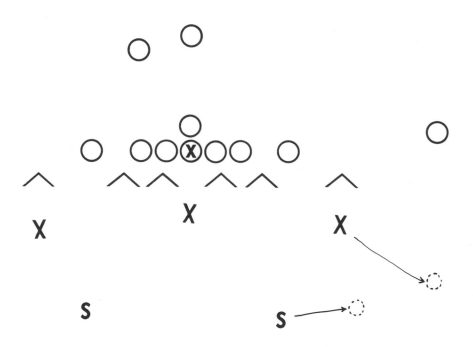

**Figure 216. Nine Man Front Against a Wide Weakside
Flanker (Normal Ends)**

Strongside flanker (normal ends). This is an extremely difficult formation to which to adjust and is usually defensed by a complete backfield rotation. The flanker side cornerman moves up to the line of scrimmage, shades the inside of the flanker, takes the quick diagonal pass away, and plays the flat territory in a passing situation. The safety to the side of the flanker moves out as a halfback in a 3-deep defensive alignment, keys the widest receiver, and has deep outside resposibility against the pass. The safety away from the flanker moves over as a safety, plays head on the remaining halfback, keys the ball, and has deep inside responsibility in a pass situation. The cornerman away from the flanker moves back as a halfback in a 3-deep alignment, keys the end, and covers the deep outside territory in case of a pass. (See Fig. 217)

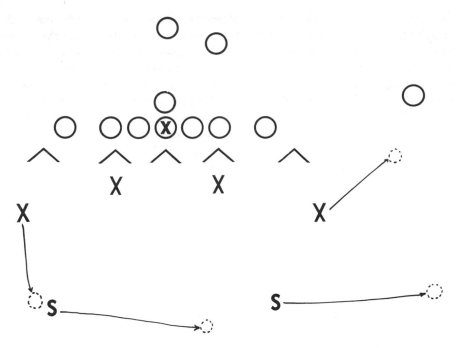

Figure 217. Nine Man Front Against a Wide Strongside
Flanker (Normal Ends)

Weakside flanker and split end. A split flanker with a corresponding split end to the weak side usually is covered by a semi-rotation toward the flanker. The split end rule is put into effect on the side of the split end. The defensive end takes away the inside territory from the nearest receiver. (Previous rules for the defensive men go into effect.) (See Fig. 218)

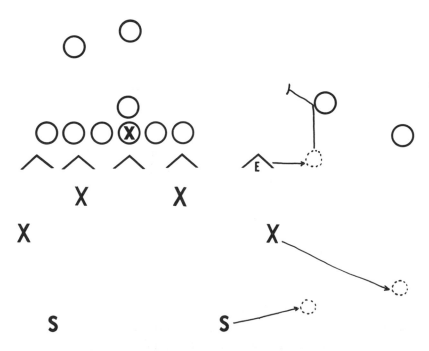

Figure 218. Weakside Flanker and Split End Against a
Nine Man Front Defense

Strongside flanker with both ends split. This is another strong passing alignment. The defense normally rotates fully to the strength. The split end away from the rotation is double covered. (Previously explained rules for the defensive men go into effect.) (See Fig. 219)

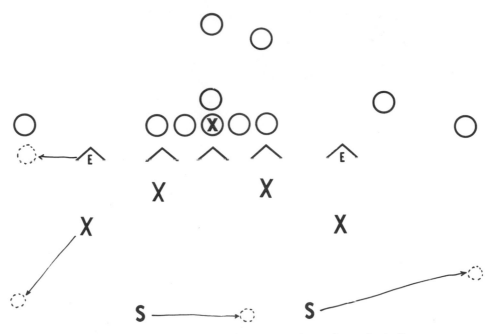

**Figure 219. Strongside Flanker With Both Ends Split
Against a Nine Man Front Defense**

Split ends double wing. This is a very new offensive formation, possessing excellent running and passing potentials. A plausible defensive maneuver from a 9-man front would be to move into the double end cover rule for both sides. (See Fig. 220)

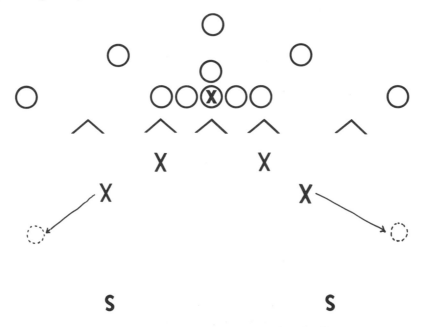

**Figure 220. Split Ends Double Wing Against a
Nine Man Defensive Front**

Use of linebackers. Split ends and/or flankers can be adjusted to by the positioning of the near side linebacker. Several linebacker adjustments are depicted below. (See Fig. 221)

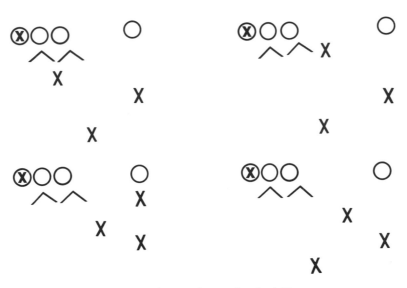

Figure 221. Split End Lineback Adjustments

Four-man line. The 4-man line accompanied by a team dispersion of four linebackers, two halfbacks, and one safety man was very popular when the T-formation first was used. It was immediately successful because of its newness. Until the T-formation came into the picture, most teams relied upon the 5- or 6-man line defense. With an offense set up to attack a traditional 5- or 6-man line, the blocking assignments became confused against this novel 4-man line. (See Fig. 222)

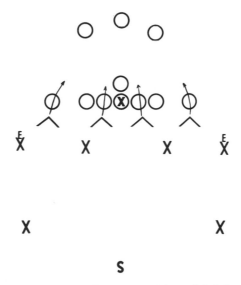

Figure 222. Four Man Line—4-4-2-1

This alignment affords excellent pass defense, using a basic zone pattern. A heavy responsibility is given the four linemen in the forward line of attack, when they are expected to rush the passer. The 4-man line is hoping that the opponent will throw the ball so that the defense can intercept it. It was not long before the 4-man line became highly vulnerable to the running attack. To compensate, coaches began stunting out of the 4-man line into 5-, 6-, 7-, and 8-man lines.

In recent years, a trend has been back to a 4-man line due to the increased use of the passing game; however, this 4-man line is now more apt to be a 4-3-2-2 defense arrangement, rather than a 4-4-2-1 alignment. The backfield can rotate toward a man-in-motion, of course. This rotation will result in a standard three deep defense. It is recommended highly that this defense be used as a stunting defense with the linebackers interacting with the front-4. Several 4-3 defensive alignments are used as indicated below. (See Fig. 223, 224 and 224a)

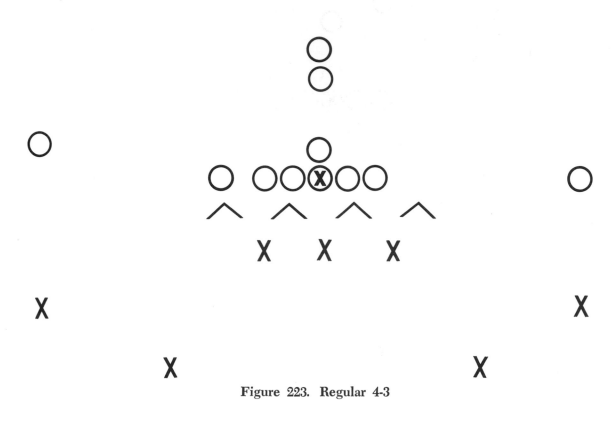

Figure 223. Regular 4-3

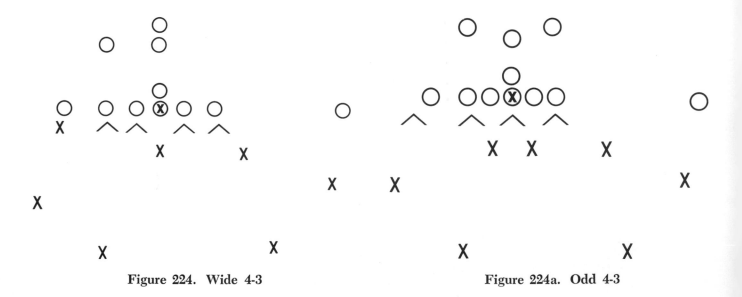

Figure 224. Wide 4-3   Figure 224a. Odd 4-3

The 4-4 alignment may have become less popular as the trend today is with a four deep secondary arrangement rather than the three deep one. The 4-4 is still used by some teams, however, with some different personnel positionings. (See Fig. 225 and Fig. 226)

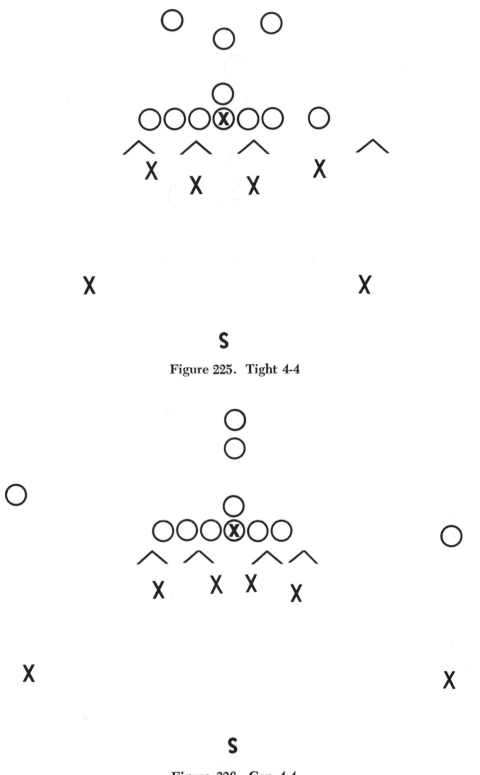

Figure 225. Tight 4-4

Figure 226. Gap 4-4

Five-man line. The 5-man line has always been a highly popular defense against all types of offensive attacks. The traditional alignment in the 5-man line defense is the 5-3-2-1 arrangement. This defense affords excellent pass defense and a strong running defense, particularly if the middle guard is a stalwart and rugged defensive man. The effectiveness of this defense is enhanced greatly by stunting maneuvers. (See Fig. 227 and Fig. 228)

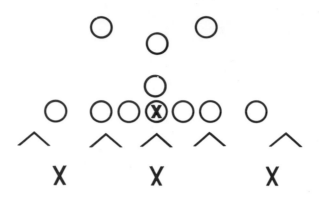

Figure 227. Regular 5-3-2-1

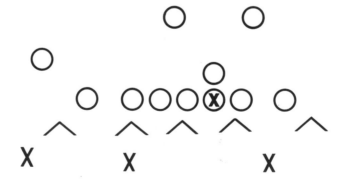

Figure 228. Wide 5-3-2-1

The 5-4-2 five-man line. In recent years, a different 5-man alignment has become popular. The defense was introduced at Oklahoma University and became known popularly in its original form as the Okie defense. This defensive pattern consists of five linemen, four linebackers, and two safety men. The inside linebackers are positioned over the offensive guards or, when outside run coverage is needed, between the two outside defensive linemen. In either case, the interior linebackers are 1 yard off the scrimmage line. The outside or corner linebackers are placed 3 yards off the scrimmage line and 3 to 5 yards outside the end lineman. (See Fig. 229 and Fig. 230)

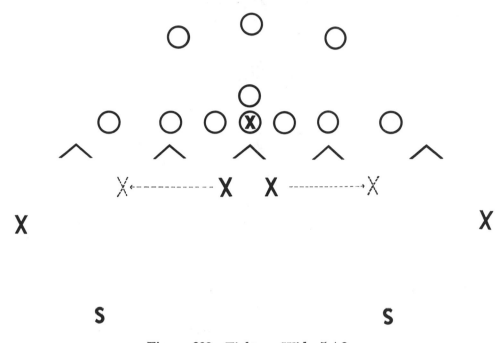

Figure 229. Tight or Wide 5-4-2

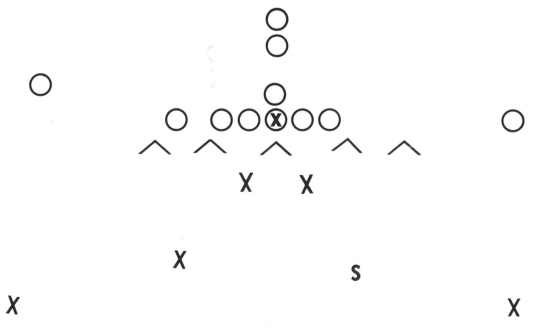

Figure 230. 5-2-4

Six-man line. Another traditional defense is the 6-man line with two linebackers, two halfbacks, and one safety man. You may recall from an earlier discussion of offense that this is known popularly as an even defense. The particular alignment affords excellent inside and outside running protection and a good 3-deep pass defense. (See Fig. 231)

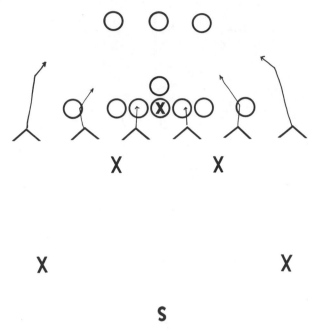

Figure 231. Six-man Line 6-2-2-1

The traditional 6-man defense can be altered to increase the strength against the running attack to the outside by a minor movement of the defensive personnel. This realignment is now known as the wide six. (See Fig. 232)

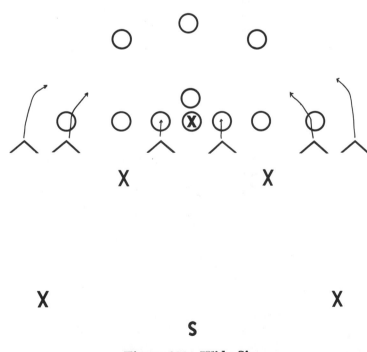

Figure 232. Wide Six

Another variation of the traditional 6-man line is used to increase the inside defensive strength against the running attack. The defensive personnel on the line are moved in closer to the center. The defense maintains its outside strength by the play of the ends who have outside responsibility. This defense is commonly called the tight six. (See Fig. 233)

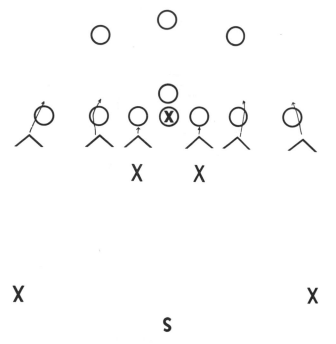

Figure 233. Tight Six

Both the tight and the wide 6-man defenses depend upon the "killing" of the offensive ends. The tackles or ends, as the case may be, have the initial responsibility of detaining the offensive end on the scrimmage line.

The six-three-two line. A modern concept of defense against the various T offenses includes the 9-man defensive front as its basic weapon. The 6-man defense is changed from an 8-man front to a 9-man front by the utilization of three linebackers. There are three popularly used 6-3-2 defensive alignments: the regular (See Fig. 234), the wide (See Fig. 235), and the tight (See Fig. 236)

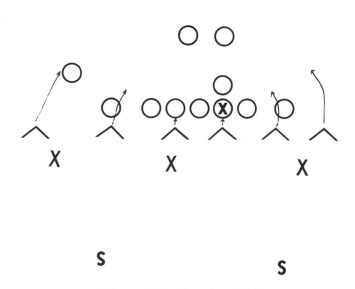

Figure 234. Regular 6-3-2

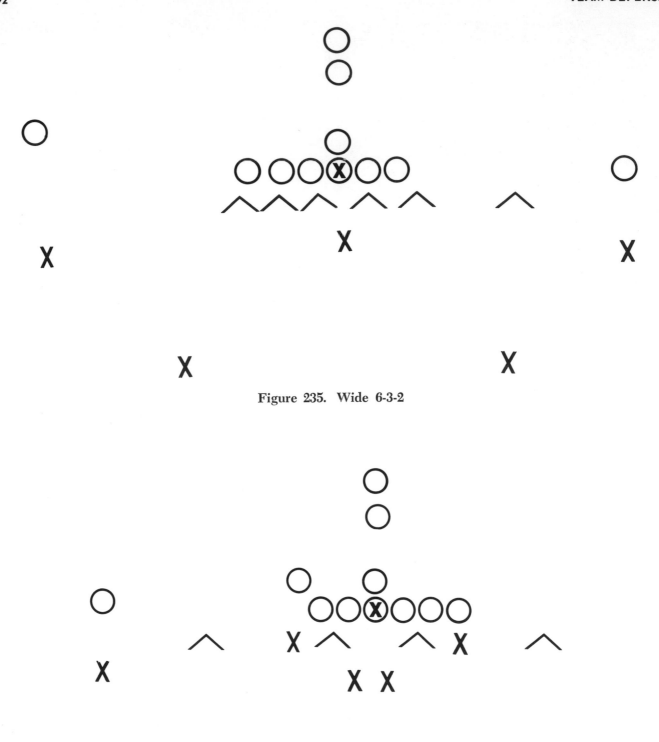

Figure 235. Wide 6-3-2

Figure 236. Tight 6-3-2

Split-six-man line. A popular defense against the split and straight T formations has the six defensive linemen playing the gaps, with the linebackers playing in the middle and a yard off the scrimmage line. The onside linebacker goes with the quarterback to the dive hole, and the offside linebacker moves directly over the center. This middle linebacker now has the tremendous responsibility of stopping counter and crossbuck type plays. Obviously these two linebackers must be strong and maneuverable. (See Fig. 237)

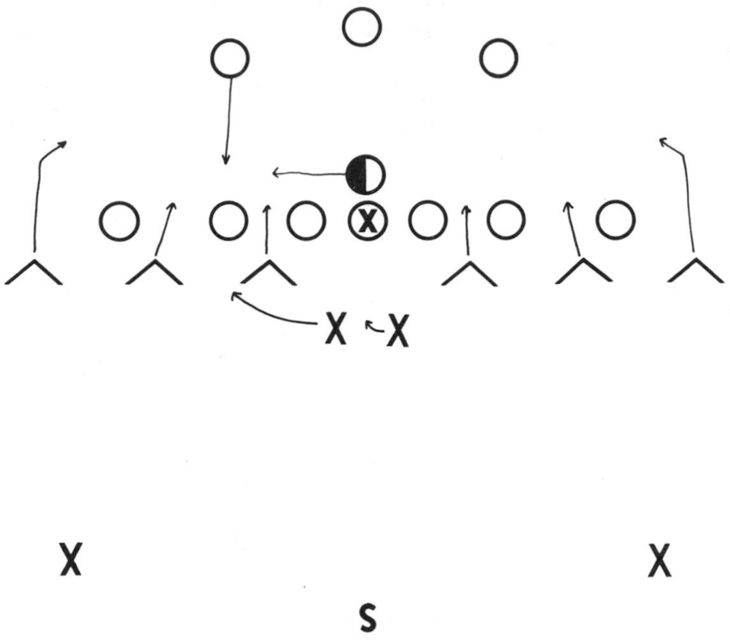

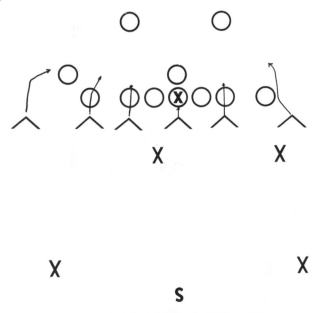

Figure 237. Split-six Man Line

Overshifted six-man line. The overshifted 6-man line is used popularly against winged or flanker T offenses. Some coaches call this the five-seven defense, as the alignment has normal five man spacing on the offside and seven man spacing on the winged side. The linebackers compensate for the offside weakness by undershifting. (See Fig. 238)

Figure 238. Overshifted 6-Man Line

The six-five goal line defense. An all-purpose goal line defense is needed that is able to cope with straight ahead power, outside runs, and short passes. The 6-5 alignment has been devised to suit this multiple purpose. Two arrangements used commonly are indicated in Fig. 239 and Fig. 240.

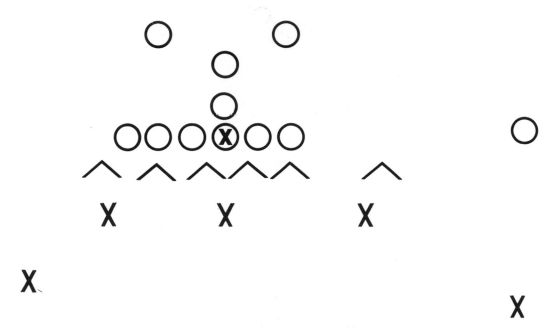

Figure 239. Tight 6-5

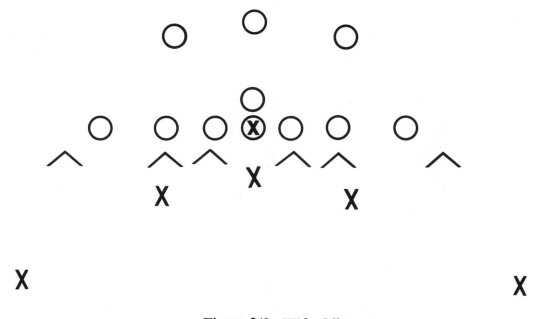

Figure 240. Wide 6-5

Seven-man line. The 7-man line is a very popular defense. It gives considerable strength to the defense against the running attack. A diamond backfield arrangement with one linebacker, two defensive halfbacks, and a safety man affords excellent deep pass protection. It is vulnerable to the short passing game. To give it more strength, the tackles "jam" and delay the offensive ends. Its primary strength against the passing attack lies in the probability of a lineman "getting to" the passer. (See Fig. 241)

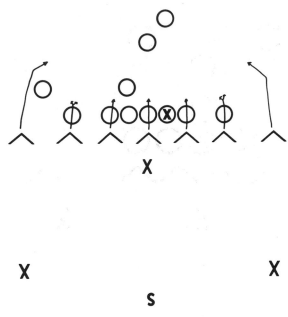

Figure 241. 7 Man Line 7-1-2-1

The 7-man line defense can afford considerable inside protection by playing the guards and tackles in the "gaps." (See Fig. 242) The former traditional alignment affords stronger protection against off tackle and end run plays.

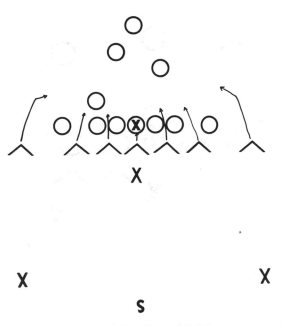

Figure 242. Gap 7-1-2-1

A 7-2-2 variation, called the seven box, sometimes is used. This box backfield alignment will increase both the strength against the running attack to both sides and the strength against the short passing game. (See Fig. 243)

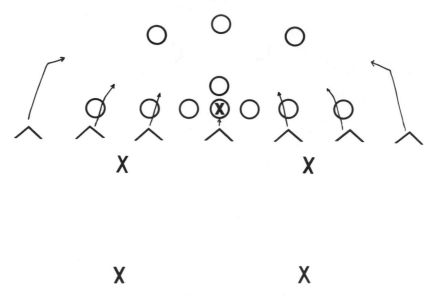

Figure 243. 7 Man Line—Box Seven

Michigan State University has used a variation of the seven box. This defense moves the ends and tackles in tighter to the center, with the onside or play running side linebacker having outside responsibility, and the offside linebacker dropping into a deep halfback position. The key for these outside linebackers is the offensive halfback nearest them. Should this man block or move in the opposite direction, the linebacker moves to the deep halfback position. In all other situations, the linebacker has outside running responsibility and flat outside pass defense territory. The inside linebackers are placed a yard off the scrimmage line between the defensive middle man and the man to his immediate outside. (See Fig. 244)

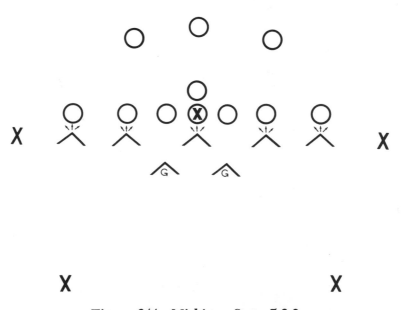

Figure 244. Michigan State 7-2-2

Eight-man line. The 8-man line with one linebacker and three defensive halfbacks is used popularly in short yards-to-gain situations, particularly in goal line stand situations. The strength of the pass defense lies

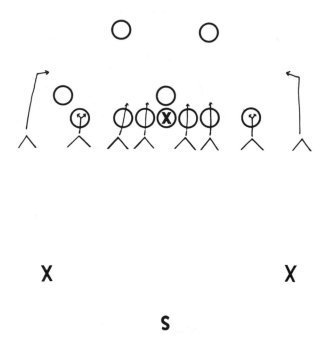

Figure 245. 8 Man Line 8-2-1

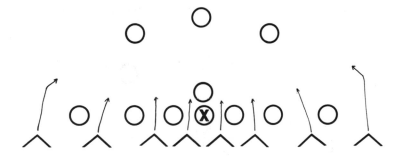

Figure 246. 8 Man Line—Gap Eight

in the facts that the ends are detained, and there is an excellent possibility that the passer will be prevented from making the pass. If a team can penetrate or run outside of this formidable wall, the chances for long gains are excellent. (See Fig. 245) In recent years, the effectiveness of this particular defense has been increased by placing the linemen into the gaps. (See Fig. 246)

A variation of the 8-man line also has been used by Michigan State University. The difference between the standard 8-man line and the Michigan State variation is the utilization of a middle linebacker rather than three deep defensive backs. This linebacker is placed in the standard 5-man line middle linebacker position. This type of defense obviously must allow for defensive mobility against anything but a balanced backfield T-offense. The key for the outside linebackers is the offensive halfback their side. If this back blocks, or moves away, the linebacker, or end, if you prefer, drops off the line of scrimmage to the deep backfield position. The key for the deep backs is the offensive end their side. If this man blocks, the deep back rotates to the middle safety position. If this man comes downfield, the deep back maintains his original position. (See Fig. 247)

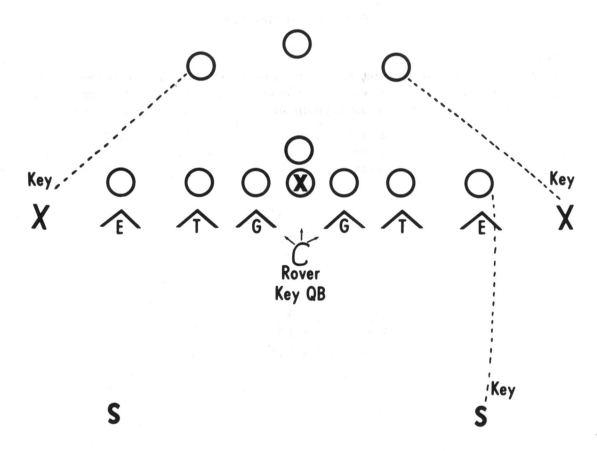

Figure 247. Michigan State 8-Man Line

Nine-man line. The 9-man line is used basically on or near the goal line, but, can be used effectively anywhere on the field. The success of this defense depends to a great extent upon the ability of the assigned men to jam the ends and slide off to the running play. (See Fig. 248)

Figure 248. 9 Man Line

Stunting Defenses

Stunting defenses are those that do not proceed by ordinary straight ahead movements from the original defensive alignment. Stunts can be used with any defensive alignment. The major types of stunts are: (1) looping; (2) slanting; (3) converging; (4) small group stunts; and (5) the shifting defense.

Looping. The loop maneuver can be a 1- or 2-man type. In the 1-man type, the defensive man—when looping left—takes a directly lateral step with his left foot. The hands are used to ward off a driving offensive man. The right foot step is made forward in a traditional penetrating movement into the opposing lineman. (See Fig. 249)

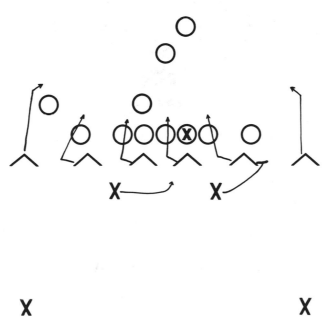

Figure 249. Looping Defense-1 Man Type

Slant Right

The 2-man loop consists of taking a lateral cross step. This step is followed by another lateral step and then a drive step into the offensive line. (See Fig. 250)

The loop maneuver must be rapid, low, and in balance. *Remember, the hands are vital factors in keeping the offensive linemen away from your body.* The loop is used to confuse the blocking assignments of the offensive line. As can be noted in Fig. 249, the offensive right guard will have considerable difficulty in his attempt to check the defensive guard head-on him. The defensive left guard should be able to stop this particular play for a loss.

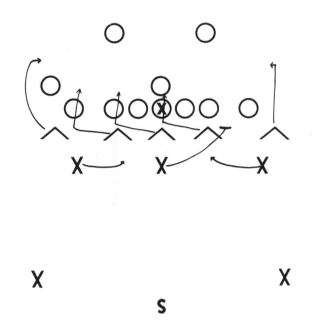

Figure 250. Looping Defense—Two Man Type

Most teams use wedge-type plays in an effort to combat the looping line. The hope of the offensive team is to catch the defense while they are moving laterally. A reminder to defensive quarterbacks: do not use the same stunt all of the time.

The direction of the looping line is compensated for by the counter movement of the linebackers.

Slanting. The slanting maneuver again is calculated to disrupt the offensive blocking assignments. To slant, the defensive linemen drive on a 45-degree angle to their right or left as the ball is put into play. Instead of driving into the man who is head-on them, they drive into the man in the next offensive position. The movement in one direction by the linemen is compensated for by a counter or compensating movement of the linebackers in the opposite direction. The slant is usually in the direction of the opponents' strength, however the defense is not weakened if the linebackers compensate adequately. (See Fig. 251)

Converge. The converge is similar to the slant. The difference between these two maneuvers is that the left side of the line slants toward the center, as does the right side of the line. This particular movement is used when an into the line play is expected. The linebackers compensate by protecting to the outside. When properly executed and unexpected, the offensive blocking assignments again are disrupted. (See Fig. 252)

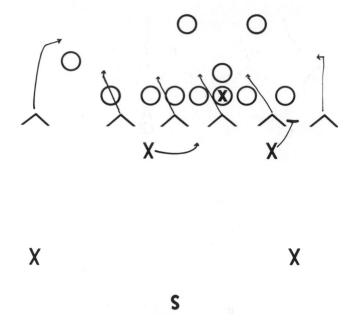

Figure 251. Slant Left

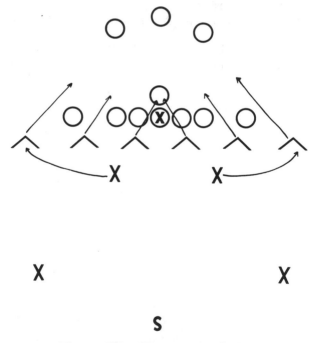

Figure 252. Converge Defense

Small group stunts. Some coaches allow the defensive end, tackle, and linebacker to use defensive tricks. This same kind of trickery can be executed by the linebacker and guard, or the linebacker and tackle. The important point in these trick maneuvers is that the assigned territory must be protected. The men must know what each one is going to do on each play. Individual movements other than the orthodox ones cannot be tolerated. Some of the more popular small group stunts are given in Fig. 253.

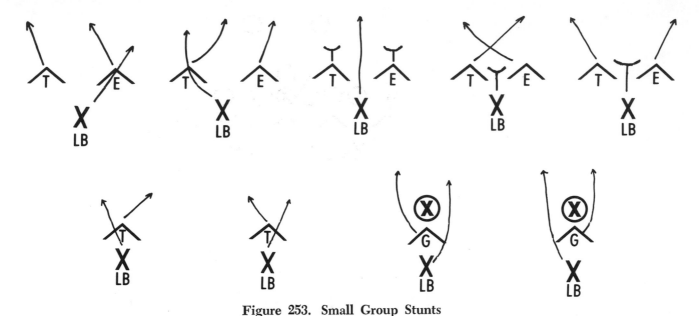

Figure 253. Small Group Stunts

Shifting or stemming defenses. Shifting defenses occur when a team starts from one defensive position and finishes in an entirely different attacking position. As can be noted in the stunting defenses before mentioned, one defensive alignment flows into another as the players execute their stunts.

The most popular technique of shifting defenses is the use of linebackers. A good example is the 4-5-2 alignment mentioned earlier. This can flow into a 5-, 6-, 7-, 8-, or 9-man defensive line simply by driving linebackers into the line.

The shifting defense, together with all types of stunts, can be very effective if used with intelligence and caution.

Chapter 13

Scouting

Scouting is of primary importance to the modern football coach. A team cannot be fully prepared for a forthcoming contest without some advanced information about the opponent. The more information about the opposition, the better the chances for an eventual victory. Scouting at the professional, intercollegiate, and, sometimes, at the interscholastic, level has become a highly specialized business. Many team victories and opponents' upsets are the direct result of elaborate scouting reports properly used by the coach and the team. Simply stated, the scouting report is an advanced accumulation of pertinent facts and data concerning some future opponent.

The detail of a scouting report can range from the sublime—complete information about the opponents' every move in practice and during a contest—to the ridiculous—nothing more than a few gathered rumors. Neither extreme seems desirable; at least the former is not very practical.

The coach must determine at what point he will stop along this range of completeness. The decision will be determined by two factors: (1) what specific use will be made of the collected information, and (2) the capacity or ability of the scouts to collect the information desired. There is certainly no sense in collecting a lot of information that will not ever be used. In addition, there is no point in asking the scouts to collect certain information that they are not capable of gathering, due to personal or situation limitations.

Who Scouts

The head football coach usually likes to see his opponents in action before his team plays them. This is to be desired as the head coach no doubt is well versed in the game of football. He probably understands what he sees and knows for what he is looking. The necessity of his being with his own team Saturday after Saturday usually makes it impossible, however, for him to do much scouting.

Many coaches use their assistant coaches as scouts. If a rank order of preference were to be made, the head coach would probably be at the top of the list and the assistant coaches next in order. The assistant coaches usually also are well versed in the game of football; however, it should be realized that the assistant may be quite inexperienced as a coach. He may have the player's view of the game, rather than the total view of a coach. If this be the case, it is highly probable that the assistant coach will not see a lot of the vital action that is taking place. It is necessary, in this instance, for the head coach to indoctrinate the assistant thoroughly in the art of scouting. The assistant needs to know specifically what to look for and how to look for it.

Some schools hire faculty or other personnel to act as team scouts. Frequently the coaches of one sport will be the scouts for another sport. Persons detached from the local school, but with a comprehensive knowledge of football and a strong interest in the team, are sometimes used as scouts.

Regardless of who the scout is, he must be thoroughly indoctrinated in the "what" and the "how" of scouting.

What To Scout For

The information desired in a scouting report will consist, as mentioned before, of information the coach can use in his team preparation for a future game. Two bits of information seem almost indispensable: (1) from what formation does the opponent run and pass, and (2) what defenses does the opponent like to use. All other information desired is supplementary to this basic knowledge.

Following are listed much of the pertinent data wanted by the coach in a scouting report:

Pre-game warm up information.

Names and numbers of players: including positions, height and weight.

Punters: including style of punt (number of steps, right or left footed), distance of punts, approximate height of punts.

Kick off man: including method of kick off used, distance and height of kicks, right- or left-footed kicker.

Extra point kickers: including distance from goal line, total distance and climb of ball.

Snap count: including most popular count (favorite number on which ball is snapped), and rhythmical timing of the quarterback.

Weather and wind conditions.

Game information.

Kick off: height and depth of kick, alignment of personnel, general movement of personnel down the field under the kick, and run back technique and succcess of opponents.

Kick off return: including player alignment, type of return (wedge, alley, etc.), criss-crosses used, lagging blockers, and run back distance.

Running offense: formation used; including normal alignment, special splits.

Standard plays used: including when used (field position, down, yards to gain, time in game), and yards gained or lost per try.

Special plays used: including when used (field position, down, yards to gain, time in game), and yards gained or lost per try.

Concentration of running attack: including holes they like to hit most frequently.

Who does the "heavy work" among the running backs.

Do they show outside running speed: including who has the speed.

Do they show inside power: including who has the power.

Particular offensive blocking or running weaknesses of personnel.

Special goal line plays: including their success.

Passing offense:

When do they pass: including down, field position, time in game, and type of pass (short, long, fast, easy).

What are their running pass patterns: including blocking protection, completions, dropped, intercepted.

What are their straight pass patterns: including blocking protection, completions, drops, interceptions.

Are there vulnerable spots in their pass protection.

What are the favorite receivers.

Does the passer run when trapped, "eat the ball," throw the ball in desperation, or throw the ball out-of-bounds.

Punting:

General formation used: including depth of punter.

Distance and direction of punt.

Who goes down under punts.

Who was blocked out in the first wave of attack (interested in men easily removed from the play).

Who made the tackle.

Pass from center: including whether it was good, slow, or off target.

Fake punt runs or passes used: including who and when.

Were any punts blocked: including who and when.

Punt returns:

What alignments do they use against the punt.

What punt blocking tricks do they use.

Can we run or pass from deep punt formation as a result of the above.

How do they attempt to return punts: including man-for-man blocking, wedge blocking, alley blocking, and criss-crosses.

How successful were they in returning punts.

Defense:

What defense was used against each offense alignment.

What were the specific situations when each defense was used: including down, field position, yards to gain, time left.

What type of backfield rotation do they use against running plays: including gang tackling.

What type of pass defense do they use: including who is involved downfield.

How did they react to flankers, men-in-motion, spreads.

Do they use stunting defenses: including what specific stunts.

How successful were the various defenses used.

Who were the weak defensive linemen, linebackers, and halfbacks against runs and passes.

Extra points and field goals:

Do they run, kick, or pass for extra points.

Distance of kickers from the center.

Speed and accuracy of center snap.

Success of kicks.

General information:

Team spirit: including whether it was level or fluctuating, high or low.

Team reaction when scored upon.

Team reaction when they score.

Team reaction when they are behind.

Team reaction when they are ahead.

Physical condition in general.

Substitutions: including when made and number made.

Injuries: including whether or not player returned to the game.

Post-game information.

Reaction of team to defeat or victory.

General impression of opponents: including whether or not they are "in our class," superior to us, inferior to us.

How To Scout

It is desirable to have scouts go to the game in pairs. One scout makes a verbal report while the other records. Sometimes scouts split this work by verbally reporting the offensive play and writing the notes for the defensive play.

The scouts should have been prepared adequately before attending the game. A preview of the previous year's report and/or movies will be a valuable asset. The scout would then know, in general, what to expect, particularly regarding offensive plays and defensive maneuvers. If the identical offense is being used, the scout records the type of play run and does not bother with particular blocking assignments. If the scout is well acquainted with various standard offenses and their particular running plays, he will usually save himself much time.

Much information about the opponents can be gathered from the game program. The scout can pick up a great deal of knowledge by staying close to the playing field during the warm-up period. This will give him an excellent chance to "size up" the team personnel and the opportunity to learn the snap signal and rhythmical sequence.

Some scouts prefer to stay at one or the other end of the field during the game. This is a good idea if the scout is in an elevated position. The running and passing offense and defense can be seen more readily from this position. If the game is played in a stadium, the press box is usually the ideal position for the scout.

Charts should be used by the scouts to record the information wanted. A note book, with the team offense drawn on each page, will expedite the recording of offensive maneuvers. This is true also of the opponents' offense, against which the defensive alignments and maneuvers can be drawn. It is much simpler and more efficient to have charts prepared in advance for the recording of the information desired.

Offensive charts. There are many ways of recording the offensive play. The chart shown in Fig. 254 is just one method suggested. This chart is arranged so as to give a maximum amount of information with a minimum of ease. The information from this chart can be summarized easily at a later date.

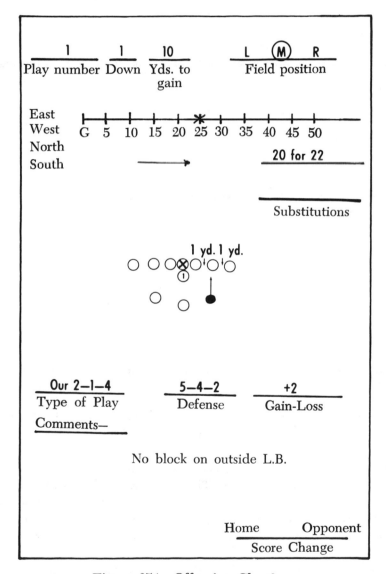

Figure 254. Offensive Chart[2]

[2]Adapted from Robert L. "Bobby" Dodd, *Bobby Dodd on Football,* First Edition, (Prentice-Hall, Inc. 1954).

Defensive charts. As mentioned in relation to offensive charts, there are many ways of gathering defensive information. The chart is particularly adaptable and desirable from the point of view of efficiency and information gathered. The defensive chart shown in Fig. 255 is another technique suggested.

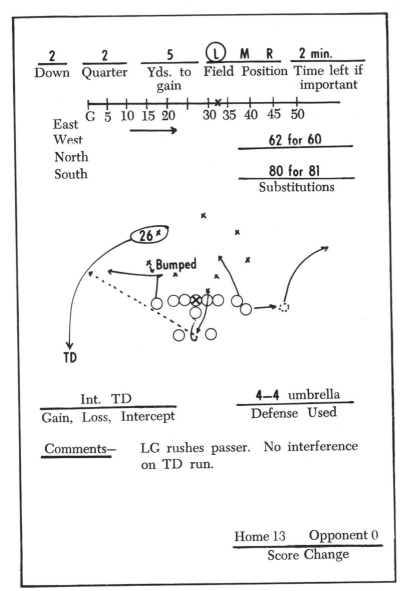

Figure 255. Defensive Chart

What To Do With The Information

As soon as feasible after the game, the scouts should assemble the information they gathered. A simple, understandable, and practical method of presenting the scouting data is by means of tables, diagrams, and charts. A narrative running account of the game is useless to the coach and team. It means that the coach must laboriously select the information he desires from the total mass of data available. The scouts who collected the data are the more logical screeners. If the coach gave them a prior indoctrination, the scouts' screening task is relatively simple. The following ideas are suggested as short cuts to data tabulation.

Personnel charts. This chart can be given to the players as well as to the coaching staff. This information is vital to all members of the squad. (See Fig. 256)

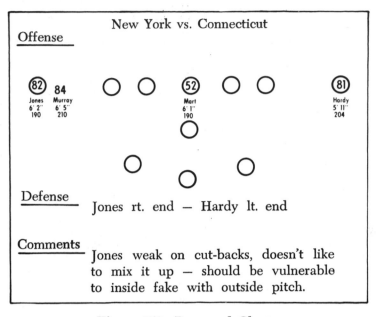

Figure 256. Personnel Chart

Statistical chart. The statistical chart gives a summary of vital data concerning the successes and failures of the team's offense and defense. (See Fig. 257)

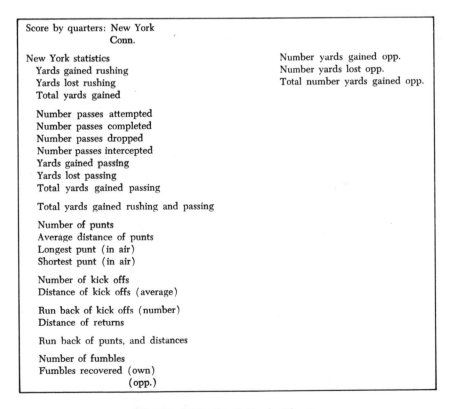

Figure 257. Statistical Chart

Running offense. The diagram of the rushing offense indicates the particular offensive hole concentration and includes the play-by-play gains or losses. (See Fig. 258) This type of chart can be made for each quarter and/or for the total half or game.

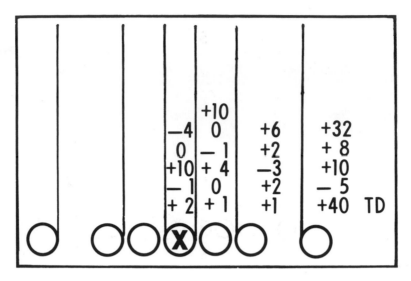

Figure 258. Running Offense

Pass plays. The pass plays chart is designed to show the area concentration of the passes. It is used also to give an account of the success or failure of passes attempted. (See Fig. 259)

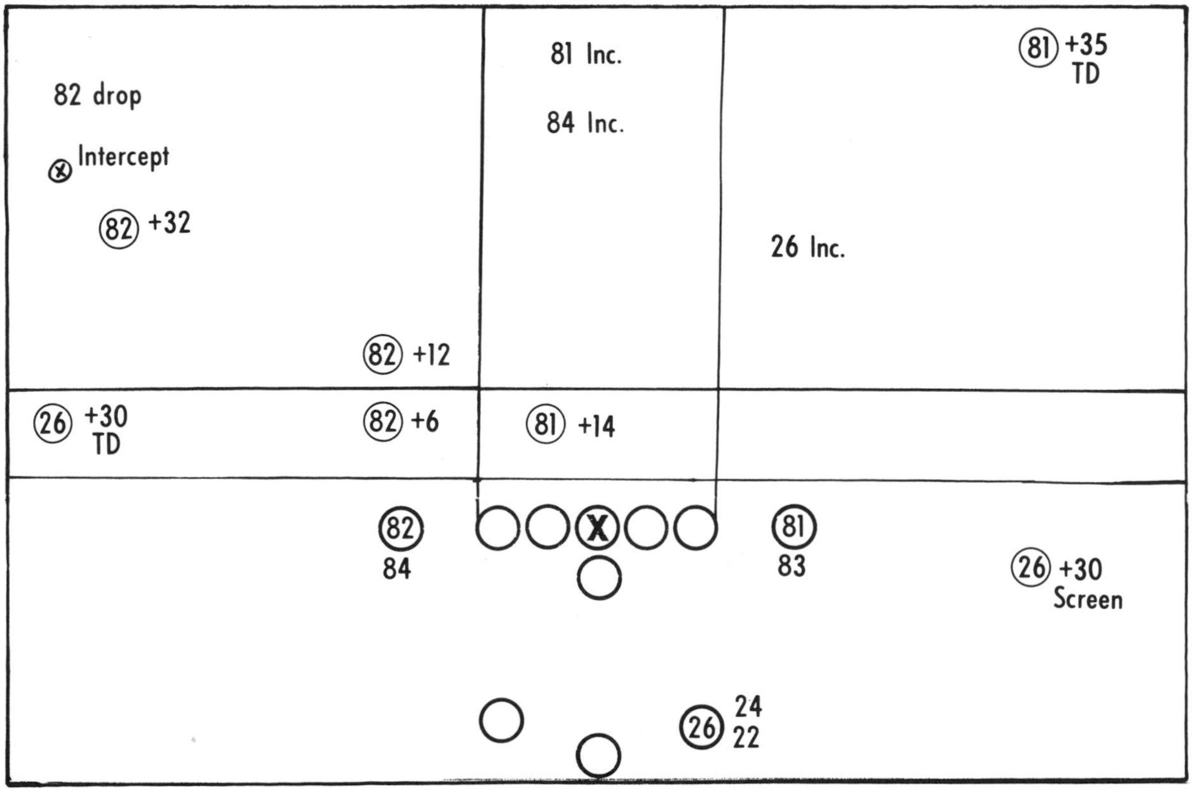

Figure 259. Pass Plays

Running plays. The section of the report related to running plays should include a diagram of each play that is different from one of your own plays. It should include also a diagram of the offense formation, opponents' defense formation, and individual blocking assignments. One such diagram is given in Fig. 260 as an example.

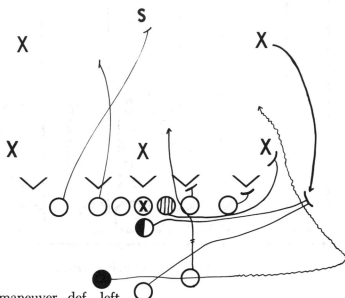

Comments: Powerful cut-back maneuver def. left end had inside resp.

Figure 260. Running Plays

Pass plays. Pass plays fall into two categories: running passes and straight passes. If the pass pattern used is identical to your own, indicate the name or number of the pass. If the pass pattern is different, diagram the path of the receivers. For straight passes, diagram the pass protection used, including weaknesses. (See Fig. 261 & 262)

Running passes—Same as our option pass. A success fully used throwback pass used late in the first half:

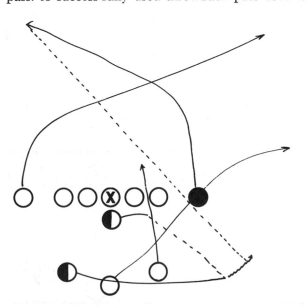

Figure 261. Running Passes

Straight passes—Used our V-out left and right, out button hook, and our screen left. Additional pass patterns are diagrammed below: the first diagram shows their standard pass protection plan —man-for-man (active).

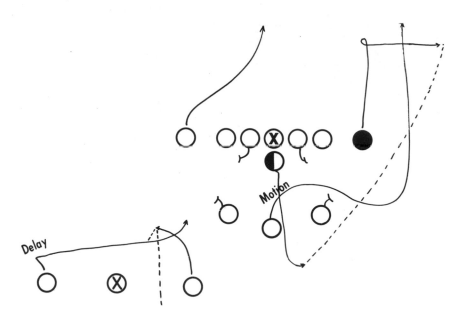

Figure 262. Straight Passes

Punting. Punting charts are of two types: punt protection and punt returns. The punt protection chart also should indicate weaknesses, if any exist. (See Fig. 263) The punt return chart should indicate who returned the punt. (See Fig. 264)

Punt protection—A standard tight punt protection plan used with ends split about three yards and kicker ten yards deep. The left tackle blocks in leaving the opp. end and tackle for the quarterback to block. The QB tries to shoulder block opp. Should be able to smother him with our tackle.

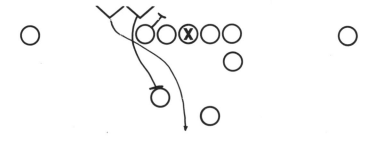

Figure 263. Punt Protection

Return of punts—A criss-cross in the backfield used with alley blocking. Heavy concentration on the ends. Halfback should be able to run up the alley formed as no one looks for him.

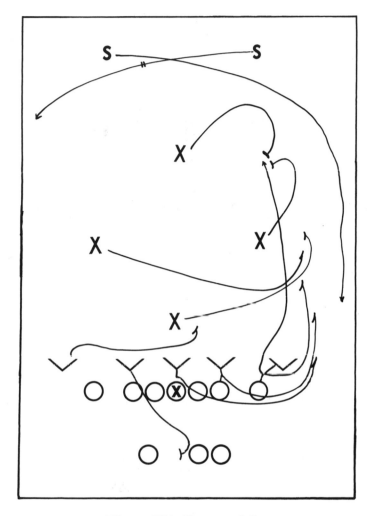

Figure 264. Return of Punts

Kick off. This page should include the kick off alignment and procedures of the team. In addition, it should show the kick off returns used. (See Fig. 265)

Kick off alignment—Down fast under kicks. Criss-cross used by end and halfback on each side. Halfback on right side, number 26, converges very rapidly. The end, number 82, stays close to sideline leaving a large gap.

Kick off return—Used wedge blocking both times with very little success.

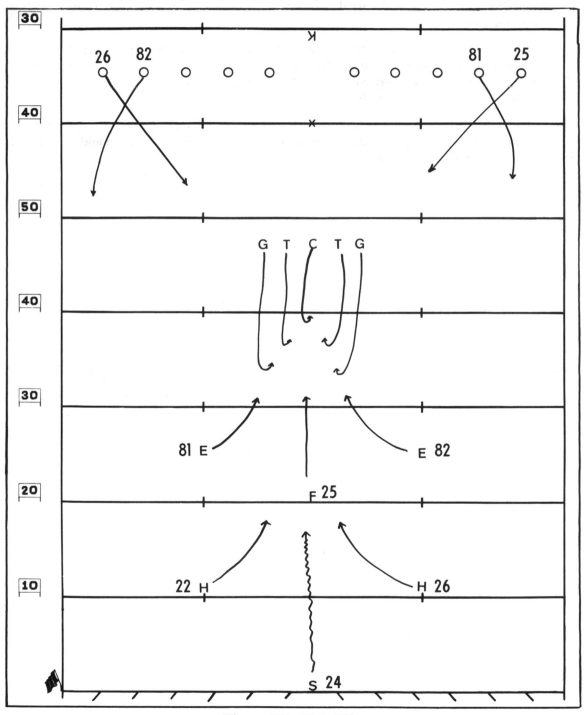

Figure 265. Kick Off

General information. The section on general information should be narrative in nature. It should include such data pertaining to team morale, injuries, and general impressions.

The Scout's Report

The scouts report to the coaching staff as soon as possible. This probably could be done best on Monday. An early report by the scouts will allow ample time for the coaches to prepare their strategy for the coming game. If the game is not to be played next on the schedule, the report should be held until the week of the particular game. The scouts should attempt to see each team twice before making their reports. This would give them an opportunity to complete the weak spots in their reports, and would show the adjustments made by the team for the second game.

The coach will want the scouts to report to the team. The best time for this report is the night before the afternoon set aside for team defensive play. The entire report is not presented to the squad; the scouts and coaches must decide what information they wish to give to the team. Particular running plays and pass patterns can be demonstrated best on the practice field.

If possible the scouts should be present at the game, to give them an opportunity to edit their report in relation to how the opponent played against your team. The final edited report should then be filed in the coach's office for use the following season.

Chapter 14

Strategy

Strategy can be defined as the combination and employment of broad scale methods for the purpose of gaining advantage in competition. The preceding chapters elaborated on individual means of gaining an advantage over the opponents. Strategy is the attempt to select, combine, and employ the isolated means properly. It is a primary task of the modern football coach. In most instances, the coach maps out the plan of strategy —both offense and defense—and then delegates the completion of the plan to members of his team. The final responsibility for the use of the strategy rests on the "broad shoulders" of the team captain(s), the offensive quarterback, and the defensive quarterback.

The Team Captain

The team captain is an extremely important cog in the football machine. He has responsibilities during the season, during the game, and during the off season. It is important that the most highly qualified person on the team be given this position of prestige and honor.

Some coaches go so far as to select the team captain. Generally, however, the coach attempts to indoctrinate the team members as to the type of person who should be the team captain, and allows them to elect their own captain. This method of selection is the more desirable democratic technique. Unless careful precautions are taken, however, the election may be based solely on popularity. The team leader should be elected on the basis of leadership, ability, and popularity.

Duties during the season. The team captain is actually the go-between between the players and the coach. This does not mean that he acts as a "stool pigeon." The captain gives to the coach the information that is vital to his team's success, and to the growth of individual personnel. A list of the duties of the team captain during the season would include items such as those that follow:

1. Be a leader—this can best be done by your outsanding example of hard work and hard play, rather than by harsh sarcastic words.
2. Talk football to your teammates; get them to think about the game.
3. Keep a mental check on the physical condition of your teammates. See that they report all injuries to the trainer or coach.
4. Be concerned personally about keeping the training rules. Try to "talk sense" to those who do not keep the rules. Only as a last resort are you to report rule infractions to the coach.
5. Discuss teammates' personal problems with the coach in private.
6. Don't pry into problems of teammates. If you are "one of the boys," they are quite apt to confide in you. Don't break that confidence.
7. If the team is upset over something done or said by a coach, don't take sides. Discuss the matter with the coach.
8. Never belittle others, including players and coaches. Always remember that your coaches are trying to help the players achieve total growth and individual success.

Duties during the game. The team captain has major duties to perform during a contest. Some of these are as follows:

1. Handle the coin tossing ceremony with poise and confidence. Carefully carry out the prearranged kick off decision of the coach.
2. Know the rules of the game in detail. Always check the decisions of the officials against this personal knowledge of the rules. Listen carefully to the penalty choices offered by the official, and be sure and confident in your selection. The captain's final choice is made in relation to the total game situation. Select the option that is the most advantageous to your team's success.
3. Be a gentleman at all times. Have your teammates report all matters concerning the officials to you. You in turn present the matters to the officials. Always address the officials as Mr. Referee, Mr. Umpire, Mr. Linesman.
4. Be an inspiration to your teammates by your aggresive, confident team play. Show a strong desire to win at all times.
5. Be certain that your team understands that the quarterback is the boss of play calling. Don't stand for unnecessary talk from teammates to the quarterback regarding the quarterback's calls.
6. Take time out only when it will work to your team's advantage.
7. Keep a watchful eye on your teammates. If any of the players are stunned or physically exhausted, notify the coach.
8. Congratulate players on fine play; give a pat on the back to those who are momentarily discouraged.

Duties during the off-season. The captain has the responsibility of talking football to team members during the off-season. He should report all serious misbehavior of teammates to the coach. The public, including the school student body, is constantly aware of athletes. Misbehavior on the part of athletes is never condoned by anyone. Help to prove the theory that it takes character to take part in sports.

The Offensive Quarterback

The offensive quarterback has the primary responsibility of calling the offensive signals. This is no easy task and requires many hours of preparation. It is the offensive quarterback's duty to comprehend fully and carry out in detail the coach's offensive strategy. The plan of strategy may be a rigid one, or one in which there is allowed considerable flexibility. This is a decision to be made by the coach. The quarterback must be as well informed of the offense, and as adept at signal calling as is the coach.

Each coach has the responsibility of personally indoctrinating his quarterbacks. This indoctrination usually is approached by a series of general ideas and a series of specific plans.

General items. A list of general information for the quarterback can be staggering in length and detail. Each individual coach will have his own ideas on the subject. The following list is partial and merely representative in nature:

1. Study your game and know it Always, All ways.
2. Have confidence in yourself.
3. You have charge of the offense. Make your team realize that you are boss.
4. If you falter, the entire team will falter.
5. Never let down mentally or physically.
6. Work with your team captain.
7. Do not call a teammate down for a misplay; the coach will do that.
8. Your teammates will react positively to you if you do your job thoroughly and in a business-like manner.
9. Know your plays thoroughly, including team assignments on each.
10. Mix the plays; do not distribute them according to friendships.
11. Do not run one back to death.
12. Confide in the coach. He is the one to go to in case of any trouble.
13. In the first few minutes feel your opponent out, even at the expense of downs.
14. Play hard and fast while the team is clicking.

15. Play cautiously if ahead in a tight game or ahead near the end of a game.
16. If one side of the opponents' line is strong, leave it alone until the players shift out of position.
17. If the coach substitutes, reason out why.
18. Do not allow the huddle to develop into a debating society.
19. Remember that fumbling is the greatest fault you can have.
20. Find out which defensive men are breaking up the plays and use plays to fool them.
21. If a good ball carrier comes into the game, settle him down with faking or interference duties first.
22. Listen to suggestions, select the best.
23. Don't waste plays without a purpose.
24. If worried, don't tell it to fellow players.
25. Don't worry about the outcome of the game to such an extent the fun of playing is eliminated.

Specific items. There is a myriad of specific facts the quarterback must know. The details will vary according to the style of offense used and the strategy plan of the coach. It seems more profitable at this point to suggest areas of information than specific facts. The coach can fill in the areas with the facts he desires. *Strategy map.* The following is a suggested strategy map for the quarterback to memorize. The coach should list in detail for the quarterback specifically what the map means. He should indicate also when a deviation from this general plan of strategy is acceptable. (See Fig. 266)

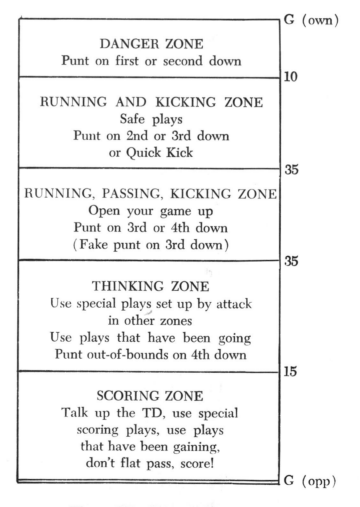

Figure 266. Strategy Map[3]

---

[3]Adapted from Dana X Bible, *Championship Football,* First Edition, (Prentice-Hall, Inc. 1947).

Vital statistics. The following is a list of vital statistics that should be known before deciding on a particular play:

Down	Position of the sun
Position on the field	Condition of individual team members
Direction of the wind	Score
Condition of the field	Time

Abilities of every player. This information is vital for the quarterback if his play decision is to be an intelligent one.

The running attack. The quarterback must know the following information about the running game:
All blocking assignments against all expected defenses
Reason for each particular play
Sequence of plays
Special plays
Scoring plays
Tactical situation when these plays are to be used

The passing attack. The quarterback should know the following information about the passing game:
All blocking assignments
Pass patterns
Choice of receivers; first, second, third choices
Screen passes
Semi-screen passes

The kicking game. The quarterback must know the following information about the kicking game:
Who and when to punt
Field goal attempts; who and when
Extra point attempts; who

Scouting report information. The quarterback should know the following information about the opponent:
Opponent weaknesses against running and passing plays
Specific plays against a particular opponent.

The Defensive Quarterback

The third and final leader on the field is the defensive quarterback. This man has the duty of selecting the specific defense to be used against a particular opponent. More than likely, he will have to make choices among several usuable defenses. The coach must school this player in the specifics of the defensive strategy to be used.

A list of information that will determine the decisions of the defensive quarterback would be endless. The following list will indicate considerations that are necessary before a decision can be made.

Standard defensive alignments. The defensive quarterback should be thoroughly schooled in the assignments of every player in all defenses. It is important he understand the theory behind each standard defense, and when each can be used most successfully. He should also know a signal system so that he can quickly indicate the proposed defense to his teammates.

Special defenses. These special defenses would include defensive stunts, indicating when they are to be used and how often.

Information about the opponent. The quarterback must know the answers to such questions as:
What do the opponents like to do under a particular set of circumstances?
What do the opponents like to do, or what have they done, under similar circumstances?
What factors of strength or weakness in the opponents' lineup can be expected to modify these assumptions?

What can the opponents do best in this tactical situation?

What are the opponents' most logical alternatives?

What are they, within reason, unlikely to do in this situation?

To Kick Off or Receive

A problem that confronts the coach and team captain at the start of every game is the decision to be made during the coin toss ceremony. The winner of the official's toss has a choice of two options: (1) whether his team will kick off or receive and (2) the goal his team will defend. The loser of the toss is given the choice not taken by the winner. Before the second half starts, the captain who lost the pre-game toss is given his choice of the two privileges, and his opponent is granted the other.

There are several factors to consider before making the final choice:

The kicking potential of your kicker.

The kicking potential of your opponent.

The wind and other weather conditions: wet or dry, sun in relation to the direction of the field.

The potential offensive strength of your team in relation to the opponent.

The potential defensive strength of your team in relation to the opponent.

The punting ability of your punter.

The punting ability of your opponent.

The psychological condition of your team: will they fumble the kick off, or fumble during the first series of
 downs; do they play better early in the game, in the middle of the game, or late in the game.

The physical condition of your team: will they tire during the latter part of the quarter, half, or end of the game.

The psychological condition of your opponent: do they start fast, slow; are they easily discouraged.

The potential of your opponent: are they superior to you, even with you, or inferior to your team.

All of the aforementioned, plus the "hunch" of the coach, will determine whether he will have his team kick off or receive. Some coaches "pass the buck" by allowing the captain to make his own decision. This is not recommended, as any blame for an incorrect decision will weigh heavily on the player. The burden of decision should rest on the coach.

In summary, the decisions as to whether or not you wish to kick off, and which goal you want to defend, are calculated ones which are based on facts and on a "hunch."

Chapter 15

Administration

Football is a game that requires industrial efficiency for its total success. The basic principles of administration—organization, deputization, supervision—are of vital concern to the modern football coach. Many "big time" coaches have stated that their duties are in the realm of administration basically, with coaching left to assistants. This is not desirable of course, but it is certainly understandable. The more the emphasis on winning, the more meticulous the administrative planning. With organization of paramount importance, the coach must devote much of his out-of-season time to careful planning. This pre-season effort will only lessen, not alleviate, in-season organizational problems.

The duties of the coach in relation to individual and team play have been indicated in previous chapters. In addition, earlier chapters have dealt with the duties of the coach regarding strategy and scouting. This chapter will concentrate on other duties of the coach: staff assignments; training rules; conditioning; practice plans; game plans; statistics of game; use of movies; and team meetings.

Staff Assignments

The coaching staff is composed of team scouts and assistant coaches. Some of these assistant coaches may be freshmen and/or junior varsity coaches.

Staff personnel are usually selected with regard to their special talents. As a minimum staff, the head coach should have a line coach and a backfield coach. Larger schools will have as many as 10 to 12 assistant coaches.

It is the task of the head coach to synchronize the staff personnel into a workable unit. Explicit assignments should be given to each staff member. It is essential that the staff coach their group of players according to the philosophy and basic principles outlined by the head coach. The staff should never improvise or change procedures without first consulting him. If the players do not seem able to handle a certain style of blocking, the matter should be discussed at a staff meeting. The final decision is to be made by the head coach and to be accepted by the assistant coaches.

The assistants should have a say in the daily practice schedule and in the offense and defense strategy plans. The head coach should listen to these opinions, weigh their merit, and then make his own final decision.

It is imperative that the head coach and assistants have respect for each other as persons and coaches so that they can work together as a unit. Differences of philosophy and behaviors are inevitable, but must be kept at a minimum.

Staff meetings at regular intervals are essential. These should be held prior to the season, during the season, and after the season. They shonuld be business-like in nature rather than proverbial "bull sessions."

Team Managers

To insure a properly functioning and well organized football squad, the coordinated effort of a staff of managers is necessary. It is wise to have two classifications of managers: varsity and assistant managers. The varsity managers usually consist of two upper classmen with one of the two designated as head manager. The assistants, at least two and preferably four, are usually underclassmen who are training for the varsity manager positions.

Most high schools and small colleges do not have a staff member known as the custodian of supplies. The coach therefore is charged with the responsibility for the care and handling of all football supplies and equipment. This task can become a full time job for the coach and can seriously hamper his coaching functions. The wise coach does the original organization and then deputizes responsibilities to other qualified personnel. He needs supervise only the following tasks: issuing of equipment; storing of equipment; cleaning of equipment; inventory of equipment; proper placing of practice equipment; proper placing of game equipment; trip planning; and the like.

It is desirable to make a check list of supplies and equipment needed for all home games and all away games. The managers then can check off each item, being sure that no equipment has been forgotten.

It should be remembered that managerial experience is excellent training for future adult life.

Physical Examinations and Insurance

It is essential that all football prospects be given a complete physical examination by a medical doctor prior to the first practice session. Most insurance policies are not effective until the physical examination has been made. Practice injuries occurring before the physical examination can readily lead to law suits against the coach. The physical examination should be thorough, and not just a rapid screening. The coach's task is to see that all arrangements are made for this all-important medical examination. It is wise for the coach and managers to be given the examination also.

It is imperative that a full coverage insurance program be obtained for the athletes. There are many reputable insurance comanies which can offer satisfactory insurance programs. Most states have an athletic insurance plan, sponsored by the State Athletic Association. In some instances, the participant pays a small premium for the insurance. It is highly desirable to have the school assume the premium cost of the athletic insurance through the budget of the board of education.

Training Rules

In many schools, training rules are traditional, to a great extent. The coach must decide first what specific training rules he deems necessary for the well-being of his team members. Secondly, he must review these training rules in relation to traditional rules, school administrative attitudes, and community attitudes. Finally, the coach must determine whether or not he can enforce these rules and what enforcements he must use.

To be a success in football, as in other athletics, the individual participant must learn to discipline himself. This personal sacrifice, conformity to rules and regulations, and individual discipline will be of great value to the individual throughout his life.

Following are listed some traditional rules for athletes:
Smoking is not permitted during the entire season.
Alcoholic beverages of all kinds are forbidden.
Nine hours of sleep are essential; the player should be in bed by 10:30 p.m.
Attendance at practice sessions and games is mandatory unless a prior excuse has been arranged.
Eat wholesome, well balanced meals. Do not indulge in sweets or in-between meal eating.

Enforcement procedures used are a major problem in conjunction with training rules. Coaches' techniques range from immediate dropping from the team to completely ignoring the infractions. It is necessary that the coach select some in-between plan. If you are not going to enforce rules, don't make rules. It is not desirable for the coach to devote his spare time to snooping and spying on his men. Have no doubt that, if a boy is breaking rules, you will learn about it, probably sooner than you wish! It would seem essential to remember that football is a game, the objective of which is not merely to win. The boy who breaks training rules should be looked upon as an individual who needs help. Only as a last resort should he be dismissed from the team. Nonetheless, the final responsibility for the handling of rule breakers rests with the coach. This is a responsibility that must not be delegated.

Conditioning

Most coaches realize that team success depends to a great extent upon the physical condition of the team members. The basic conditioning work is undertaken during the early fall practice. Once the season gets under way, team practice must be devoted to team work and offense and defense polishing. Conditioning will pretty well take care of itself through the actual practice.

Early fall conditioning. There are two basic considerations with which to cope in the conditioning program: musclar strength and endurance and cardio-vascular endurance. There is a great deal of interest today in the potential of weight training as a pre-season conditioner. The principle behind the modern weight training concept is the doing of several repetitions with weights that can be handled with relative ease, rather than attempting to lift maximum load. The exercises used are standard weight lifter's exercises: clean and press (light weight); heavy press; squat; pullovers; wrestler's bridge; sit-ups; curls; rowing exercises; and supine press.

The basis of weight training as a pre-conditioner lies in the principle of overload. The use of weights during exercise speeds up the conditioning program by making the muscles do an above-normal amount of work in a short period of time. Much loss of time and general muscular soreness could be avoided if the players devoted some of the late summer time to weight training.[5]

The actual exercise program should be undertaken with snap and precision. A slow methodical period of exercise will tend only to bore the players, and will result in their developing sloven undesirable habits. The standard exercises of push-ups, sit-ups, toe touching, lateral bends, jumping jack, toe bouncing, and arm circles should be done with speed and timing, not necessarily until exhaustion. Grass drills are a vital part of the conditioning program, as they aid in general muscular development, endurance and reaction speed. It is desirable to have chinning bars or vertical climbing ropes available. This type of exercise is unsurpassed for shoulder and arm development.

The employment of short sprints generally is preferred to long distance runs. It is profitable, however, to end practice on alternate days with a long distance run. Charging sleds, blocking dummies and tackling dummies all play an important part in the conditioning program. Individual fundamental drills in tackling, fumble recovery, pass defense, punt returns, and kick off returns all aid immeasurably in the athletes' total conditioning.

The extent and type of pre-practice exercises should be determined in relation to what is to take place during the actual practice session. It is not necessary to devote much time to running and leg exercises if the planned practice will consist primarily of running activities.

Conditioning During the Season

The problem of conditioning during the season is, in reality, one of maintaining present condition. The team should be at a high level of physical fitness by the first game. Regular exercises are necessary during the season, but these should be short, snappy and varied. Much of the exercise needed will result from the actual performance of game skills in various drill sessions. The coaches and trainer should emphasize maximum short bursts of speed in all drills.

Practice Plans

Considerable thought should be devoted to the practice sessions by the entire coaching staff, including the trainer. It is recommended that the practice sessions be run with precise timing. No more than two hours should be devoted to practice. The most efficient method of planning practice sessions is by itemizing what is to be done during the particular session, and how much time is to be devoted to each item of business. A written practice program should be made out for each day's session, and all coaches should have a copy of the program before going on the field. A copy should be posted on the players' bulletin board so that they will know what to expect. A manager actually should be in control of the time element of the practice. He should notify the coaches when they have spent the alloted time on a specific activity. Only the head coach can decide, on occasions, to spend more time than is scheduled on some phase of the program.

Scrimmages should be held twice weekly prior to the first game, usually on Wednesday as a controlled scrimmage, and Saturday as a regular game scrimmage. The extent and number of the scrimmages will depend to a great extent on the experience and caliber of players. The less game experience and the poorer the caliber, the more time needed for scrimmage sessions. In the final analysis, all real learning takes place during a scrimmage session. A player may know the fundamentals perfectly in drills and dummy scrimmages, but prove completely inept in actual combat.

The following is a sample of a daily practice session:

3:00   Mass exercises

3:10   Group work
       Backs: fumble recovery—5 min.
            tackling dummy—5 min.
            blocking machine—5 min.
            live tackling—5 min.

       Linemen: fumble recovery—5 min.
            blocking machine—5 min.
            tackling dummy—5 min.
            live tackling—5 min.

       Ends: fumble recovery—5 min.
            blocking dummies—5 min.
            tackling dummy—5 min.
            live tackling with backs—5 min.

3:30   Group drills
       Backs and ends: ball carrying—5 min.
                 pass patterns—5 min.
                 pass defense—10 min.

       Linemen: 2 on 1—5 min.
              3 on 2—5 min.
              defense stunts—10 min.

3:50   Group drills
       Backs: with centers, polish ball handling
            in various plays—10 min.

       Linemen: offensive play maneuvers against
            dummies—10 min.

4:00   Team drill
       Dummy scrimmage with air dummies—15
         min. Use three offensive teams

4:15   Team scrimmage—30 min.
       Use three offensive teams for this of-
       fensive scrimmage.

4:45   Punt return practice—5 min.

4:50   Extra point scrimmage—5 min.

4:55   Wind sprints

5:00   End of practice

Once the season has started, most coaches stop using scrimmages. This is dependent, however, upon team performance. An inexperienced team needs the scrimmage session as a part of its total learning program. Some coaches use Wednesday as an offensive scrimmage period and Thursday as a defensive scrimmage period. If the team is in excellent physical condition and is quite experienced, it is suggested that it should not have any practice on Friday prior to a Saturday game. This procedure will depend upon the prevailing circumstances, however.

Game Plans

The strategy involved in offense and defense has already been discussed. Space here will be devoted to pre-game warm-up drills, bench management, and substitutions.

Pre-game warm-up. The usual amount of time devoted to the warm-up session is 20 minutes. Three to four minutes should be devoted to stretching and limbering up exercises, followed by a couple of short sprints. The team then is dispersed for individual skill practice in passing, centering, punting, place kicking, ball handling, blocking, charging, and tackling. The team usually leaves the field, or huddles for last minute instructions, about 10 minutes before game time. Two or three minutes before kick off time should be devoted by teams to running signals. *Remember, the pre-game warm-up is just that, a warm-up period, not a conditioning period.*

Bench management. It is important that the coaches and players know where they are to sit on the bench when they are not otherwise occupied. It is a good idea to group players by positions, so thta an interchange of information can take place. This positioning can be arranged by several different methods. The following pattern is merely suggestive.

Quarterbacks—on the center of the bench next to the coach.
Guards—on the right side of the quarterbacks.
Tackles—on the right side of the guards.
Ends—on the right side of the tackles.
Centers—on the left side of the quarterbacks.
Right halfbacks—one the left side of the centers.
Fullbacks—on the left side of the halfbacks.
Left halfbacks—on the left side of the fullbacks.

Substitutions. Many coaches prefer to have the coaches who have been working with certain specific positions make their own substitutions, feeling that this will give prestige to the assistant coaches. This prestige, in turn, would be a great help to the assistant coach in getting 100 per cent effort during the practice session. The assistant coaches' freedom to substitute can cause a great deal of misunderstanding and confusion, however. Most coaches prefer to approve or disapprove all substitutes suggested by the assistant coaches. In the final analysis, the head coach has the responsibility for his team.

Game Statistics

A football game is an exciting, fast-moving encounter involving a large number of people. It is humanly impossible to recall all the action that has taken place and the performance of each player after the game is over. Much of this information can be compiled after the proper collection of game statistics.

The coaching staff will want to know specific information as suggested in the following list:

A. *Offense*
Where did the team make the greatest gains rushing?
What particular holes produced the fewest gains?
What particular plays produced the smallest gains?
What yardage did the various backs gain rushing?
Who fumbled, and under what conditions?
What were the results of each pass play?
Who seems to be the best pass receiver?
What noticeable player errors were made on offense?
What particular plays were called, and under what circumstances?
How was the kicking game?
How successful were the various plays against specific defenses?

B. *Defense*
What particular defenses were used, including the circumstances involved at the moment?
Where did the opponents make the most rushing yardage, and through what particular holes?
How successful was the passing defense, including at what point were most of the completions made?
Who made and/or missed tackles?
How successful were punt and kick off returns?
Were opponents' punts or kicks blocked, by whom, and under what circumstances?
Number of opponents' fumbles recovered?

C. *Season totals*
Average yards gained by rushing for each player.
Average number of pass completions by each quarterback and other passers.

Number of passes caught and average yards gained by each receiver.
Average yards gained by each specific rushing play.
Average yards gained by each specific pass play.
Average distance of punts for each punter.
Number of punts blocked for each punter.
Average distance of kick offs.
Average return of kick offs, including what specific return used.
Average distance of punt returns, including specific return used.
Number of field goals made and/or missed.
Number of extra points made and/or missed.
Total points scored by each player.
Total number of yards gained rushing.
Total number of yards gained passing.
Total number of points scored.
Total number of points scored by opponents.
Number of games won and lost.
Number of fumbles made, including number recovered.
Number of fumbles made by opponents, including number your team recovered.

This partial listing of desired and usable information points up the tremendous administrative task confronting the coaching staff. It must be gathered efficiently and assembled meaningfully.

There are many possible methods of gathering this information. The following technique has been used succesfully.

Offensive information. This data can be gathered efficiently by means of a play-by-play account of the game. One particular person, usually a team manager who has been thoroughly schooled in the team offense, is assigned to collect this data. He should be near the quarterback and head coach to enlist their help, and to gather their comments. (See Fig. 267)

Down and Distance	Field Position	Ball Carrier	Play	Results	Comments of Coach
1—10	Opp. 45 M	Royston	2—4—8	+12	Cut back left
1—10	Opp. 33 R	Berg	2—1—5	+5	Poor fake
2—5	Opp. 28 R	Brem to Zirpolo	Dive Rt. Pass	+8	Good Call
1—10	Opp. 20 M	Berg	Dive Rt.	+2	Hit outside

Figure 267. Offensive Chart

Defensive information. A play-by-play account of the defense should be kept also. This account is by a manager who is well versed in the team defensive strategy. This manager should be seated near the defensive quarterbacks and coach. (See Fig. 268)

1–10	Opp. 35 R	7–1–2–1	St. T	Off tackle left	Good call
2–7	Opp. 38 M	7–1–2–1	St. T	Pass Rt. flat	Poor call, should have expected pass
1–10	Opp. 49 R	Gap 8	St. T	Sweep left	OK

Figure 268. Defensive Chart

Additional chart (offense and defense). In addition to the two charts discussed and shown, a running account of the game should be kept. It is a good idea to have the man responsible for this chart in some elevated position, preferably the press box. He will chart the offensive and defensive play of the team. (See Fig. 269) This information is very useful at half time as it shows the "complexion" of the game. The information is valuable also as a review for the offensive and defensive quarterbacks after the game. All charts should become a part of the coach's permanent files.

Brockport vs. Cortland   1969   1st quarter

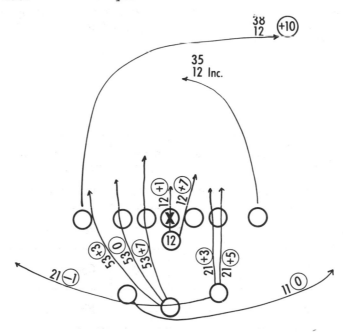

Figure 269. Offense-Defense Chart

Movies

Movies can be a valuable asset to the coaches and team members. The movies will give a detailed account of the total game action. There are two general uses for game movies: (1) review by coaches and (2) review by the team members.

Review by the coaches. It is important that the coaching staff meet on Monday to review the movies of the previous game. These movies will indicate clearly where additional work is needed, and will show the relative worth of particular personnel under fire. The assistant coaches should keep notes of comments about the players for whom they are particularly responsible. Notes should be kept concerning suggested blocking and/or play changes. This latter information can be carefully scrutinized by the coach and will help him make his final decision.

Review by the team. There are two ideas about using movies for team members. Some coaches prefer to merely run through the films to give the players a general impression of their own play. The movie is stopped and reversed only when requested by the players.

The other idea is to make the showing of the movies an educational experience. The coach who uses this technique constantly stops and runs the movies back, pointing out specific player mistakes. He also mentions different cuts or movements the players should have made under certain circumstances. If not properly handled, the team humor can get out of hand during this kind of showing. Unless the players are properly conditioned to this technique, many sarcastic and painful remarks may be made during the players' free time.

The coach should think carefully before he decides which of these methods he wishes to adopt. In the final analysis, the total amount of learning by the players will determine which of the methods should be used.

Team Meetings

Team meetings are essential. The number of meetings and their length will differ according to circumstances. An intelligent, alert, successful team does not need to meet as often, or for so long a period of time, as do other teams.

Some coaches prefer to meet with the team members every day for a short session. Other coaches would rather meet only once or twice a week for longer sessions. It is necessary to meet in order to review the previous game, preferably as a part of the Monday practice. Another meeting should be held the day before the practice to be devoted to defense. At this meeting, the scouting report will be given.

The primary consideration to be given is to the attitudes of the players. Meet often and long enough to impart pertinent information, but not often and long enough to stifle the team interest.

Off Season Organization

Equipment and supplies. As soon after the season as is humanly possible, the coach, together with the team managers, needs to make a complete inventory of all the football equipment and supplies. The equipment must be checked for worn out items, and items that need reconditioning. Consideration should be given to the replacement of depleted supplies, and to new equipment or supplies that are desired. This is easiest done by keeping a running inventory of equipment and supplies throughout the regular season. The post season inventory then becomes a simple matter of checking through the regular season inventory.

The materials that need reconditioning should be sent as soon as possible to one of the reliable reconditioning firms. This will allow ample time for the materials to be returned prior to the arrival of the new football season.

Before the opening of the season, the football equipment should be properly marked with an identification code. The equipment should be arranged on individual shelves so as to make its distribution an efficient and simple process. Each item should be separated as to kind and size for ease of handling.

New equipment also should be ordered promptly. It is recommended that quality be considered when purchasing athletic equipment. Quality equipment from a reliable firm is the key to satisfaction and economy.

Planning for the next season. The post season period is the time when the coach and his assistants review the previous season to consider personnel changes and/or additions. At this time, the coaches need to give careful consideration to the desirability of making changes in both their offenses and defenses in light of past season experiences and incoming potential personnel. A delay in thinking about the changes desired in offense and defense until the start of the new season usually results in no changes—unwanted status quo. The running comments made during the regular season games, together with the perusal of game movies, will give the coaches many ideas as to ways to strengthen their total team play.

The coaches need to make a careful review of their pre and regular season practice plans. It may be that unsatisfactory drills and procedures are being used, thereby hampering the precision of the offense or defense. Poor organization can lead to a rapid deterioration of team skill and/or morale.

Personal improvement. It is necessary and desirable that the football coach keeps up-to-date in his field. He should watch as many university and professional games as possible. These games usually continue after the completion of the high school schedules. Many valuable ideas can be obtained from such game viewing. The coach should read all new literature available from the various presses. It behooves the coach to attend some off-season coaching clinics. These usually are sponsored by colleges and universities and have the nation's outstanding college coaches as the leaders. These coaches offer many ideas and "tricks of the trade" that can help the less experienced coach immeasurably.

Postlude[4]

Misconceptions frequently arise regarding the educational values of competitive athletics. It is certain that athletics provide opportunities for the development of "character." They abound with circumstances favorable to the development of sociological concepts necessary for adequate democratic living: understanding of competition, cooperation, leadership, "followership"; respect for authority; respect for people, regardless of race, color, or creed; sportsmanlike conduct. These endless values are purely potential at best, however.

Educationally speaking, the great number of values attributed to athletics are not automatic or inevitable, as is sometimes assumed. The values are there as a result of the social setting of athletics, to be absorbed, ignored or rejected by the individual participant. It is difficult, probably impossible, to predict or even safely generalize about the impact of athletics upon the athletes, because of the tremendous difference in individual personalities. Each individual will react negatively or positively, depending upon his personal nature and the environmental forces surrounding him. One person may gain much from his association with athletics, another may remain relatively unaffected, and a third may be severely distorted by his experiences. The direction of the learning, the effectiveness of the learning, and the carry-over or transfer of the learning to other than controlled athletic situations, are of primary concern to educators. To say that victory is of no significant importance would be nonsensical. Victory and defeat are valuable basically for their contribution to the total process of education for the participant. The cliché—The important thing is not whether you win or lose, but how you play the game—has considerable meaning.

Athletes learn concepts of living, attitudes and behavioral patterns through various environmental circumstances. Social pressures from within the athletic group frequently contribute considerably to individual learning. Pressures from within the particular athlete result in personal and social adjustments. Pressures from external sources—parents, siblings, other relatives, friends of the same or opposite sex, interested community members—often directly chart the course of education. Of singular importance is the effect of the adult leaders associated with the athletic teams. The reactions of the individual performers often are related directly to the degree of control of the adults' competitive feelings. Lack of emotional stability in competitive situations among adult leaders will frequently result in ineffective or negative learning on the part of the athletes.

The athletic coach is in a strategic position for the dissemination of democratic behavioral concepts because of the unique atmosphere of athletics. Why are athletics unique in comparison with other types of school situations? The answer lies in the high emotional appeal of athletics. The emotional appeal radiates from within the athletes, from within the school population, and from within the community.

Sociological and democratic principles can be taught by a variety of techniques. These behavior patterns generally can be remembered and adhered to in a non-emotionalized setting. Conflicts between what is known

---

[4]Clifford Wilson, Education Potential of Interscholastic Athletics, New York State Journal of Health, Physical Education, and Recreation, Vol. 9, Dec. 1956.

to be right and the actual behavior of the individual readily arise under emotional stress, however. The adolescent may realize that controlled verbal discussion is a most adequate and desirable problem-solving technique; however, in an emotionalized setting the fists frequently replace the voice.

Adults view this adolescent problem-solving technique with dismay, wondering, "Why?" Conversely, many adolescents wonder, "Why?", when they observe the frequent violent reactions of adults in emotionalized settings. If we are to expect much transfer of socially-accepted democratic patterns of behavior from the controlled school atmosphere to the out-of-school environment, attention must be given to emotional stability.

Athletics, by their very nature, present a constantly emotionalized environment. The extrinsic pressure for success from the school and community populations, the intrinsic desire for self or ego satisfaction, assure a constantly emotionalized setting. The coach thus must be more than a technician, an offensive and defensive strategist. These are certainly attributes necessary for success, but first of all he must be a student of human relations, an educator of outstanding insight and perception of the interactions of people. IIe must be all this if adequate education is to take place with any hope of success in teachnig desirable behavioral patterns that will be adhered to in out-of-school situations.

The coach, by arbitrary techniques, can cause the members of his particular team to react and behave in clear-cut stereotyped patterns. The basketball player can be forced to abide by the official's decisions meekly or violently. The runner can be taught to "elbow on the turn" or to respect the running rights of his opponents. The football player can be taught to return illegal violence with illegal violence, or to capitalize on the emotional upheaval of his opponent. These stereotyped behaviorisms may be adequate for particular athletic competitive situations. Regardless of the direction of the forced behaviorism, however, the probability of any successful transfer of this behavior to other than athletic situations is highly questionable. Consequently one may rightfully inquire, "Where is the educational value of athletics?"

A forced response by threats or violence is worthless at best. To dismiss a player from the squad because of his lack of emotional control in an athletic contest obviously is harmful to the player, the team, and, no doubt, to society. To locate the cause of the player's apparent frustration, to help him realize his problem, to help the player learn to overcome his handicap, are the desirable types of correctional approaches. Domination and arbitarary decisions by the coach frequently supersede all other types of educational techniques. These methods may lead to more victories, but, unfortunately, also to less significant learning for future transfer. One cannot expect the adolescent to learn by merely "showing him the way." For the learning to be significant, the learner must understand the *why*, not just the *how*. Obviously, if athletics are to contribute to successful living, the coach must be concerned with the members of his team as individuals.

There are certainly more than immediate values to athletics. If a coach is to expect any carry-over of his training to other than athletic competition, he must teach for it. He must relate his teachings to basic problems and their solutions, rather than to aggressive "do this or else" techniques. The coach must understand and use psychological principles of adjustment and guidance techniques if he is to expect any semblance of adequate learning in his team personnel. Without insight and concern, the athletic experience serves only as another stereotyped behavioral situation with little, if any, lasting value.

Coaching at the high school and junior high school levels is a precarious and extremely serious business. Coaches at these levels have responsibilities far greater than do the college and university coaches. A highly selective screening job is done at the college and university level, leaving the meek, the maladjusted, the frustrated and the confused would-be-athletes behind. This is not true at the public school level. There, of necessity, the coach handles the "run of the mill," the below average as well as the few well-adjusted and well-rounded athletes.

The majority of public school athletes will discontinue sports' participation upon graduation. Consequently, if the educational values of athletics are to be for the mass rather than the select few, public school coaches must be of the highest caliber. It becomes mandatory that the public school coach be highly skilled in human relations and in the psychology of adjustment. His is a task without equal in the educational life of these students.

Glossary

The following slang terms are commonly used in modern day football:

belly play—An offensive backfield maneuver in which the quarterback places the ball into the stomach area of another backfield man and moves with the man to the line of scrimmage.

blast through—Over-power your opponent by sheer strength. A maneuver used frequently by a backfield man when he cannot avoid contact with a tackler.

blitz—A term describing the driving penetration of defensive linemen after the passer.

boys—A term of respect used by some coaches when referring to their team members.

bread-and-butter plays—Primary plays of the offense that are relied upon to continuously gain yardage.

bull session—A discussion period carried on by players about anything in general and nothing in particular.

day light—A space between the defensive players large enough for the ball carrier to run through.

deep men—This usually refers to the defensive halfbacks and safety man.

dive play—An offensive maneuver in which one of the backfield men, other than the quarterback, carries the ball on a straight ahead play.

dog an end—Run alongside the end within blocking distance as he goes down under a punt by his teammate.

down the throat of the kicker—To run back a punt to at least the point from which it was punted.

draw play—A play which appears to be a pass play, causing the defensive linemen to converge on the passer. The passer than hands the ball to a waiting backfield man, who carries the ball through the first daylight he sees.

ease in the ball—As the ball contacts the receiver's hands, he allows them to continue momentarily with the ball in the direction of its present momentum.

eat the ball—This occurs on an attempted pass play where the quarterback can find no open receiver, and has no opportunity to run with the ball in an effort to evade the onrushing opponents.

eat-up the clock—Slow down the tempo of the game to allow the time to pass with as little action as possible.

floaters—Linemen who do not penetrate past the line of scrimmage when on defense, but drop behind their own scrimmage line to follow the path of the ball carrier.

flood an area—A maneuver used against a zone pass defense calculated to place two or more offensive pass receivers in an area protected by one defensive halfback.

freeze the tackler—So maneuver deceptively when carrying the ball to utterly confuse the tackler as to what direction the ball carrier eventually plans to run.

gap—The space between two offensive linemen.

getting to the passer—Penetrating through the offensive blockers to be able to tackle the passer.

get into a rut—Repeating a particular play or maneuver, very frequently while ignoring other maneuver or play possibilities.

give—A maneuver in which the quarterback hands-off the ball to another offensive backfield man.

give ground—The defensive maneuver of a halfback who backs up on pass defense as an offensive receiver comes straight down the field toward the defensive man.

head-on—The alignment in which one defensive opponent is directly in front of an offensive player.

heavy ball—A nose down ball which hits the receiver's hands with seemingly extra force.

hit the ball—The maneuver of recovering a fumbled ball.

hit the line—The maneuver of carrying the ball on a play inside the opponents' defensive end positions.

jam the ends—Preventing the ends, by legal tactics, from going out into the secondary to receive the pass.

keep—A maneuver in which the quarterback fakes the ball on an offensive play to a teammate, and then proceeds to carry the ball himself.

keep the defense honest—Attempt to keep the defense from guessing what offensive maneuver your team plans to utilize, thus eliminating strong defensive maneuvers against your desired offensive maneuver.

key men—Certain offensive men to be watched by certain defensive men which will indicate what defensive movement will be employed.

key plays—Primary plays in the offensive repertoire.

kick step—A short, quick back step with one foot before moving forward, used to delay momentarily the forward movement of the player. This maneuver generally is used by halfbacks.

knee snap—The rapid extension of the leg, causing the instep to meet the ball with maximum force when punting.

leave your feet at home—The mistake of moving forward rapidly by the extension of the hips, knees, and ankles and not following up this initial action with short driving, chopping steps.

leg kick—The mistake of attempting to punt the ball without the use of knee snap.

light ball—A nose up ball which seemingly hits the hands of the receiver with but little force.

limp leg—The technique of relaxing one leg as the opponent blocks into it, causing the blocker to pass on by the defensive man.

loosen up the defense—The offensive technique of either throwing passes or running end runs in an attempt to cause the defense to stop concentrating their defense against your into-the-line plays.

lost soul—A defensive or offensive player who does not know his assignment on a particular maneuver.

off arm—The arm not carrying the ball, or the arm away from the quarterback when receiving a hand-off.

over—A man lined up directly in front of one of the opponents.

pass and a prayer—A desperation pass made in the hopes that it will be completed.

pay off—The successful completion of a team offensive maneuver.

perfect pass—A pass that is so timed as to drop into the waiting arms of a fast-moving receiver.

pitch-out—A lateral pass maneuver usually made by a quarterback to a halfback who is swinging wide around his own end.

pulling—The maneuver of a lineman causing the lineman, usually a guard, to move along behind his own line of scrimmage.

red dogging—A term used to describe the crashing action of linebackers.

ride—The belly play maneuver of the quarterback, who places the ball into a teammate's stomach and then moves with the man to the scrimmage line.

running room—The space between two defensive linemen sufficiently large enough for the ball carrier to run through.

size up—This simply means to look over the situation.

shake loose—So block the defensive personnel as to allow the ball carrier ample opportunity to progress with the ball.

stop cold—Prevent the opponent from moving the ball forward on an offensive play.

talk sense—An attempt by common sense reasoning to make a person understand the reality of a situation.

trap—The offensive maneuver of allowing an opposing lineman to penetrate into your backfield, and blocking him just before he tackles your ball carrier.

up the alley—The maneuver of carrying the ball down the center of the playing field.

wide open football—The style of offensive play that utilizes many passes and lateral passes in its schedule.

Index

Administration, 221-230
Angle of pursuit, 60
Army, 92, 112
Automatic plays, 80-81

Backfield
    alignments, 62-63, 83-119
    defense rotation, 181-183
    individual offense, 21-41
    team offense, 62-68
Ball carring, 34-40
    eluding tacklers, 36-40
    hand-off, 35, 65-66
    receiving ball, 34, 65
    shifting ball, 37-38
Belly maneuver, 63, 65
Bench management, 225
Bible, Dana X, 110
Blaik, Earl, 110
Blanchard, "Doc", 91
Blocking
    brush, 12
    charging, step & lunge, 46-47
    cross, 72, 118-119
    cross body, 12
    double team, 72, 116-118
    man-for-man, 9, 117-120
    man head-on, 47
    man on inside to outside, 47
    reverse body, 14
    roll, 16
    rules for, 134-141
    screen, 11
    shoulder, 9-10
    single leg or crab, 14
    trap, 69, 73, 117, 120
        avoiding, 59
    wedge, 120, 124
Bootlegs, 131
Bread-and-butter plays, 120
Brush block, 12
Buck lateral, 85
Button hook pass, 145-146, 149

Center, 47-49
    blocking of, 48

hand position, 47
single wing, 47
stance, 47
T-formation, 48
Change of pace, 41
Charging
    defensive, 49-57
    lunge, 46
    offensive, 46
    step, 47
Check-out pass, 152
Check signals, 81
Chicago Bears, 91
Conditioning, 223
Converge, 201-202
Counter plays, 128
Cross blocking, 118-119
Cross body block, 12
Cross buck, 121-124
Cross pass, 150
Cross step, 38
Cup blocking, 143

Davis, Glenn, 91
Deep pass, 153
Defense, individual, 41-45
    against trap, 59
    end play, 60
    forearm shiver, 52
    hand shiver, 52
    in and out, 57
    limp leg, 57
    line, 49-60
    one against two, 57
    over-the-top, 57
    pass, 41-45
    roll out, 57
    split, 57
    stance, 49
    submarine, 57
Defense, team
    backfield rotation, 177-180
    eight- and nine-man front, 177, 180
    eight man line, 197-198
    five man line, 188-189

four man line, 185-187
huddle, 174
odd and even, 128, 169
nine man line, 198-199
pass, 41, 174-177
    combination, 177
    man-for-man, 176
    theory, 174
    zone, 174
pursuit, 59-60
selection of, 172
seven man line, 195-196
six man line, 190-194
standard, 177
split ends, 180-185
strongside flanker, 182, 184
straight, 172
stunting, 172, 199-203
    converge, 201-202
    looping, 199-201
    shifting, 203
    slanting, 201
    small groups, 202-203
teaching of, 173-174
theory of, 171
weakside flanker, 182-183
Delay pass, 154
Desire, 171
Dodd, Robert L. "Bobby," 207
Double team block, 72, 116-118
Double wing, 5, 86-88
Double winged-T, 6, 101-103
Draw plays, 131-132
Drop step, 64

Eligible receivers, 2
Eluding tacklers, 36-40
End-around, 133
Equipment
    off-season organization, 228
    wearing apparel, 1

Faurot, Don, 96
Field goal
    definition, 4
    blocking, 170
    protection, 170
    score, 3
    technique, 28-29
Field judge, 4
Flag pass, 148
Flair pass, 151
Flanker, 110, 180-185
Fly pass, 153
Football
    definition, 1
    educational potential, 229-230
    history, 1
    officials, 4
    rules, 2-3, 91, 156
Forearm shiver, 52
Free ball, 18, 28, 30

Fumble, 18
Fundamentals
    backfield
        defensive, 41-45
        offensive, 20-40
    general, 7-19
    line
        defensive, 49-69
        offensive, 46-49
    team play
        defensive, 171-185
        offensive, 46-49

Game
    length, 2
    plans, 224-225
    starting, 2
    statistics, 225-227
Goal lines, 2
Goal posts, 2

Halas, George, 91
Hand-off, 65
    fake, 66
Hand shiver, 52
Hash marks, 2
High-low block, 72
Huddle
    defensive, 174
    offensive, 77-78

I-formation, 6, 30, 104-106
In and out pass, 149
Individual running technique, 36-40
Insurance, 222
Interceptions, 42, 44
Iowa Pre-Flight, 96

Kerr, Andy, 86
Kick off
    alignment, 155-156
    on side, 30
    return, 155-161
    rolling, 30
    rules, 2, 156
    technique, 29

Lateral pass, 66-67
Line, basic maneuvers, 116-119
Linesman, 4
Lonesome end, 110
Look-in pass, 153
Looping, 199-201

Managers, 221-222
Man-for-man blocking, 117-120
Maryland University, 96
McCay, John, 104
Meetings, team, 228
Michigan State, 114, 138
Missouri University, 96
Monster man, 177

Movies, 227-228
Multiple offense, 114-115
Munn, Clarence "Biggie," 114

Naked reverse, 132
Numbering systems, 74

Offensive formations, 4-6, 82-115
    double wing, 6, 86-88
    double winged-T, 6, 101-103
    I-formation, 6, 30, 104-106
    multiple, 114-115
    short punt, 89-90
    single wing, 82-86
    slot-T, 6, 96-99
    split-T, 6, 32-33, 96-98
    spread, 6, 111-113
    T-formation, 6, 91-111
    tandem-T, 6, 99-101
    variable, 115
    wishbone-T, 7, 107-109
    winged-T, 6, 93-95
    Y-formation, 107-109
Oklahoma University, 96
Optional run or pass, 145
Out and in pass, 149
Overloading pass, 152

Passer, attributes, 20
Pass defense, 41-45
Passing
    concepts, 142
    receiving, 21
    techniques, 20
Pass plays, 145-154
Pass protection, 142-144
Physical examinations, 222
Pitch outs, 66-67
Pivot, 39
Place kick, 28-29
    blocking of, 170
    protection, 170
Players, names and positions, 2
Playing fields, dimensions, 2
Pointing, 9, 69, 77
Postlude, 229-230
Post pass, 148
Post-power block, 72
Power through, 42
Practice plans, 223-224
Pre-game warm ups, 224
Pulling linemen, 68-69
Punt
    blocking, 163-165
    catching, 28
    protection, 162
    quick kick, 27, 162
    return, 166-170
    technique, 24-27

Quarterback
    hand-off, 34, 65

    hand position, 32
    reverse-out, 62
    roll-out, 63
    stance, 32
    step-out, sprint out, 62
Quarterback sneak, 130
Quick kick, 27, 162
Quick pass, 146
Quick play, 81
Quick trap, 73

Receiving the ball
    from center, 34
    from quarterback, 34, 65
    from passer, 21
    from kicker, 28
Referee, 4
Reverse body block, 14
Reverse-out, 62
Reverse play, 125-127
Ride, 62, 65
Roll block, 16
Roll-out, 63
Rover man, 177
Rules, 2, 3, 91
Rule blocking, 135-141
    defensive alignment, 134
    Michigan State, 138-140
    number system, 135-136
    player options, 141
    zone or area, 136-138
Running plays, 116-134
    bootleg, 131
    counter, 128
    cross-buck, 121
    draw, 131
    end run, 121
    off tackle, 121
    quarterback sneak, 128
    reverse, 115, 119
    special, 132-134
    straight ahead, 121
    sweep, 128
    trap, 117-118, 125

Safety, 3-4
Sally Rand, 132
Scoring, 3
Scouting, 204-215
    charts, 208-215
    how, 206-208
    report, 215
    what, 205
    who, 204
Screen block, 11
Screen pass, 146, 151
Shaughnessey, Clark, 91
Shift, backfield, 78
Short punt, 89-90
Shoulder block, 9-10
Shoulder charge, 57
Side step, 38

Sideline cut pass, 148
Signal systems, 75-77
    defensive, 174, 219
    offensive, 75-77
Single leg or crab block, 14
Single wing, 6, 82-86
Slanting, 201-202
Slot-T, 6, 96-99
Southern Methodist University, 111
Spinning back, 63-65
Split end, 110, 183-185
Split line, 96, 110
Split-T, 6, 32-33, 96-98
Spread formation, 6, 111-113
Sprint out, 62, 129, 131
Staff assignments, 221
Stance
    defensive, 49
    four point, 49
    fundamentals, 7
    semi-upright, 30
    split-T, 32
    three point, 7-9, 32, 46, 49
    upright, 30
Stanford University, 91
Step-out, quarterback, 62
Starting count, 79
Statistics, game, 225-227
Statue of Liberty, 134
Stiff arm, 38
Straight ahead plays, 121
Strategy, 216-220
    automatics, 79-80
    check signals, 81
    defensive quarterback, 219, 220
    map, 218
    offensive quarterback, 217-219
    quick plays, 81

starting count, 79
    team captain, 216
    to kick off or receive, 220
Submarine charge, 52
Substitutions, 2, 225
Sweep plays, 121, 129

T-formation, 6, 91-93, 110-111
Tackling, 16-17
    head-on, 16
    rear, 17
    side, 17
Tandem-T, 6, 99-101
Tatum, Jim, 96
Texas Christian University, 111
Touchdown, 3
Trailer pass, 152
Training rules, 222
Trap block, 69-71, 73, 117-118, 120
Trap plays, 125-126
Try-after-touchdown, 3-4
Twenty-five second count, 3

Umpire, 4

V-out pass, 147
Variable offense, 115

Warner, Blenn (Pop), 86
Wilkinson, "Bud," 96
Winged-T, 6, 93-95
Wishbone-T, 6, 107-109

Yards-to-gain, 2
Y-formation, 6, 107-109

Zone flooding, 150